Artful Therapy

Artful Therapy

Judith Aron Rubin

WILEY

John Wiley & Sons, Inc.

Published by John Wiley & Sons, Inc., Hoboken, New Jersey.
Published simultaneously in Canada.

For general information on our other products and services please contact our Customer Care Department within the U.S. at (800) 762-2974, outside the United States at (317) 572-3993 or fax (317) 572-4002.

Wiley also publishes its books in a variety of electronic formats. Some content that appears in print may not be available in electronic books. For more information about Wiley products, visit our website at www.wiley.com.

Library of Congress Cataloging-in-Publication Data:

Rubin, Judith Aron
    Artful therapy / Judith A. Rubin.
        p. cm.
    ISBN 0-471-67794-9 (paper/dvd)
        1. Art therapy. I. Title.
RC489.A7R833 2005
615.8'5156—dc22
                    2004057102

Printed in the United States of America

10 9 8 7 6 5 4 3 2 1

Contents

Contents

Contents

Contents

.

Illustrations

Chapter 1

Chapter 2

Chapter 3

Chapter 4

Chapter 5

Chapter 6

Chapter 7

Chapter 8

Chapter 9

DVD Contents

A Note to the Reader/Viewer

Illustrations, not Instructions

Because the book covers a great deal of ground, the DVD is meant to illustrate rather than to instruct. In order to show a wide variety of examples, I have opted for breadth rather than depth. Another reason for the brevity of most of the film clips is to minimize the likelihood of revealing any sensitive information or material about the participants.

Although the majority of the illustrative clips are from unfinished film and tape materials, some are excerpts from finished works, a few of which may still be available for purchase. I have therefore included any relevant information, as well as a listing of those individuals and institutions who have generously given permission for their inclusion (see Acknowledgments).

About Confidentiality

Although not all of the people on this DVD are patients, it is important to note that many were, and that they agreed to be photographed for the purpose of professional education. Since this book is meant for those in the helping professions, I trust that viewers will respect the privacy of anyone allowing themselves to be filmed, and will maintain the same kind of confidentiality normally accorded to any clinical material.

Chapter 1. Overview

Chapter 2. Why Add Art?

2.1 Animal Artists
- A. Congo the Chimpanzee Painting a Picture
- B. Chimp Painting
- C. Dolphin Painting
- D. Elephant Painting

2.2 Art Comes Naturally
- A. Creating in the Sand
- B. Early Interest in Images ("Going Home")
  Therapist: Maxine Junge, Ph.D.
- C. Creating with Chalk
- D. Early Absorption in Art

2.3 Cave Paintings
- A. Interior—Lascaux (France)
- B. Simulation—Altamira (Spain)

2.4. Art When Speechless
- A. "Shock"
- B. "Confusion"

2.5 Traumatic Memories ("Visual Memories")
  Therapist: Janice Hoshino, Ph.D. (Filmmaker: Rachel Lordkenaga, M.A.)

2.6. The Dark Side
- A. "It's My Fault" (Witch)
- B. Angry Dragon
- C. Bill is Angry at Sue ("We'll Show You What We're Gonna Do!")
  Therapist: Judith A. Rubin, Ph.D.

2.7 Some Things are Easier to "Say" in Art
- A. My Family—All Stuck Together
- B. Talking about Family Dynamics Using Clay
  Therapist: Shirley Riley, M.A.
- A. What People Can Tell You Through Art ("Listening to Children")
  Therapist: Robert Coles, M.D.
- B. Permissible Regression ("A Brush with Life")

2.8. In Art Everyone Can Talk at Once
- A. Working Individually in a Group ("Art as Therapy")
- B. Working Together in a Group ("Arts and Environment")

2.9 Some Things are Easier to "See" in Art
- A. A Family Draws Together Silently
- B. Two-Headed Dragon
- C. Two-Faced Guy (Brought in by a Patient)
- D. A Monster Inside Us ("Multi-Arts Resource Guide")
- E. A Woman Discovers Aspects of Herself ("Art Therapy: The Healing Vision")
  Therapist: Robert Ault, M.F.A.

C.   Looking at the Painting
D.   "Sea Mist"

4.4 To Talk or Not? Active Listening

A.   Child Talking while Drawing ("Stevie's Light Bulb")
     Therapist: Sarah Dubo, M.D.
B.   Adolescent Talking while Painting
     Therapist: Judith A. Rubin, Ph.D.
C.   Therapist Initiating a Topic ("A Boy's Anger")
     Therapist: Violet Oaklander, Ph.D
D.   Talking about the Assigned Theme ("Mothers and Daughters")
     Therapist: Shirley Riley, M.A.

4.5 To Create or Not? Working Alongside

A.   With an Individual ("Art Therapy: Beginnings")
     Therapist: Edith Kramer, D.A.T.
B.   With a Family
     Therapist: Judith A. Rubin, Ph.D.
C.   With a Group
     Therapist: Kit Jenkins, M.A.

4.6 Interviewing During the Process

A.   About Getting Mad ("A Boy and His Anger")
     Therapist: Violet Oaklander, Ph.D.
B.   About the Art
     Therapist: Judith A. Rubin, Ph.D.
C.   About Coming to a Clinic
     Therapist: Judith A. Rubin, Ph.D.

Chapter 5. After the Process

5.1 Reflecting on the Art and the Process

A.   A Title
     Therapist: Andrea Ramsey, M.A.
B.   Framing
     Therapist: Judith A. Rubin, Ph.D.
C.   Writing
     Therapist: Dayna Block, M.A. (Open Studio Process Group)
D.   What Do you See? ("The Scribble")
     Therapist: Mala Betensky, Ph.D.
E.   Describing a Picture
F.   Tell Me About It ("Listening to Children")
     Therapist: Robert Coles, M.D.
G.   How Would This Story End?
     Therapist: Janet Bush, M.S.
H.   Group Members Interview Each Other (RAW Art Works)
I.   Responding by Moving
     Therapist: Arthur Robbins, Ed.D.

Chapter 9. Art in Child Therapy

Chapter 10. Art in Family and Group Therapy

Chapter 11. Using Other Art Forms

Chapter 12. Using Mental Imagery

Chapter 14. Using Art Therapists

Acknowledgments

Thanks to the following for permission to excerpt:

ABC News Archives
"Tender Hearts"

Gladys Agell, Ph.D.
Videotape of the Ulman Personality Assessment Procedure

Sandra Graves Alcorn, Ph.D.
Tape of Interview with Child After his Mother's Sudden Death

Simone Alter-Muri, Ph.D.
"Creative Arts Therapies at the Pace School"

American Art Therapy Association
"Art Therapy: Beginnings"

Peter Amman, Ph.D.
"Sandplay with Dora Kalff"

Doris Arrington, Ph.D.
Videotape of Russian Orphans

Robert Ault, M.A.
"Art Therapy: The Healing Vision"

James Babanikos, Ph.D.
"Color My World"

Lore Baer, M.A.
"Art Therapy Is . . ."

Acknowledgments

Mary Blaylock, M.A.
"Clinical Art Therapy With the Family," "Going Home"

Lila Bonner-Miller, M.D.
"Lila"

Ian Brownell, Bushy Theater
"Across the Threshold," "Arts and Environment"

Fran Burst-Terranella, Filmmaker, Burst Video/Film, Inc.
"Lila"

Janet Bush, M.A.
Art Therapy Session in a School

Lucia Capacchione, Ph.D.
Television Interview

Mildred Lachman Chapin, M.Ed.
Interview with Patient

CBS News Archives
"The Big Picture" (60 Minutes), "The Healing Art" (Sunday Morning),
"The Face of Violence" (Sunday Morning), "Middletown, U.S.A." (48 Hours)

C.G. Jung Educational Center of Houston
"At the Threshold: A Journey to the Sacred . . ."

Selma Ciornai, M.A.
Videotape of Art Therapy Workshop in Brazil

Karen Clark-Schock, Ph.D, Hypnotherapist and Art Therapist
Television Interview

Claire Clements, Ed.D.
"Art Therapy Teleconference"

CNN ImageSource (Joel Suttles)
Videotape of Judith Scott at Creative Growth Arts Center

Barry M. Cohen, Ph.D.
A Diagnostic Drawing Series Interview

Robert Coles, M.D., Child Psychiatrist
"Listening to Children"

Irene Corbit, Ph.D., Art Therapist
Photo-Art Therapy Class Videotape

Carol T. Cox, M.A., Art Therapist
MARI Interview

David Crawley, KDKA-TV
News Segment on Art Therapy at the Pittsburgh Center for the Arts

Expressive Media, Inc.
"Art Therapy Has Many Faces," "Beyond Words: Art Therapy With Older Adults," "Children and the Arts: A Film About Growing," "The Green Creature Within: Art and Drama in Group Psychotherapy," "We'll Show You What We're Gonna Do!: Art With Multiply-Handicapped Blind Children"

Family Communications, Inc. WQED-TV
Excerpt from "Mister Rogers' Neighborhood"

Carolyn Grant Fay
"At the Threshold: A Journey to the Sacred Through the Integration of Jungian Psychology and the Expressive Arts"

Robert Frye, Bolthead Communications
"The Journey of Butterfly"

Jerry Fryrear, Ph.D.
Videotape of Photo-Art Therapy Class

Robin Gabriels, Ph.D.
Med*Source Program on Art Therapy for Asthma at National Jewish Center

Linda Gantt, Ph.D. and Louis Tinnin, M.D.
"Diane's Intensive" at the Trauma Recovery Institute

Sondra Geller, Ph.D.
Art Therapy Sessions at George Washington University Counseling Center

Nancy Gerber, M.A.
Videotape of a Brief Art Therapy Screening Evaluation (BATSE)

Lani Gerrity, Ph.D.
Puppet Session with Adult Therapy Group

Eliana Gil, Ph.D.
"Essentials of Play Therapy With Abused Children"

Glaxo Wellcome, Inc.
"Stress: My Special Box"

Frank Goryl, Ph.D.
Videotape of Clay Workshop Led by Linda Gantt, Ph.D.

John Graham-Pole, M.D.
"Color My World"

Janet Greenwood, Ph.D.
"Gestalt Art Experience With Janie Rhyne"

Acknowledgments

Guilford Press
"Essentials of Play Therapy With Abused Children"

Mary Ann Hayden-Shaughnessy, M.A.
"Creative Expression in Recovery"

David Henley, Ph.D.
Videotape of Chimpanzee Painting

Ellen Hiltebrand, Ph.D. and Glaxo Wellcome
"A Healing Journey"

Chris Holmes, Chris Holmes Productions
"Drawing From the Fire"

Ellen Horovitz, Ph.D., Julia Productions, Inc.
"The Cognitive Art Therapy Assessment"

Paula Howie, M.A.
Videotapes from Walter Reed Hospital

Simcha Jacobovici, Associated Producers, Ltd.
"A Child's Grief"

Irene Jakab, M.D., Ph.D.
"Family Video-Art Therapy"

Kit Jenkins, M.A.
Videotapes from RAW Artworks

Deborah Slavitt Joost, M.A.
Picture of Art Therapy at the Addison Gallery

Maxine Junge, Ph.D.
"Going Home" (Clinical Art Therapy With the Family)

Georgiana Jungels, M.A.
"Anna Shafer and Her Art"

Martin Kalff, Ph.D.
"Sandtray Therapy with Dora Kalff"

Edith Kramer, D.A.T.
"Edith Kramer: Artist and Art Therapist"

KQED-TV
"Without Words"

Helen Landgarten, M.A.
"Lori: Art Therapy and Self-Discovery"

Majie Lavergne, M.A.
"Art as Therapy"

Myra Levick, Ph.D.
"Aspects of Art Therapy"

Barbara Ann Levy, M.A.
Videotape of Dolphin Painting

Rachel Lordkenaga, M.A., Powerful Pussycats Productions
"Visual Memories: Japanese-American Internment and Art Therapy"

Laura Loumeau-May, M.P.S.
"Tender Hearts" (ABC News Archives)

Cathy A. Malchiodi, M.A.
Videotape of Shirley Riley at Opica Day Treatment Center

Janos Marton, Ph.D.
"Ooh La La! The Living Museum"

Russell Meares, M.D.
Slide of Ainslie Meares, M.D.

Ann Mills, Ph.D.
DDS Session with a Woman

James Minson, M.A.
"The Transition of Indigenous Guatemalan Youth Living in Foster Care as Assisted by Glass Craft Training and Practice" Masters' Thesis DVD

NBC News and the Hebrew Home and Hospital for the Aged in Riverdale
"Art and Art Therapy at the Hebrew Home" (Today Show)

Aina Nucho, Ph.D.
"Art Therapy With Adults"
"Luis and the Big Fish"

Violet Oaklander, Ph.D. and Max Solomon, MaxSound Productions
"A Boy and His Anger"

Pedro Orrega, City-TV
"Ooh La La! The Living Museum"

Pabst-Verlag
"Impulse Der Kunst"

Ralph Rabinovitch, M.D.
"Stevie's Light Bulb: Graphic Art in Child Psychiatry"

Acknowledgments

Andrea Ramsey, M.A.
Individual Art Therapy in a Hospital

Trudy Manning Rauch, M.A.
"Psychimagery"

Patti Ravenscroft, M.A.
Family Art Evaluation

Shirley Riley, M.A.
Videotape of Family Art Therapy in Holland, "Mothers and Daughters"
(Clinical Art Therapy with the Family)

Arthur Robbins, Ph.D.
Videotape of Individual Art Therapy Session

Natalie Rogers, Ph.D. and Allyn and Bacon
"Person-Centered Therapy" (Therapy With the Experts Series)

Oren Rudavsky, Filmmaker
"Dreams So Real"

Glen Salzman, Filmmaker (Cineflix)
"A Brush with Life"

Ellen Speert, M.A.
Videotapes of Art Therapy Workshop and TV Show on Phototherapy

Buddy Squires, Filmmaker
"Listening to Children with Dr. Robert Coles"

Aaron Strong, Filmmaker
"Isaac's Interpretations"

Arthur Ulene, M.D.
"When Children Grieve"

University of London
"Art and Psychiatry"

Very Special Arts, Massachusetts
"Multi-Arts Resource Guide"

Evelyn Virshup, Ph.D.
"Suicide: A Teenage Dilemma"

Harriet Wadeson, Ph.D.
Videotape of Couple Art Therapy

Diane Waller, Ph.D. and John Beacham, Ph.D.
"Art Therapy," "Art Therapy and Children"

Irene Ward-Brydon, M.A.
"Creative Growth Art Center"

Truus Wertheim-Cahen, M.A.
Dutch Film about her Work in Art Therapy

Ann Sayre Wiseman, M.Ed.
"Nightmare Help"

Carol A. Wisker, M.A.
"Breaking Barriers"

Olenka Woloszuk
Footage from "Olenka's Workshop"

Alice Rae Yellin and the New Orleans Museum of Art
"Passionate Visions"

Preface

The truth of the matter is that art therapy is not a discipline, it's . . . a modality. Art therapy is a way of getting there. It operates as a modality because you can adapt it to any theory.

HELEN LANDGARTEN (in Warren, 1995, p. 3)

During more than 40 years as an art therapist, I have spent a good deal of my professional time teaching clinicians from other fields how to add art to their own armamentaria. Yet, although I've written four books for art therapists, and one for the general public, I have never specifically addressed my colleagues in other clinical disciplines.

This book and its accompanying DVD are therefore designed for those who are not art therapists, but who would like to be able to include art in their work. It is for practitioners who have never used art, as well as for clinicians who have done so, but who would like to have additional guidance and support.

Artful Therapy is especially for those in other mental health disciplines, like psychology, psychiatry, social work, counseling, and psychiatric nursing. The audience also includes workers in related fields, such as rehabilitation, activity therapy, speech and language therapy, recreation therapy, and occupational therapy.

The book is addressed as well to those from a variety of backgrounds who do play therapy, marriage and family therapy, and pastoral counseling. And it is for people who work in other human-service roles, such as child life specialists, child care workers, psychiatric aides, and mental health associates.

I have one simple reason for wanting to write this book and to make the

DVD that goes with it. It is that I am thoroughly convinced that the addition of art can serve to deepen and enhance anyone's clinical work.

I do not mean to imply that you will become an art therapist by reading this volume. Like any other clinical discipline, art therapy requires a substantial amount of specialized study: usually 2 years of full-time postgraduate training, including 700 hours of supervised clinical work. Becoming registered and, later, board certified involves thousands of hours of additional supervised practice, as well as passing a national exam.

Rather than turn you into an art therapist, I hope to help you to expand your existing repertoire, in order to open new avenues of expression for those you serve. To the extent that you are able to embrace the ideas and approaches presented in this book, I know that you will be rewarded when you put them into practice.

Although I imagine that this volume will appeal to those with artistic interests, it is not necessary to be either an artist or an art lover. For, as you will learn to explain to your patients, creating art in the context of diagnosis and therapy is not about "art" in the usual sense. It is certainly not about learning how to make art with technical proficiency.

Rather, it is about adding another language to the communication between you and those you serve, so that they may express themselves even more fully. In short, those of you who assist others mainly through talking can easily add pictures as well. And, if you already have some art materials in your therapy space, I hope to help you to make even better use of such media and the messages they generate.

The audience for this book, then, includes all therapists, whether you see individuals, groups, or families, and regardless of the setting in which you see them. For no matter where human beings are served—whether in a school, a hospital, a clinic, a shelter, a jail, a church, an emergency room, or a nursing home—art is always a potentially useful addition to a clinical toolbox. The primary goal, then, is to help you use art in your own therapeutic work. Because it is so closely related, I have included a chapter on the use of mental imagery, with or without art.

In addition to helping you use visual modalities yourself, I shall also open the door to the world of art therapy, so that you and your patients can have access to the expertise of this group of specialists. Although art therapy has been a defined profession in the United States and Great Britain since the 1940s, there are still many misconceptions about it, some of which I will try to dispel.

My goal is to help you to be more familiar with those for whom art is not a second language, but rather the mother tongue. Once you have an educated understanding of art therapy, you can then decide whether you want to collaborate with, hire, consult with, or refer someone to an art therapist. Just as art can be a valuable tool in your own work, so can this group of specialists be a resource for you and your clients.

Finally, while the emphasis in this book is on the visual arts, I have also included a brief description of how you might use other expressive modalities—like drama, photography, creative writing, and music—as helpful adjuncts. Since I, like some of you, am untrained and unsophisticated in all of them, I have noted elementary materials and activities that I have found useful in my work.

I have had the privilege of working closely with many talented dance, drama, and music therapists from the beginning of my career. It was only through their example and generous permission that I hesitantly added some of their materials to my own therapy room. They did for me what I hope to do for you—to help you become less afraid to open additional avenues of expression for your patients.

Most of the book is about what can be done with artistic media in the settings in which you do your work. An additionally useful aspect of all creative modalities is that they can be used away from the office as well as in it. For that reason, I've included a chapter about assigning the arts as homework, as well as prescribing them as therapeutic activities. All of the arts are relevant for between-session bridging and as healthy pursuits, both during and at the end of treatment.

Since my energy and time for in-person workshops and classes will not last forever, and since the number of people who can attend them is inevitably limited, I am delighted that there is a way to reach practitioners through print.

In order to help the ideas in this book come alive for you, I've also created a visual accompaniment in the form of a DVD, which illustrates some of what is on these pages in color and action. Because this book is addressed to non-art therapists, the DVD includes live footage of clinicians from a variety of other fields using art in therapy with individuals, families, and groups.

Art therapists work hard to convince their patients that anyone can create art. I hope to persuade you that anyone can provide art materials as another avenue of expression. When you integrate the arts and mental imagery into your own work, I think you will agree. At least that's what I've found in over 40 years of teaching people from other disciplines how to incorporate art activities into their practice. I hope that your experience will be equally satisfying.

CHAPTER

1

Overview

Background

A Psychiatric Hospital

In 1963 I became the first art therapist at the Western Psychiatric Institute and Clinic, working individually with youngsters who had been diagnosed with childhood schizophrenia. Although the label today might be different (e.g., autism, pervasive developmental disorder, or Asperger's disorder), there was no question that they were severely disturbed children.

Before I started seeing them, there had been some anxiety on the part of the staff about whether the children would be able to use art materials appropriately, rather than eating or throwing them. Happily, each child was able to find a way to use the art sessions productively, given a choice of media and surfaces. The many different ways in which they responded to the opportunity were impressive, ranging from performing calming repetitive movements with body and brush, to graphically organizing their perceptions, to expressing previously unknown feelings and fantasies.

It was soon apparent that some of those whose language was hard to understand were able to communicate remarkably clearly through art. This was dramatically true for Dorothy, a 10-year-old whose speech was frantic, garbled, and virtually incomprehensible (DVD 1.1). She began by drawing very competent pictures of birds (1.1A), then painting them (1.1B). But until she drew and painted first a monster (1.1C), then a bird devouring a human being (1.1D), the treatment team had been unable to decipher the fantasies behind her bizarre behavior of flapping her arms and making squawking sounds. In fact, it was only after her bird and then her cat fan-

1

tasies (1.1E) were expressed and explored in visual form that Dorothy began to draw human beings: the other children on her unit (1.1F).

Despite her social isolation, it was evident that she had been observing these youngsters, who were instantly recognizable to everyone who knew them (1.1G). Although her group portraits were rather stiff at first, they soon included a good deal of action and a clearly defined environment (1.1H). It was during this period that Dorothy began, for the first time, to relate to the other children, and we can only speculate that making the drawings was a rehearsal for live social interaction.

Even the few children on the unit with normal speech began, in their art, to express feelings and fantasies that helped the staff to understand their often puzzling symptoms. This was true for Randy, a 12-year-old who suffered from Encopresis (DVD 1.2).

He was a sweet and affectionate child, whose aggression—which he denied but which was manifest in his explosive symptom—first came out symbolically. After drawing a picture of Mars (1.2A) with constellations named "The King" and "The Queen," Randy embarked on a book, "Our Trip through Outer Space," (1.2B) in which a Martian and I traveled together from one planet to another.

This was followed by some realistic paintings, including one of his "School on Fire" (1.2C), one of the "School Burning Up" (1.2D), and one of a "Dinosaur and Volcano" (1.2E). After expressing some of his pent-up rage, Randy turned to an elaborate oedipal fantasy in which he and I went on a trip, this time on Earth, and as clearly romantic companions.

In the course of this second journey, the Randy character became less Martian and more human, appearing at one point to have won me, who I believe represented his mother in the transference. This was evident in a picture of Randy as a Scotsman holding me on what looks like a leash (1.2F), presumably to keep me from falling while dancing. The eventual resolution, however, was a healthier one. In the final picture/story (1.2G), the woman rejects a sailor, "because she already had a boyfriend," the boy accepting the reality that mother belongs to father. What was interesting was that during his work on the picture series, Randy's symptom gradually went away.

Because his psychiatrist was also seeing him for both individual and family therapy, we cannot be sure what role, if any, the art had in his recovery. Both his doctor and I felt, however, that art therapy had had a positive impact on Randy and on his progress in treatment. Since Dorothy's severe language problems had prevented her from communicating effectively with her psychiatrist, the role of the art in her case was clearly vital. When Professor Erik Erikson was presented with her history and that of her treatment at a grand rounds 4 months after art therapy had begun, he felt that it had been critical to her increasing relatedness, and urged that it be continued.

A Child Study Center

At the same time that I was seeing the schizophrenic children, I was working with after-school groups at a child study center run by the Department of Child Development. There, we found that some children who were very shy were able to whisper in paint what they could not say in words. Youngsters who were impulsive were often able to settle down and focus, and some of the boys and girls whose self-esteem was low, blossomed artistically in this nonjudgmental atmosphere where, unlike in art class at school, there were neither assignments nor grades.

My colleagues—at both the hospital and the child study center—soon began asking for help in using art themselves. They wanted to know what materials to buy, as well as how to get the children to use them. It wasn't long before I also found myself, in addition to working with the youngsters, training other staff members. Some requested individual consultation, while others wanted to meet as a group and to work with materials. My first adult students in 1963, therefore, were teachers, child care workers, occupational therapists, social workers, psychiatrists, and psychologists.

An Institution for Disabled Children

In 1967 I started an art program at a residential treatment center for orthopedically disabled youngsters (DVD 1.3). The staff members, like those in the hospital, had been extremely pessimistic about the capacity of these severely impaired children to use art materials with any degree of success. We were pleased to discover how very many of them were able to be creative through adaptive modifications of tools, media, and work surfaces (1.3A). It was soon evident that art provided these youngsters with a pleasurable outlet, as well as a place to learn new skills, to develop their potential, and to enhance their fragile self-esteem.

Although the staff had feared that art would discourage them because of their poor fine-motor control, the children's excitement about the art sessions was evident from the first (1.3B). In fact, because it was so popular, an extra period in the art room became one of the most frequently chosen rewards in a newly instituted behavior modification system, even though it cost the most tokens.

Art was also a place where both conflicts and capacities were revealed—as with the deaf-mute girl (DVD 1.4), thought to be profoundly retarded, who first demonstrated (1.4A) her normal intelligence in pictures (1.4B). As a result, she was able to return to the classroom and to speech therapy, using a "talking book" of drawings to communicate with others (1.4C), long before she was able to master sign language (1.4D).

On the basis of her success, the psychology and speech therapy departments both requested in-service training so that they, too, could use art with the children they were treating. Soon, sessions on art activities were requested by the child care workers, the occupational therapists, and the nurses, all of whom found that it helped them to better achieve their goals.

A Child Guidance Center

When I became the first art therapist at the Pittsburgh Child Guidance Center in 1969, the psychiatrists, psychologists, and social workers on the staff were naturally curious about this new clinical modality. I invited them to watch the art sessions through the one-way observation windows used for trainees. I also let it be known that I was interested in our working together, and eventually did so with some of them as co-therapists with families or groups (cf. Chapter 14, pp. 230–233; Rubin, 1981b).

After several months of a part-time pilot program, there was steadily growing interest in referring patients for assessment and treatment. In addition, however, some clinicians were eager to learn how to incorporate more art into their own work. I therefore ended up consulting with many of my colleagues, to enhance their comfort in using art with the children and parents they saw.

In 1970, a psychologist and I designed a family art evaluation and presented it at a general staff meeting (Rubin & Magnussen, 1974). The interest was so keen that we soon formed a family art study group in which we trained other clinicians to conduct the evaluation, reviewing their videotaped sessions at our 2-hour weekly meetings. Observing their ability to use what they learned, and to modify the procedures to fit their needs, was an important learning experience for me (cf. Chapter 10, p. 152).

Pretty soon, the social workers requested a course in using art materials with the activity groups they were leading. There was also a series of meetings with the psychologists on the use of projective drawings in assessment. The psychiatric consultant to the clinic's therapeutic preschool requested an art therapy group for the mothers (DVD 1.5), to which the latter (1.5A) responded more positively (1.5B) than they had to a purely verbal group (1.5C). The teachers of these severely disorganized students wanted consultation in helping the children, whose controls were weak, to use art materials constructively.

Responding to requests from people working with troubled adolescents in the community, a psychologist suggested that we design a course in art for self-awareness (DVD 1.6). We did so, training workers from many different fields to use art activities with groups of teenagers—first experiencing the exercises (1.6A), then trying them out with teens, then returning for group supervision on their work (1.6B).

The director of research invited me to work with his department on what became a series of studies of children's drawings related to diagnostic issues (cf. Chapter 14, pp. 233–234). These were all two-way situations, in which I learned at least as much as they did.

Consultation to Other Institutions

My job at the Pittsburgh Child Guidance Center was half-time in Direct Service and half-time in Community Service, otherwise known as Consultation and Education. That meant that I could consult to other institutions in the community, which greatly expanded the clinic's ability to reach parents and children in the wider geographic area.

In the hospital across the street, which, like the center, was run by the Department of Psychiatry, the occupational therapists soon requested a series of classes. They wanted to deepen their use of art media, which at that time were central in their work. Because they had excellent art and craft supplies and equipment, and were seeing most of the patients in the hospital, helping them to be more creative and reflective in their approach to art activities had an impact on the majority of those being treated on the inpatient units.

Shortly after that, the staff of the then-new day hospital asked for consultation on the use of art in group therapy. We began by having the patients make collaborative murals, inspired by an early book on art therapy in a New York day hospital: *Murals of the Mind* (Harris & Joseph, 1973). I ended up both observing the social workers leading the groups, and working alongside them.

The work of an art therapy intern at the children's hospital next door to the center stimulated a long-term collaboration with the pediatricians on art activities for their waiting rooms, something we had already instituted at our clinic (see Figure 1.1). For a number of years, I met for a series of workshops with the graduate students in child development and child care who conducted evening play programs for the children in that hospital. Their interest was in making the recreational art activities as therapeutic

1.1 Waiting-Room Art Activities

as possible, especially for those youngsters who had long hospital stays. Later, when a Child Life Department was formed, I conducted regular training sessions on the use of art media for its staff members.

I eventually found myself giving talks and workshops, as well as teaching courses for those who worked in other mental health centers (see Figure 1.2). They were offered not only at the clinic, but also in the community, in a wide variety of settings, including universities. For those who attended, I created a mimeographed handout entitled "Some Ways to Use Art in Therapy," which listed basic art materials; how to offer them; how to decide what to do, depending on diagnostic and treatment goals; and how to look at the art work that was evoked. I had forgotten that handout, which I used with other clinicians for many years, until I started work on this book. *Artful Therapy* is clearly a logical extension of those early efforts to share the wealth (so to speak) with those in other fields who wished to add a creative dimension to their therapy.

Perhaps the most important thing I learned from these experiences was that if people are well trained and knowledgeable in their own disciplines, they are able to incorporate art activities in ways that are therapeutically relevant. And, as is true for art therapists as well, they inevitably do so in

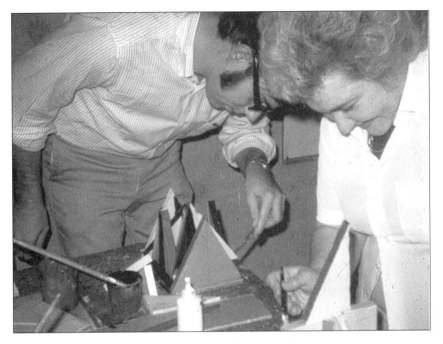

1.2 Course for Child Care Workers

ways that fit their theoretical outlooks as well as their preferred styles of relating.

Where Can You Use Art?

The kind of basic materials recommended in this book, most of which are only minimally messy, can be used in almost any place where you might be helping someone. In addition to using them in an office, you can offer art to people of all ages not only in clinics and hospitals, but also in schools, shelters, prisons, and rehabilitation centers, even in their own homes (DVD 1.7).

Just as art is possible with people of all ages—as soon as a child can hold a marker and not put it immediately in the mouth—so it is possible to make it available in virtually all kinds of settings, including outdoors, as with the wall mural done by adolescent gang members in a project facilitated by their leader (a woman who had also been in a gang). The theme of the mural is their dreams for the future (DVD 1.8).

Naturally, as with any kind of psychotherapy, it is ideal to have a space that is private, protected, and quiet—and if there's a sink in the room or

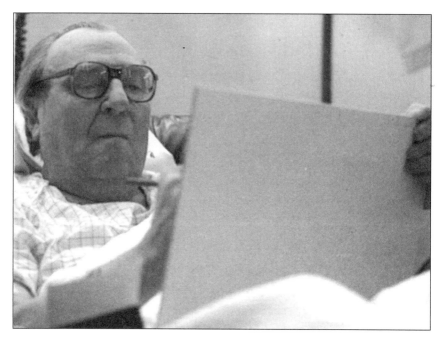

1.3 Patient Drawing in Hospital Bed

nearby, it helps to allay anxiety about getting dirty. Even when there is no private work space, however, and even if the table is mahogany and the floor is carpeted, you can easily protect both work and fallout surfaces with newspaper or plastic cloths.

Although some settings, like a shelter or a hospital ward, are unavoidably noisy, crowded, and full of interruptions, it is really amazing how people of all ages can concentrate on making a drawing or a collage when they are genuinely engaged in the process (see Figure 1.3). I once had a book called *Art Is a Quiet Place*, which is what often happens, even with otherwise disorganized individuals.

I once had the good fortune to accompany my colleague, art therapist David Henley, on a visit to a zoo where he had been going for weekly art sessions with the animals. While there, I had the pleasure of observing a gorilla named June create a crayon drawing, which I treasure as a memento of the visit (DVD 1.9). June's drawing itself was unremarkable, like any young child's scribble (1.9A). But watching her concentrate on the activity for a full five minutes in a large cage full of noisily playing apes was astonishing (1.9B). Although I have often seen human beings similarly absorbed in the act of drawing, I felt like I was witnessing firsthand the primal pleasure of a deep engagement in the creative process. This organization of the organism's faculties in such purposeful, focused activity is one of the broadly therapeutic aspects of art activities.

It is therefore not surprising that art has always provided a refuge (DVD 1.10), and that making even a simple drawing can be a way of escaping a painful situation (1.10A). The children in the Nazi concentration camp of Terezin were enabled to create by a teacher named Friedl Dicker (1.10B), whose art classes were an island of peace in a sea of despair[1] (Jewish Museum of Prague, 1993; Makarova & Seidman-Miller, 1999; Volavkova, 1962; 1.10C).

Frederick Terna, one of the few child artists surviving the death camps, spoke about the experience during a reunion 50 years after he was liberated from Auschwitz:

> It was one of the moments of total privacy—when one is in front of a piece of paper, that rectangle or square, the world does really not exist. That is, I am the total master of that little paper; I can do with it what I want. My oppressors here—the Nazis, and the Gestapo, and SS—could do whatever they wanted. When I was in front of that little piece of paper, I was my own boss. (1.10D)

Even now, people of all ages spontaneously turn to art to cope with overwhelming traumatic events (see Figure 1.4). This was evident in the many art expressions—such as community shrines, murals, and picture-messages by individuals of all ages—following the terrorist attacks of September 11, 2001.

1.4 Drawing about September 11, 2001

When Can You Use Art?

With *when*, as with *where*, the possibilities are virtually limitless. Like words, art materials can be always available, to be used as desired. This is common in child therapy, where art media are among those normally present in a well-equipped playroom. Art can also be introduced selectively, as indicated by your own notions of how best to further the therapeutic work.

Art is often found in assessment because it is quick and, when intelligently utilized, can be a rich source of diagnostic information. It is also helpful in the course of therapy, regardless of whether the treatment is long or short term. Because of its efficiency and its ability to tap rapidly into important concerns, art is especially well suited to brief therapy.

Whether it becomes an always-available mode of expression or a selectively introduced intervention, art can be used at any stage of treatment. The decision about when, how, and why in any particular clinical instance is up to you, just like a decision about whether to request specific memories or to introduce any other adjunctive technique, such as hypnosis.

Art is especially helpful in *crisis intervention*. Some events are so devastating that words fail, and images become the best way to say what presses for release. Because art is portable, it is possible to take crayons and paper anywhere people need help, whether in a home, a hospital, a shelter, or a school.

Here are a couple of examples in which art was useful in helping people cope with crises: After the 1995 terrorist bombing in Oklahoma killed and injured hundreds of innocent people, survivors experiencing posttraumatic stress found that art was especially therapeutic (Jones, 1997). When a brushfire destroyed many homes and injured a number of people in northern California, the team that did group therapy with the children at a local school found that art was especially useful in helping them get in touch with their feelings about the event (DVD 1.11).

With Whom Can You Use Art?

Although as an art therapist I can see potential benefits for many different kinds of patients, there are people for whom art is especially helpful. While words are inadequate for all of us in trying to express certain ideas and feelings, for some people, words are less easily available, and for others they often get in the way. These are the people for whom using art materials can definitely open up new possibilities in therapy.

A variety of patients cannot or will not speak, whether the cause is organic, as in aphasia, or psychological, as in elective mutism. Those who are painfully shy might be able to talk, but can be so frozen with inhibition that precious little can be accomplished in verbal therapy. For all such patients, adding art can open a vital avenue of communication.

Paradoxically, another group of patients for whom art offers a welcome channel is those who are highly verbal—who use words to hide, and who do it all too well. Intellectualization and rationalization are wonderful defenses, but when they don't allow people to know what they're feeling and what their fantasies are, they can get in the way of psychotherapy. Similarly, for those who isolate affect, who talk about it but do not actually feel it, art can help them get in touch with the unruly emotions of which they are so afraid.

Just as children find making art easy and natural, so do adults who are temporarily or permanently regressed. When my colleague and I started a program of creative arts therapies throughout a large psychiatric hospital in 1981, we found that art was the most popular modality, probably because it was less threatening than movement, drama, or music, in all of which people felt more exposed.

As we had expected, art therapy was welcomed on the child and adolescent units. But we had not anticipated that it would be so appealing to adults who were in an acute phase of their illness—those suffering from various kinds of psychoses, including schizophrenia, depression, bipolar disorder, and serious personality disorders. This is not so surprising if we recall the universal phenomenon of the spontaneous art of the mentally ill (DVD 1.12)—presumably, an effort to stay in touch in some way (1.12A)—long before the advent of antipsychotic medications or art therapy programs in mental hospitals (Jakab, 1998; MacGregor, 1989; Morgenthaler, 1921; Prinzhorn, 1922; 1.12B).

A similar motive is probably present for most of those doing what has come to be known as "outsider art" (Cardinal, 1972; Hall, Metcalfe, & Cardinal, 1994; DVD 1.13). There seems to be something that relieves tension and provides grounding, in the very making of something concrete. The impulse to create is a compulsion for most of these self-taught artists, like Howard Finster (1.13A), and is evident in their use of any available material, whether it be Nellie Mae Rowe's chewing-gum sculptures, or Jimmy Lee Sudduth's mud paintings with natural dyes from grass and flowers (1.13B).

Since creating art seems to be an inborn human capacity, it is possible to add the option in your work with almost anyone. As noted, it is especially useful with those whose language or reality-testing is limited. It is also remarkably helpful for those whose mastery of verbal expression actually gets in the way of their efforts to feel better through psychotherapy.

Children of All Ages

Although the majority of children you see for therapy have probably developed some language, they do not have the vocabulary or the expressive range of adults. Moreover, most are comfortable with drawing, painting, and modeling, which they do quite naturally. Thus, like playing with dolls or toys, making art is a familiar expressive activity, and one in which a great many youngsters are quite fluent. For these reasons alone, it's important to provide even the most articulate children with a broad range of possible media.

The quality of materials like crayons or paper is important, because youngsters press hard and scribble vigorously. And since their verbal abilities are more limited, the variety of materials offered needs to be greater than is necessary with adults and older adolescents. Chapter 9 focuses on the use of art in work with children and adolescents.

Adults Young and Old

While adding art may not seem as compelling when you are working with articulate adults, I think you will be pleasantly surprised at the many ways in which it can enhance treatment. Just as art in therapy is not only for children, so it is not only for those who are regressed. The worried well, the average neurotic, and those who suffer from dysthymia, cyclothymia, personality disorders, low self-esteem, and anxiety disorders are as good candidates as those who are nonverbal or psychotic.

Older adults, whether they are suffering the normal losses of aging or have a specific disability, enjoy the opportunity to have a visual as well as a verbal "life review" (Butler, Lewis, & Sunderland, 1998; DVD 1.14). Photographs from the past are helpful, and can be placed in collages, arranged in sequence, or used in memory boxes (1.14A, 1.14B).

Drawings of memories are another way to look back, and to put things in order. Anna Shafer, an elderly woman who attended an art group at a local community center, became quite excited about drawing, doing it every time she was free. She used it not only to reminisce, but also to fantasize (DVD 1.15).

After all, you can do anything you want to in art, unbound by realistic considerations. Age brings inevitable losses of loved ones, of societal roles, of health, and of mobility—all the more reason that being able to imagine freely in art is extremely therapeutic. Moreover, if there is any neurological deficit or memory loss, drawing can be used not only diagnostically, but also as a way of organizing otherwise confusing perceptions and events.

Indeed, I hope that you will consider using art with all people who are willing to try, whether they are in their 20s or their 80s. In fact, I suggest that you experiment with offering materials to all of your clients, so you can see for yourself who might benefit and how. The following are some groups not mentioned earlier who respond well to art, though the list is far from exhaustive.

People Who Are Resistant and Suspicious

Those who are able to talk, but who are openly resistant to verbal therapy, may be somewhat more receptive to drawing. Despite the anxiety of most adults about their artistic abilities, even wary and hostile patients can become engaged, especially if the art activity is presented in a nonthreatening way.

When I worked in the outpatient clinic of a community mental health center, as well as on the inpatient units of its hospital, I found that people with less formal education were often suspicious of verbal therapy, fearing that a therapist could play with their minds, so to speak. Yet they were sometimes more willing to use markers than to talk. The indirectness of art has an appeal for many, perhaps because it is concrete and thus makes it easier to *see* things.

People with Developmental Delays

Those suffering from delays in development, whether they are of organic or psychological origin, can often benefit significantly when you add drawing and other art activities to your behavioral, cognitive, or psychodynamic treatment. In fact, including art can sometimes make psychotherapy possible for those for whom it would otherwise be inaccessible.

As noted earlier, art can be used with anyone who can learn to use materials constructively. If you are working with people who, for whatever reason, are unable to symbolize, you will find that drawing can be helpful. Making images can even be an avenue toward higher functioning (Wilson, 1999, 2001). Certainly, there are many times when words alone are of limited value.

People with Communication Problems

Anyone who has problems with verbal communication, whatever the cause, is a good candidate for "art as a second language."[2] This includes those who are autistic, hearing impaired, or brain damaged. Elective mutes and deaf-mutes may be able to speak to you only through drawings. And the universal language of art can be a godsend with recent immigrants when you do not speak the same language.

Those with chronic mental illness can often tell you even more about how they are feeling through art than in words. In the 1960s, psychiatrist Mardi Horowitz (1983) discovered that "interaction painting" enabled him to communicate with acutely regressed catatonic patients.

When people's capacities for speech are temporarily or permanently impaired due to a trauma, it is especially vital to provide them with other ways to communicate. It does not require any special training or skill—you don't need to be an art therapist to offer an aphasic patient a pencil after he or she has had a stroke. Nor do you need to be an art therapist to give crayons to a person with Alzheimer's disease.

People with Eating Disorders and Substance Abuse Problems

Patients suffering from eating disorders are obsessed with a distorted body image, which can be represented concretely in a drawing, a painting, or a sculpture. Being able to externalize such imagery is, in itself, helpful. It is rare that an anorexic, for example, is able to see how emaciated she is; but she can sometimes perceive what has happened to her body when she represents it (see Figure 1.5).

In addition, as they frantically pursue an attempt at magical control of

1.5 Distorted Body Image by Anorexic Girl

the body, these patients are usually not in touch with the powerful feelings and fantasies they are working so desperately to master. Because what is repressed can be expressed in images more easily than in words, art is one way to get in touch with the affects and ideas behind their symptoms. Moreover, using art materials can satisfy the intense need of such patients to be in control. The availability of media can also be experienced as a kind of feeding, with the therapist as provider of something taken in and then used by the patient for him- or herself.

Those who suffer from the equally oral and addictive problem of substance abuse also respond positively to the use of art as part of their therapy. There are probably good developmental reasons that people with such disorders, often due to unresolved issues from early periods of life, find nonverbal modes of expression to be so congenial. Since art therapy is very popular with both of these groups, it is worth adding art to your treatment of such patients.

Victims of Abuse

Whether the abuse happened in childhood or adulthood, it is often repressed and unavailable to both patient and therapist. Even if they might remember, victims have usually been threatened with reprisal if they tell anyone what happened. The traumatic events may be totally unconscious, or they may have been suppressed out of fear.

With repressed memories of physical, psychological, or sexual abuse, the image can be a gateway to what was largely a nonverbal event, especially when it occurred before the person had language. Psychiatrist Mardi Horowitz (1983) found that the common posttraumatic stress symptom of flashbacks could sometimes be alleviated by drawing the *unbidden images* and then discussing the drawings.

You can also suggest drawing significant places, people, or events related to the trauma, as a way of helping people reach beyond repression for what they want to remember. Although some therapists fear opening up such tender subjects, it turns out that survivors often welcome the opportunity, because they are able to process and come to terms with such events only by reexperiencing them. Art offers a safe and concrete way to begin the reexposure necessary for ultimate healing from Posttraumatic Stress Disorder (PTSD; Steele, 2003).

People with Dissociative Identity Disorder
(Multiple Personality Disorder)

If you read the story of *Sybil* (Schreiber, 1974), you may recall the drawings made by her "alters" of different ages and personalities, each with his or her own artistic style. Christine Sizemore, the woman whose story was told in the film *The Three Faces of Eve*, also found painting to be very helpful in the work of integrating her subpersonalities (Sizemore, 1977). In Chapters 11 and 14 you will find descriptions of therapy with Elaine, whose art helped her to express, and then to work through, the traumas that had fragmented her personality into many alters—each formed at a different age in response to a traumatic event that was, by definition, too much for her ego to handle.

People with Medical Problems

Patients' drawings can sometimes provide a useful window on the mind for those involved in their treatment. For example, the structural (formal) aspects of drawings can help identify the extent and nature of organic impairment. Judy Wald (1989, 2003), who worked with people suffering from Alzheimer's disease, observed that their progressive cognitive deterioration (DVD 1.16) was often hidden by their ability to mask symptoms with well-learned compensatory behaviors, but was painfully visible in their drawings (1.16A), especially when viewed over time (1.16B).

Drawings can also help others to understand patients' feelings about their illnesses and the treatments they are undergoing. A child psychiatrist, for example, asked a boy with juvenile diabetes to make a picture about his disease. By making the drawing and then describing it to the doctor, Eddie was able to say much more than he could have using words alone (DVD 1.17).

A pediatric neurologist invited children to represent their migraine headaches in pencil drawings. He eventually offered them colored pencils and markers, recognizing the expressive value of color. What is most promising is that these drawings helped his colleagues in the differential diagnosis of migraine, which is hard to determine in these youthful sufferers (Carl Stafstrom, personal communication, May 15, 2002; cf. also DVD 8.1).

A speech therapist invited stutterers to draw pictures of their feelings before, during, and after a stuttering episode (Bar & Jakab, 1969). As with showing what it's like to wheeze (Gabriels, 1988), or drawing one's asthma as a creature (as proposed by art therapist Robin Gabriels; DVD 1.18), making such pictures evokes ideas and feelings that the patients could probably not have verbalized. In both instances, repeating the task at intervals allows the treatment team to monitor the progress of patients' abilities to cope with their disorders.

The new field of alternative or integrative medicine is discovering that the shamans who made fetishes and created sand paintings to heal the sick were onto something significant. From the early work of physicians like Carl Simonton (1978) and Bernie Siegel (1986) with cancer patients, to the studies of Jeanne Achterberg (1985), to the present developments in psychoneuroimmunology, there has been considerable support for the possibility that both mental imagery and drawing directed toward the disease and the healing process can affect the immune system (Malchiodi, 2003a & b).

People Who Are Bereaved

You might not have thought of using art with patients who are dealing with unresolved grieving, but if you consider how often images are part of normal mourning, it makes sense. A Toronto psychologist, working with a group of children who had lost family members, asked each child to make a picture of the person who had died (DVD 1.19)—a powerfully evocative task (1.19A). As with most uses of art in therapy, she then invited them to share their pictures with the group (1.19B). She also asked them to draw "the weather inside" (1.19C) and to talk about it (1.19D).

Young children often turn to art spontaneously (DVD 1.20A), as do some adults. Adults who have lost people can also be helped by such art tasks, especially in a group of other mourners. Memorials are found in all cultures. Thus it is not surprising that creating something concrete would be helpful, like the clay head of my father made by my nonartist mother the summer after his death (1.20B), or the totem carved out of a tree trunk by a rural man (1.20C) after the death of his young wife (see Figure 1.6).

In a New Jersey town that had lost many people to the terrorist attacks of September 11, 2001, an artist invited survivors to participate in a sculpture in memory of the victims (DVD 1.21), which he called *The Memoria Project*. The mother of one young man expressed how good it was to be "finally doing something."

Another local artist made portraits of those who had died (DVD 1.22), using photographs supplied by their families. It is noteworthy that, even though the color photos were accurate visual records of their loved ones, there was something uniquely valuable for survivors in the colored-pencil drawings.

The Purpose of This Book

Although I know of no data on the frequency with which non-art therapists invite art work, I suspect that many of you have done so in the past, perhaps while in training, and that you may still do so, either routinely or occasionally.

1.6 *Memorial by Bereaved Husband*

If you have never explored having patients create images, the purpose of this book is to persuade you to give it a try. And if you already do so, the aim of this book is to help you to invite art-making even more comfortably and effectively.

Almost everyone who treats children uses art, though unfortunately, not always with ease or effectiveness. Without guidance, it is all too easy to buy inadequate materials, or to feel stuck over what to do or say once something has been made with them. Even though children are usually willing to create, they are often quite disinterested in talking about their art.

I have known many therapists who have attempted to solicit art from adolescents and adults with little or no success. I have also known many who, though they persuaded their patients to create, were then uncertain about how to help them learn more from the experience. While it can be extremely fruitful, interviewing patients about their creations in a productive way is not easy.

This book is not neutral. In fact, it is rather evangelical. To the uninitiated, the message is: "Try it, you'll like it. The water's fine, and you can walk in slowly or dive in, whatever suits you best." To those who already have art materials and are using them, the message is: "Don't be afraid to explore the use of art in your work even more fully." To both groups, it is: "You don't have to be an art therapist to add art materials and activities to your clinical work."

The questions of *where*, *when*, and *with whom* are, however, not the core of this book, which focuses on *why* and *how* you should include art in your work. In the next chapter, I will note some of the many reasons for adding art to your clinical armamentarium; and in the subsequent chapters, I will focus on how to do so effectively.

Notes

1. Friedl Dicker, in addition to being an artist and teacher at the Bauhaus, was also the mentor of Edith Kramer, one of the pioneers of art therapy, who escaped from the Nazis at the very last minute. Dicker was not so fortunate; she died in Auschwitz.

2. Art therapist Susan Orr gave this title to a videotape she made some years ago about her work with a girl who had been sexually abused. She also uses it as the name for her practice (personal communication, June 9, 2000).

CHAPTER

2

Why Add Art?

One cannot use a left hemispheric key to open a right hemispheric lock.
—LEY (1979, pp. 950–951)

We experience it [a dream] predominantly in visual images; feelings may be present too, and thoughts interwoven in it as well; the other senses may also experience something, but nonetheless it is predominantly a question of images.

Part of the difficulty of giving an account of dreams is due to our having to translate these images into words. "I could draw it," a dreamer often says to us, "but I don't know how to say it."
—FREUD (1916–1917, p. 90)

At this point you may be thinking that art activities might indeed be possible, probably interesting, perhaps enjoyable, and potentially relevant to your work. But with therapy time so limited, and the cost so high, why add art? If you see adolescents or adults, you are more likely to question the value of introducing art activities. Even if you treat children, you are probably comfortable with the games, toys, and drawing materials you already offer, and may well wonder why you should consider introducing the inevitable mess and possible mayhem of chalk, paint, or clay. After all, art materials cost money, art activities use space, and making art takes up valuable treatment time.

Although the growth of art therapy in the last half century is indirect evidence of its value, there are also good reasons that it has developed as rapidly as it has, not only in the United States, but around the world. They explain the expansion of the discipline itself and argue for its inclusion in the work of other therapists. While I cannot cover all of them, I shall note those that seem most important, in order to answer the question of why you should consider adding art. In the film *Art Therapy Has Many Faces* (Rubin, 2004), the most relevant section for this chapter is the one entitled "Why Art Therapy Has Grown So Fast."

Art Is a Natural Way to Communicate

Anthropologists, who have demonstrated that chimps can learn sign language, have also introduced many of our animal cousins to art-making (DVD 2.1) with surprising success (Morris, 1962). Perhaps even more remarkable than their ability to learn how to draw or paint is that they can become deeply engaged in the process (2.1A), like June in Chapter 1, or Sophie, another artistic gorilla, shown in Figure 2.1. Equally impressive, however, are the individual styles that are visible among chimpanzees, elephants, dolphins, and other mammals (2.1B) who have learned how to make art (2.1C). The artwork of different animals is easily identifiable, just as with humans (2.1D).

2.1 Sophie Doing a Drawing

Moreover, children all over the world, in both primitive and sophisticated societies, take naturally to making marks and shapes (DVD 2.2), first in sand (2.2A), and later (2.2B) with art materials (2.2C). Long before human beings developed alphabets, written communications were in pictorial form, such as pictograms and hieroglyphics. Since these forms of expression are as much a part of our biological heritage as making the sounds that eventually become language, it seems only logical to make them available in a process that involves knowing and accepting the whole self.

Making Art Relieves Tension

If you are someone who doodles, you know how relaxing it can be. Just playing with a marker on a sheet of paper, or fooling around with a piece of plasticine clay, can help reduce tension and anxiety in a patient of any age. For some, playful activities with art materials also loosen the tongue. It is remarkable how much more freely certain inhibited patients can express themselves in words when they are also working with art media. I have also observed that stutterers are sometimes more fluent while painting, drawing, or squeezing clay.

Thus, encouraging most patients to play with art media, even if their products are not immediately revealing, almost always relaxes them. To be able to reduce tension, without using more potentially threatening techniques like relaxation or hypnosis, is extremely valuable. After all, the more comfortable people are, the more easily they can communicate with you in words, the usual coin of psychotherapy.

Parenthetically, not only do such playful art activities enable verbalization for many, but the creations made while fooling around with markers or clay often reveal ideas and feelings of which the person is unaware. Indeed, you may not have thought of doodles as containing important messages, but if you take a closer look, you will find that they often do. As Ernst Kris observed, "The ideas hidden in 'doodles' are often ideas of which the ego wants to liberate itself" (1952, p. 307). There is less inhibition about what is being expressed, precisely because the context is a casual one.

Much of Our Thinking Is Visual

Studies of thought processes long ago revealed that visual thinking makes up a substantial part of our mental life. Paying close attention to internal images can therefore provide relevant clinical information, one that is often neglected. Thinking in images is also a way to conceptualize working in art. When a person makes a drawing, he or she is engaged in what

22

psychologist Rudolf Arnheim (1969) called "visual thinking." Creating art is a way of externalizing ideas so that they can be viewed, and can then stimulate new thoughts and feelings.

Just as the act of making a work of art is another kind of thinking, so the act of creating and then looking at the product is, as art therapist Pat Allen (1995) said, *Another Way of Knowing.* Psychiatrist Irene Jakab expressed a similar idea when she said that art psychotherapy gives clients the opportunity "to listen with their eyes" (personal communication, September 20, 2004).

A Picture Is Worth a Thousand Words

Just as a chart or graph enables us to grasp trends and relationships more clearly than we can through words alone, so a picture or sculpture can do the same. You may even have given patients visual feedback yourself at times, drawing a sketch or a diagram to convey an idea that was difficult for them to get in words, but easier to grasp—to "see"—in an image (Gladding & Newsome, 2003).

Or you may have had a patient bring you an image that was not literally representational, but that symbolically captured the essence of something he or she was trying to convey. A woman who had come for treatment following a traumatic hospitalization gradually began to value psychotherapy, something she would not have undertaken had it not been a condition for discharge. Although she preferred not to use art materials, she responded well to being asked if there was a mental image that went with something she was talking about.

One day she brought in a greeting card with the picture of a small creature dangling from the end of the sharp-toothed mouth of an alligator (Figure 2.2). She said it epitomized her relationship with a sadistically controlling man, in which she felt trapped, though she wanted to extricate herself. Although she had talked at length about the involvement and her feeling of helplessness, the vividness of the image conveyed the essence of her dilemma in a way that was extremely helpful to our work.

The Magic Power of the Image

We do not know why the artists of Lascaux and Altamira crawled into tight spaces hidden deep in caves to work on their paintings by the light of oil lamps (DVD 2.3). We can only imagine that the making of such images helped them to feel more powerful in the face of overwhelming natural forces over which they had no control. We can also assume that when hu-

2.2 Patient's Image of a Relationship

man beings carved fertility figures or fetishes, when they painted protective symbols on mummy cases or made sacred icons, they were calling on what art historian and psychoanalyst Ernst Kris called the "magic power of the image" (1952, p. 200).

The magical thinking behind faith healing, sand painting (Reichard, 1977), and voodoo effigies is not exclusive to primitive cultures. It is present in us all, not only in children, but in that part of the adult mind not accessible to rational thought. I believe that it is the source of the placebo effect, and the success of many kinds of mind-body approaches to healing.

Some Things Are Easier to "Say" in Art

To put it simply, there are many things people can say in art that they can't put into words, no matter how articulate they are. These include images from dreams, which do not translate well, as well as feelings or thoughts that are ineffable—beyond words—one of the reasons for the very existence of the arts.

Overwhelming Affects

One day, Mrs. Lord, a normally articulate young woman, entered her session saying she had almost not come in that day, because she was too distraught to speak. I asked if she could draw what she was feeling, and she quickly agreed. Using thick poster chalks on black paper, she energetically made first one, then another picture (DVD 2.4). Later, she was able to give them titles: "Shock" (2.4A) for the first and "Confusion" (2.4B) for the second.

Only then was she able to talk about her distress, as expressed in her art. Discharging the affect in the physical activity of drawing had helped her to master her anguish, relieving some of the pain she was feeling. In addition, even though the pictures were abstract, their intense colors and expressive designs gave form to emotions that had been flooding her in an inchoate, disorganized fashion.

Preverbal and Forbidden Memories

Art is especially helpful in expressing *preverbal memories*—events that occurred before the patient had language, and that are encoded in the body as well as in images. A woman who had been abused recalled another part of the narrative of a trauma that had occurred when she was 2 years old. When art therapist Linda Gantt asked her to draw it, the patient said that she didn't know what to draw, and Gantt replied gently, "Well, just let your hand remember" (see DVD 8.6B).

Although events like sexual or physical abuse may have occurred after a child had language, he or she was forbidden to disclose them. But, as Cohen and Cox (1995) have shown, art is a perfect way of "telling without talking." This makes drawing a critical modality for those who have buried incidents out of fear, whether the memories are suppressed (hidden but accessible) or repressed (unconscious).

Mardi Horowitz (1983), a psychoanalyst and psychiatrist who did considerable research on image formation, used both art and mental imagery in therapy with people suffering from PTSD. He hypothesized that there are good neurological reasons that people can gain access to otherwise unavailable material by visual means.

Psychiatrist Louis Tinnin (1990, 1994), medical director of the Trauma Recovery Institute, has also proposed physiological explanations for the effectiveness of art in therapy with survivors, citing the fundamental biological processes involved in nonverbal communication, mimicry, and the placebo effect. This may be why drawing about their traumatic internment during WWII was helpful to some Japanese Americans (DVD 2.5).

The Dark Side

One of the reasons art is so helpful is that some materials, like finger paint and clay, permit making and then destroying an image. It is possible to be safely aggressive with other art materials as well, as when the artist creates an angry or ugly image of someone he or she is mad at (see Figure 2.3). While they are sometimes explicit, expressions of darker human impulses are often initially disguised.

The dark side is more easily expressed in art, precisely because the aesthetic and psychic distance provided by the symbol allows people say things long before they are ready to own them. Even when such "bad" thoughts and impulses are conscious, it takes a long time for most people to put them into words, because they are so deeply ashamed.

Since art is essentially value free, people can begin to express those disowned aspects of the self—what Jungians call the *shadow*. It is naturally difficult to represent what has been rejected; but if the unacceptable thoughts, feelings, and impulses can be seen and accepted, the individual is then free to use his or her energy for more constructive goals.

This was true for a woman in her late 30s who, despite four substantial periods of psychotherapy, feared that she was incurable. She was resistant to using art, but agreed to doodle, since she often did so. She was so self-conscious that I offered to leave the room. When she looked at her drawing

2.3 Angry Picture of Mother

26

(DVD 2.6) and was asked whether it reminded her of anything, she replied with shock that it looked like an evil "witch" (2.6A).

She then confessed that she was sure that she was really bad at the core, and that this frightening image, which she entitled "It's My Fault," reflected that ugly truth. During the following years of therapy, there were many references to the witch inside, whose appearance had been vivid, and who eventually was replaced by a more balanced sense of herself as both good and bad (see also DVD 2.6B, C, and D).

Complex Feelings and Situations

It is possible to represent—in a single picture space—complex relationships that are virtually impossible to put into words (DVD 2.7). This is one reason drawings or sculptures of the family are helpful (2.7A), as they are so different from verbal descriptions (2.7B). In art, you can also represent different times and places in the same pictorial space (DVD 2.8). These can be *simultaneous*, as in a "life space" (2.8A) picture (Rubin, 1974), which is very different from talking about what's going on at that moment in time.

The events, places, and people may also be *sequential*, as in a "life line" (see DVD 7.7A), a topic for which many art therapists have suggested variations (Landgarten, 1981; Martin, 1997; Rhyne, 1995; Rubin, 1974). Drawing a pictorial representation of a life is not the same as giving a verbal history; and looking at a lifetime on one piece of paper is a far different experience from thinking back over what has been verbally recalled.

In a similar fashion, a single work of art can express and synthesize apparently incompatible affective states, such as love and hate (Figure 2.4). Ambivalence about loved ones is such a deeply troubling source of mental anguish that it is most helpful to be able to look at it pictorially, to see both the good and the bad in a single image that can be taken in as a whole (cf. Figure 2.3; see also DVD 2.9B, C, D, and E).

In Art, Everyone Can Talk at Once

Although several people cannot talk simultaneously and still hear each other, different individuals can all work on their art at the same time (DVD 2.8). Art therapy is therefore especially valuable for groups, especially those that already exist—whether in a home (a couple or family), an institution (a group), or a community (gang members). People can work independently (2.8A) or jointly (2.8B), making the use of art efficient as well as powerful.

2.4 Self as Both Good and Evil

When they are creating individual images, participants can express themselves privately and therefore less self-consciously. In addition, while they are working with art materials, conversation typically becomes more natural and spontaneous, giving you a more accurate sense of how members interact with others (see DVD 10.8D).

Some Things Are Easier to "See" in Art

Patients who have excellent verbal defenses do not necessarily have similarly effective mechanisms for screening out unwanted ideas and feelings in their art. This was true for an articulate mother who saw, for the first time, how she dominated other family members only after a nonverbal, joint drawing exercise (DVD 2.9A).

Although the others had been trying to give her the message for months, she had been unable to hear what they were saying. But when her hand was visible in everyone else's space in a nonverbal family drawing, she could finally see what they had been trying to tell her. The joint picture was displayed at their request during weekly sessions for at least a month, a vivid and powerful point of reference, allowing them to finally deal with issues of power and control in the family (cf. Chapter 10, p. 161).

In other words, by adding art, you are enhancing the possibility that patients can express ideas (2.9B) and feelings (2.9C) that they may not be able to say in words (2.9D), or that they can see by looking at images better than by talking (2.9E).

Art Tends to Accelerate Therapy

Despite the time involved in the creative process, art often reduces the amount of time required to get to important issues. I once had an experience that provided a natural experimental situation in which this hypothesis could be put to the test. It happened early in my career, before I knew anything about conducting psychotherapy and could only offer patients the opportunity to work with art materials and to reflect on what they had created.

Doctor Mann, a child psychiatrist, had been seeing a depressed mother and her equally sad daughter for individual psychotherapy and play therapy for a year, but with little progress. The mother seemed to be stuck, due to intellectualization and denial of affect, and the child seemed unable to move forward by herself. He therefore decided to refer each of them for adjunctive art therapy. Since we were at the same outpatient clinic, we could work in tandem, exchanging patients after 45 minutes.

Afterwards, Dr. Mann and I met for a half hour, during which time we shared what had transpired. Early in our collaborative process, which lasted for 8 months, Dr. Mann called the artwork a "preview of coming attractions." And indeed, it was. Ideas and feelings that were first expressed symbolically in the patients' art and associations to it would usually not surface in verbal or play therapy until weeks, sometimes months, had elapsed. Most important, their therapy, once stalled, started to move ahead.

Even when the clinician is working alone, the art is usually the first place that previously unconscious material is expressed, and it is often visually obscure until its representation and meaning become clearer. This first image-step is not simply revealing; it may well provide a necessary basis for the word-step that is eventually taken (cf. Wilson, 1999). Freud once defined thought as "trial action." It may well be that expressing forbidden ideas in art is a similar kind of rehearsal for consciously knowing and exploring them in words.

Whatever the explanation for this phenomenon, it is probable that it accounts for some of the effectiveness of including art in therapy, as well as for its ability to speed up the treatment process. Unfortunately, it is difficult to prove that art accelerates treatment, because it is so hard to quantify all of the variables involved in any psychotherapy, or to hold them constant for any kind of reliable research study. Nevertheless, such an impression is often expressed by art therapists and non-art therapists alike.

Art Can Overcome Treatment Impasses

Some of the adults I saw in private practice were reluctant to use art. However, if we both felt that treatment was stalled, the patient would usually agree to experiment with materials. We were often rewarded with unexpected breakthroughs, usually in areas that had been stubbornly resistant. After the session described in the following section, this woman's therapy resumed its previous momentum.

Hannah Reveals Her Secrets

Hannah, a woman in her early 60s, had asked for a double session (90 minutes) because it had taken her so long to open up in her first experience of psychotherapy. Though deeply ashamed and hesitant, after several months she finally risked disclosing that she had been sexually assaulted as a child, and that her rejecting mother had refused to listen when she tried to tell her about it.

Hannah then decided to take another risk—of using art materials—though she was very afraid of what might come out (DVD 2.10). Using clay, she modeled a powerful head of a dog. As she looked at the finished sculpture (2.10A), she said that it looked "very sad," and that maybe it had something to do with the sadness inside of her, the depth of which she had only begun to know.

Having enjoyed using the clay, Hannah then wanted to draw. Developing a drawing from a scribble, however, turned out to be a more frightening experience. In the picture that emerged (2.10B), her inner chaos, confusion, and rage—which were clothed so well by her socially appropriate behavior—were made visible. She didn't like the oral-aggressive head, which she saw as a "monster."

I privately thought to myself about how "hungry" she was, not for the extra time she had requested, but for what it probably stood for—nurturance and maternal "supplies." While shocked by her inner hunger and anger, Hannah was also relieved to be able to see them and to begin to explore them with someone else. The visual message conveyed by both art expressions enabled her to gradually give up the rigid defenses that had greatly constricted her emotional range, allowing her therapy and her life to move forward once again.

Art Reduces Self-Consciousness

Whatever people are saying in their art, it is less direct and therefore more private than expressing something in words. And because art allows for symbolic disguise, some messages can be hidden without the person realizing their meaning until he or she is ready to do so, and is therefore less self-conscious about what has been "said" (DVD 2.11).

Moreover, when the creative process is finished, there is now another object in the room: patient(s), therapist, and product(s). In individual therapy, for example, looking at a picture together (2.11A) is radically different from looking at each other. This phenomenon can make doing psychotherapy considerably less difficult, especially with people who have trouble maintaining eye contact or talking about themselves.

Similarly, discussing a picture is different from discussing personal matters, even when there is some awareness of the connection. When participants in group or family therapy look at their artwork together (2.11B), the presence of the products is helpful in much the same way (2.11C). Whether they have worked independently or jointly, their discussion of the art produced is typically more comfortable than talking directly about themselves, each other, or their interpersonal interactions (see Figure 2.5).

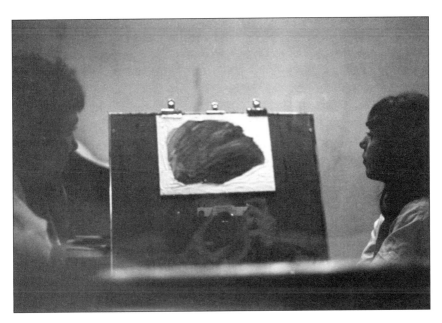

2.5 Art Therapy Reduces Self-Consciousness

Art Is Concrete and Lasting

Unlike words, glances, or body movements, art expression is concrete and physical. This gives it a very special and valuable role in any therapy, whether individual, couple, family, or group (DVD 2.13). Because of its otherness, it can be looked at and referred to, literally and in memory, from one week to another—indeed, over the entire course of treatment (2.13A). The value of art products in reviewing what happened in the course of a session (2.13B), during a past session (2.13C), and over a period of time (2.13D), becomes eminently clear once you've used them in that way.

Art's concreteness is also helpful during interruptions in therapy. Patients often find that continuing to doodle in the pad they usually use in your office is a comforting way to maintain the connection. Sometimes taking a cherished picture home allows them to provide themselves with a transitional object, a concrete and powerful way of coping with the separation.

Art Enhances Integration

There is evidence that creative processes involve the use of both cerebral hemispheres, and that in fact, they require communication between them. This may turn out to be one of the most persuasive arguments for incorporating art into your work: that it may actually facilitate neurological integration.

Although our understanding of the brain is still in its infancy, it makes sense that it is probably related to psychological integration. Many patients, as well as most artists, report that being deeply involved in a creative process creates an altered state of consciousness and, most often, a sense of well-being that is hard to put into words, but remarkable in its power.

Given recent technological developments that allow researchers to see some of what's happening in the brain through various imaging techniques, it is not unrealistic to expect that some day the biologically based therapeutic effects of art activities will be experimentally confirmed. In fact, according to Cathy Malchiodi (2003a), from her perusal of the literature in both neuroscience and psychoneuroimmunology, that has already begun.

What Next?

The question of *why* you should consider introducing art into your work, however, is not the core of this book, which focuses on *how* to do so. That is because you will be able to make useful judgments about where, when, and with whom to use art only if you have mastered the *how* of doing it. You can't invite anyone to do something unless you are comfortable doing so.

I also believe that my arguments about *why* you should do it, while perhaps intellectually persuasive, will carry weight only when you see for yourself how very useful art can be in helping those you serve. And, in order to do that, you've got to feel comfortable with making art a part of your work.

The following three chapters deal with just that, beginning with what you need to do in order to get started, how to go about inviting patients to create, what you can do while patients are working, and finally, what you can do after the creative process is finished to extend the experience through reflection. The general principles covered in these three chapters can be applied in a variety of situations.

CHAPTER

3

Inviting Art-Making

Getting Started

Before you can use art materials in your practice, you need to obtain them, arrange your space so that people can use them, and—most important—get to know them yourself. In this chapter I shall describe what you ought to keep in mind when you are buying supplies, when you are setting things up, and when you are getting acquainted with art materials. In the film *Art Therapy Has Many Faces* (Rubin, 2004), the most relevant part for this section is the one entitled "Setting the Stage."

You may want to consider asking an art therapist to be your consultant at this stage, though it is not essential. I mention this option mostly because I have enjoyed serving this function for many colleagues in a variety of settings, sometimes individually, sometimes as a group. One advantage is that you not only have someone to help you with the nitty-gritty of getting started, you also have someone to call on at later stages, when you may have questions about the issues that arise as your patients use art materials and create products with them.

Buying Supplies

The Importance of Quality

Early on, I discovered that one reason non-art therapists sometimes have problems getting people to use art supplies is that, through no fault of their own, they've purchased materials that don't work very well. So one of the secrets of success is buying supplies of reasonably good quality. Inexpensive materials more often than not confirm my grandmother's warning that you get what you pay for.

You don't have to buy costly artists' supplies. What you will need are those in the middle range, and you can generally depend on brands that have been supplying educational institutions for many years—Binney & Smith, Prang, Sakura, or Artista, to name a few.

There are several catalog-based companies that offer a good range of art materials (see Table 3.1). Since they market only functional supplies, even their budget-level items are sufficiently sturdy for your purposes. You will probably pay less if you use such catalogs. If you prefer to shop in retail stores, however, stick to well-known brands. Art supply stores tend to stock materials that are of higher quality because of their artist clients, but these are not necessary for your purposes.

The reason that it is essential to offer decent materials is that they work, they are satisfying, and they don't cause the kinds of unnecessary frustrations that poor-quality ones do. What you want to avoid are such things as crayons that are weak in color no matter how hard you press, markers that dry out too soon even though you put the tops on right away, and drawing paper that tears with a minimal amount of pressure.

Materials that don't do what you want them to do quickly lose whatever appeal they might have had. Even if patients continue to use them, they allow much less to be said than materials that can be used effectively.

I have supervised or consulted to many therapists during their training who were eager to use art with their patients. Alas, they would often bring in paintings that looked washed out. I wasn't surprised to learn that they were made with watercolor sets from a drugstore, which simply didn't have enough pigment in the paint to make a mark saturated with the hue. The same was true for inexpensive brushes, crayons, and markers as well.

Typically, when those same trainees borrowed or purchased better materials, they were amazed by patients' increased interest in using them. They were also surprised by how much more people could express in their art when the materials were no longer an obstacle, but instead facilitated the expression of their ideas. The investment, while slightly greater, is well worth it. Happily, good materials last longer than poor ones, so in the long run, they are actually more economical.

I hope I've convinced you of the importance of good-quality materials. If you can imagine having an office in which, because of the acoustics, you could hardly hear each other, that would be analogous to trying to use poor art materials for expression. It just doesn't work well for either patient or therapist. If you happen to have the opportunity to compare inadequate materials with good ones, you will instantly see the difference.

Table 3.1   Basic Art Materials and Supplies

Activity	Supplies
Drawing	Pencils (soft drawing pencils, colored pencils) Crayons (wax and oil-based) Chalk (thin and thick) Markers (thin and thick)
Painting	Watercolors, gouache Tempera (liquid, tempera markers, cakes) Finger paint (need glossy paper) Acrylics (can be used on sturdy paper or cardboard) Brushes, short-handled (small, medium, large; flat, pointed)
Modeling	Plasticine (oil-based clay) Water-based clay (red and gray) Other clays (Sculpey, Model Magic, Fimo, etc.) Dough (best part is mixing) Clay tools (can use pencils and/or craft sticks)
Construction	
Two-dimensional	Collage: papers of all sorts, especially picture magazines
Three-dimensional	Craft sticks, tongue depressors, wood scraps, soldering wire, pipe cleaners, etc.
Miscellaneous	
Surfaces	Cardboard, papers (white, colored construction)
Attachment	Glue sticks, Elmer's, tape, staples, etc.
Tools	Scissors

Sources of art supplies
Dick Blick Art Materials: (800) 447–8192, http://www.dickblick.com
Nasco Arts & Crafts: (800) 558–9595, http://www.nasco.com
Sax Arts & Crafts: (800) 558–6696, http://www.sax.com
Triarco Arts & Crafts: (800) 328–3360, http://www.triarco.com

The Importance of Choice

In my opinion, you will be most likely to succeed in persuading your patients to use art materials if you give them choices, even if they are minimal. It helps people to be able to select things, whether it is the size or color of paper or clay, the type of drawing or painting medium, or the tool to be used.

Choices enable people to create in a way that feels comfortable to them, and are therefore most likely to foster honest self-expression. In addition, having options really does help patients to feel more in charge. It allows them to select materials they find appealing, and to handle the task—whether free or specific—in a way that feels more manageable to them.

Basic Art Materials

In Appendix A you will find detailed information about the different kinds of materials you can obtain, along with where you can purchase them (DVD 3.1). It will amplify and explain the list in Table 3.1, and should be consulted before you actually buy anything. If you have little space or want to begin minimally, you can start with some drawing paper and a few kinds of drawing materials, like oil crayons and markers.

If you see children, it is best to offer a greater variety and to be even more concerned about sturdiness (cf. Chapter 9). Below is a list of recommended supplies for work with adolescents and adults, with optional items in square brackets. As you will see when you read Appendix A, there are other possibilities as well, but this is a good place to start.

Papers
- White drawing paper (loose), 60–80 lb. (by the ream or smaller package)
  1 package each: 9″ × 12″, 12″ × 18″ (individuals and couples)
  [1 package 18″ × 24″ (couples, families, groups)]
- Construction paper, assorted colors
  1 package each: 9″ × 12″, 12″ × 18″
- Pads of white drawing paper, 9″ × 12″ or 11″ × 14″ (individuals)

Drawing materials
- Pencils
  Soft drawing pencils, no. 2 and no. 4 (also Ebony pencils) + good eraser
  Set of colored pencils, 12–24 colors
  [Charcoal pencils or sticks]
- [Pens
  Roller or felt-tip drawing pens (black) in 2 sizes]
- Crayons
  Set of oil crayons, 16–24 colors
- Markers
  1 set each of thin and thick felt-tip watercolor markers, 8–16 colors
- [Pastels
  Set of Alphacolor pastels, 12–24 colors]

Painting media
- Paints
  Set of oval water colors, 16 colors

Set of tempera paints in 2 oz. jars, 8 assorted colors
- Brushes (short handles)
  Set of 3–6 pointed brushes, assorted sizes
  Set of 3 flat brushes, assorted sizes

Modeling materials
- Set of plasticine clay, assorted colors (Modeline, Clayola, etc.)
- [Bag or package of earth clay, brown or gray]
- [Set of assorted clay tools]

Collage materials
- Old picture magazines and postcards
- Glue, tape, and stapler
- Scissors

Setting Things Up

Working Surfaces

Tables are ideal as work surfaces for all art media, but they are more easily available in some work settings than in others (DVD 3.2). As long as a table isn't wobbly, it can be used for creative work (3.2A). Although there is an optimal height for the greatest working comfort, I have been surprised that patients are able to use even coffee tables remarkably well when there is no alternative. If you do not have space for a table, you can use a piece of cardboard or a pad of paper as a work surface for drawing. For messy materials, a plastic tray with raised sides, like those used in cafeterias, is useful (3.2B).

If you see children, families, or groups, you probably already have a table with sufficient workspace. If you are buying one, be sure that the top has a washable surface. If you need to use a table you don't want to stain, simply cover it with a temporary or permanent covering of paper, plastic, or vinyl—any smooth surface that can be cleaned or disposed of.

Easels, like tables, are not essential, but are highly desirable. If you don't have enough space for a floor easel (Figure 3.1; 3.2C) a wall or table easel (Figure 3.2) is another option (3.2D), and can be stored in a closet when not needed. Some therapists also store folding tables for occasional use.

Displaying Art Materials

If you plan to offer only one material, you have no need to worry about displaying media. If, however, you want to offer a choice, you can do it either orally or visually. In general, people have an easier time making a selection when they can see the materials (see Figure 3.3). If you have

3.1 A Standing Easel

enough space, you may want to have the most commonly used art supplies, like papers and drawing materials, visible all the time, to enhance the likelihood that patients will use them spontaneously.

If you store supplies in a closet, you can simply open it, and if you have visible shelf or display space, you can direct people's attention there. In either case, you will want to be sure that the various options are visible, and that their location is known. Whether all or some of your art supplies are visible at any time, it helps to be *consistent* about where they are located, in order to promote the possibility of independent decision-making and autonomous creative functioning (DVD 3.3).

It is also important that the materials be *organized*, so that finding what people are looking for does not interfere unnecessarily with expression. You can use any scheme that makes sense to you, and—as with location— be as consistent as possible.

3.2 A Table Easel

Storing Art Materials

This problem can seem formidable, until you realize that there are numerous ways to solve it. With paper, for example, I found that I used the least amount of space by putting different sizes and types in vertical letter files. Such an arrangement also enables patients to easily select the size, color, and type of paper they want, and it can hold picture magazines as well. If that doesn't work for you, you might want to examine your other storage options, such as closets. Sometimes the easiest thing is to buy or build shelves into all or part of a closet to accommodate art supplies.

Drawing and painting materials can also be placed on bookshelves, or in any of the many kinds of sectioned plastic containers sold in hardware stores—whichever suits your space best. If you need to carry art supplies from one place to another, plastic containers with handles provide light transport.

Storage of plasticine is fairly simple, since the boxes are small and comparable to boxes of drawing materials. If you decide to offer water-based earth clay, all you will need for storage is a plastic garbage can with a secure lid, and twist ties to be sure the plastic bags that hold the clay are sealed.

3.3 A Choice of Paper Colors and Sizes

Cleaning Up

Pastels are powdery and messy, and the very quality that allows colors to be blended—which can be *so* very satisfying—will also cause the chalk to get on people's hands. All types of modeling media will dirty the hands, too, even if tools are used. While most drawing materials and paints don't necessarily get on the hands, they certainly can. Paint will need to be removed not only from hands, but also from brushes after use.

So if you offer art materials, it helps either to have a sink that is accessible, or to put water into a large container. Moist towelettes, like baby wipes, are another option for the waterless office, as is hand sanitizer in a pump dispenser. Paper towels are essential in any case, whether on a roll or in a package.

Learning by Using Art Materials

Perhaps the easiest way to explore media is to take an art class, ideally one in which you can try out a variety of materials. Another alternative is to join with other clinicians and invite an artist, art teacher, or art therapist to offer one or more workshops in the use of simple media, which don't require technical training, and which you can then provide to your patients.

If neither of these is feasible, I suggest that you try out each of the materials you want to make available to your patients. If possible, it's best to conduct this exploration with other people, who can be family, friends, or colleagues. If you approach each medium as if it were a new person you want to get to know, you will find out a lot about the material itself, as well as how it feels to encounter it for the first time.

I also suggest that you do at least two things with each kind of art material you plan to offer to your patients:

1. First, you should *just fool around,* playfully exploring the material's properties, without worrying about making anything in particular.
2. Second, it is useful to try to *represent a theme or idea,* especially one you may want to request from patients (like a self- or family portrait).

Although you can always try things out by yourself, one reason to do your investigating with other people is that you can see what it feels like to be watched while you make something. It's also extremely useful to *interview* each other about what you've created, in order to experience being interviewed. If you'd rather not answer questions, you can simply see what it feels like to tell someone else whatever you want to say about what you've created.

After you have conducted such experiments, on your own or with guidance, you will be better acquainted with the materials you plan to offer others. You will also have a taste of how it feels to work while being observed, how it feels to tell someone about what you've done, and what it's like to be questioned about your creation.

Introducing Art to Patients

How you invite people is absolutely critical to your success in helping them to become engaged in the creative process. If you are truly convinced that using the materials will help you to help them, which is of course the main reason to offer art, you will probably be able to sell them on the idea of giving it a try (DVD 3.4).

If you are also persuaded that they will be able to use the materials—which you will be if you've had a successful experience yourself—your optimistic expectations will have a significant and positive impact on their willingness to explore art-making, especially if there are choices (3.4A).

Indeed, if you are comfortable with sharing the fact that you are not an artist, and have explored making art yourself before asking them to do so, that will go a long way toward encouraging their participation. If you have tried doing with materials whatever you are asking of your patients, this will also help you to be more sensitive to any frustrations they may experience. In the film *Art Therapy Has Many Faces* (Rubin, 2004), the most relevant part for this section is the one entitled "Inviting Expression."

Making a Good Case for Art

You can probably bypass this step with children, most of whom who are likely to want to draw, paint, or model simply because these are familiar and appealing activities (3.4B). Although young children are generally uninhibited about using art materials, by the time most people reach their teens, they have had more uncomfortable experiences than pleasant ones with art (3.4C).

It makes sense, therefore, that they deserve a persuasive reason for using it in their therapy. How you make the case for doing so depends partly on your rationale. Regardless of when in the process you invite a patient to use art materials, it helps to have some clear ideas of how and why doing what you're suggesting will help you to help that individual.

Although there is no single, generic rationale applicable to all situations, the reasons noted in the last chapter may be helpful in your "sales pitch"—and of course, you may think of others as well. Most important, be clear about why you want your clients to use art, and then tell them honestly and directly, in language they can understand (3.4D).

For example, if you're asking an adolescent to draw or model her family, you might note that it's a way for you to get to know some of the people in her life better, which will then help you to help her. Since most teens want you to see things from their perspective, asking her to show you her viewpoint is usually appealing.

Similarly, if you're asking an adult to draw a dream he has just described, you can explain that it is yet another way to learn what the dream might be expressing, especially because it *is* largely a visual experience. Whatever topic you ask someone to draw, you can make the point that representing something is very different from talking about it. You can also add that together you will be able to learn a great deal from looking at and discussing what they have created.

Even if you are simply inviting an inhibited patient to doodle on paper or squeeze some plasticine, you can explain that this mundane activity may well lead the two of you in surprisingly productive therapeutic directions. If you add that people think visually as well as verbally, and that pictures give us clues to things we may not be able to put into words, it makes exploring their own imagery like solving a puzzle, an intriguing adventure.

You may also want to remind them that art really is another language, but one they're already familiar with, from dreaming and imagining. Finally, since exploring ideas and feelings in images may even help you to bring them the relief they seek more rapidly; this argument might be the most powerful of the lot.

Reducing Anxiety

Rather than try to sidestep patients' self-consciousness, it is best to acknowledge openly that what you're asking them to do might feel really awkward. It is especially useful to ask what worries or discomforts they're aware of. Most people will tell you that they "can't draw [or paint or model]," and that they feel inadequate.

It's important to stress that using creative materials in therapy has nothing to do with being artistic. What is true is that, regardless of whether they enjoy art, it is simply another way of trying to understand the issues that brought them to treatment.

In addition to feeling uncomfortable, most people also fear being exposed and not knowing what they have revealed. They assume that you can read things in their art of which they are unaware. Happily, art therapists are in substantial agreement that the patient, not the therapist, is the ultimate expert about the meaning of his or her art.

Of course, visual creations may contain messages that are not yet conscious to the artist. For art therapists, however, the meaning of anyone's sign or symbol can be known only through the patient's own ideas and associations. In fact, discovering meaning is not some mysterious, secret reading of the patient's art by the therapist, but is rather a collaborative effort involving both people. Knowing this can make using art materials much less threatening.

It generally works best to ask simply that people try it, with the understanding that after doing so a few times they may decide not to continue, or they may find that creating something can be both fascinating and fun. If they really hate using art materials, it is best not to pressure them, but to leave it open as an option for the future.

For that reason, it's always best to begin with a relatively nonthreatening kind of activity, like playing or fooling around with a piece of colored plasticine selected from an assortment of colors. Wetting a paper and using watercolor or tempera on it, making dots and lines in a playful way, is also an easy way to begin the process of creating.

Another simple way to start out is to use some sort of *visual starter*, like a dot, a line, a blot, or a squiggle, from which to develop an image. Choosing a picture from a magazine, cutting or tearing it out, pasting it on a piece of construction paper, and writing a title or phrase to describe it is another easy way to begin.

Some people get stuck when invited to use whatever they wish and to make whatever they want. If so, you can assist them by asking whether they want to draw, paint, or model. Once the category is chosen, you can give them more specific options; for example, if they say they want to draw, you can ask if they want to use pencils, markers, crayons, or pastels.

If they are having trouble deciding what to make and ask for a topic, you can suggest that they fool around with the material and see if that gives them any ideas. If they want to draw but are stuck, you can suggest that they develop a picture from a scribble (cf. DVD 7.3E). But whatever you do, you'll want to encourage people to let you know whatever they find diffi-cult or anxiety provoking, both during and after the process.

Any discussion of their products also needs to be as nonthreatening as possible at this early stage. It should be brief, relying mostly on whatever people choose to tell you about what they have made. This is not the time for a lot of questioning, as your goal in the beginning is to help them get used to working with art materials as part of therapy. For them to want to do more, the earliest experiences should be as pleasureable and unthreat-ening as possible.

Deciding What to Do

Clarifying Your Goals
Diagnostic

In order to decide what to do, which media to offer, and how, you need to first clarify your goals. Many times your goal is primarily diagnostic. If it is, for example, to assess someone's perception of his or her family, request-ing a family drawing would clearly be in order. On the other hand, you may want to find out how a person sees him- or herself, in which case a self-portrait makes sense.

If you want to ascertain a patient's ability to function independently, then a free-choice procedure works best. On the other hand, if your goal is to explore a person's response to regression, you might ask him or her to try finger paints. Or, to clarify the interaction between family members, a proj-ect that requires them to work together will give you the most information.

Therapeutic

On the other hand, your goal might be primarily therapeutic, such as helping a constricted individual to become freer. In that case, activities like developing an image from a scribble, or closing his or her eyes and report-ing whatever imagery arises might work.

If you want someone to feel less inadequate, to increase his or her self-esteem you would look for an activity with a high potential for success. Examples would be modeling designs with Fimo clay, making a collage using magazine photos, or creating a torn tissue-paper collage with thinned white glue and brush on white drawing paper.

Or, if your goal is to help someone release aggressive impulses, activities that invite pounding, such as hammering nails, punching clay, or using tempera markers to make dots, might be useful. On the other hand, if your goal is to help a couple to become aware of their interaction patterns, a nonverbal dyadic drawing might be best.

As with interviewing someone about his or her art, which is discussed more fully in Chapter 4, trial and error is generally the best way to proceed. In other words, if the first method you try to meet a goal doesn't work, try another. Of course, you do this all the time in verbal therapy, as well, trying different interventions to accomplish your ends, until you feel something has worked.

The Elements Available in Art

In deciding what to ask people to do, the prime consideration is always the goal or purpose you want to achieve. To meet such goals, you have three main elements at your disposal, which can have varying degrees of structure or specificity: the medium, the theme, and the manner of working.

The Medium

The first is the medium offered, which can be an open choice from among two or more alternatives (e.g., drawing or painting), the specified use of a class of media (e.g., drawing materials), or a request to use a specific material (e.g., pastels).

Art media, as you will discover when you try them yourself, differ along a number of relevant dimensions, including how controllable they are, how messy they are, how fluid they are, and other factors relevant to therapy. These considerations influence what works best for which task (cf. Lusebrink, 1990).

For example, if you want to assess the degree of elaboration in someone's drawing, media like drawing pens, colored pencils, or fine felt-tip markers will allow the person to represent details. On the other hand, if you want someone to cover a large area rapidly, a medium like thick poster chalks or broad felt-tip markers would work best.

The Theme

The second element is the theme, which can be open-ended, such as "Do what you want," or more or less specific, as in "Draw a feeling" or "Represent anger." This is the area where your verbal therapy experience is highly relevant, since you will have a sense, not only of what you want people to deal with, but also of how well they are able to do so at any point in time.

For that reason, it is important to be creative, but also careful, about how direct are the themes you request from particular clients at any moment. When in doubt, it is best to stay at a more symbolic level. This is fairly easy to do in art, which allows for a substantial degree of disguise. For example, if your goal is to help someone to become aware of anger at his or her mother, a request to draw a witch might be more fruitful than asking for a picture of the parent herself.

The Manner

The third element you have at your disposal in deciding what to do is the manner in which the task is to be accomplished. It can relate to the interaction, as in "Choose a partner and draw each other"; the time, as in "Do a one-minute gesture drawing"; or the method, as in "Model a piece of clay with your eyes closed." If you have one or more goals clearly in mind, it can be fun to try to think of activities with art media that will help you accomplish them.

As in verbal therapy, there will also be times when a patient presents you with an opening that you will want to take advantage of. You can't really plan in advance for such opportunities. But the more you use art materials with clients, the easier it will be to think of ways to make the most of those unpredictable moments, when people are more open to change. An example would be asking someone who has just drawn a picture to enlarge a portion of it, so that he or she can focus on a particular element.

Making Sure They Understand the Task

Even though you may think there is no ambiguity in what you have asked your patients to do, please don't assume that they have understood you without checking it out. No matter what you've requested, even if you have demonstrated it yourself, it is wise to ask whether there are any questions before they get started. Because they may not be able to easily see the choices that are available (of materials or paper sizes, for example), you might need to show—as well as to state—what the options are. In fact, it is generally best to do both: to point to the materials as you say what they are, so that whatever confusion or anxiety may be present, your patients have been informed as well as possible.

As for the task itself, even something as simple as a free choice can trigger enough anxiety that the person isn't sure whether they are supposed to select from among the drawing materials available, or to choose whether to draw, paint, or sculpt. Similarly, a theme like "a family," because it is emotionally loaded, can stimulate many questions.

Be prepared for these, so that you know how you will answer if the client asks, for example, "Do you want me to draw *my* family?" or "Do I have to include myself?" and so on. When it comes to tasks that require people to interact with others, it is especially important to ask for any questions they may have, and to do so in a way that genuinely invites inquiry.

What about Resistant Patients?

Even with your very best efforts to make the introduction of expressive media nonthreatening, you will certainly run into some individuals who flatly refuse. One possibility is to suggest that they try it just once, before completely rejecting the idea. However, if they are still firm, there are a number of other options.

First, you can ask if they mind if *you* use art materials, even though they have said no to doing it themselves. Generally, people are willing to allow you to do so, as long as you remain attentive to what they're telling you. If you are casual and playful, patients may be stimulated by your activity to start using media themselves.

Another alternative is to ask people to respond to something, such as a photograph or an art reproduction. Asking for reactions rather than creations can be a more comfortable way to ease reluctant patients into the visual arts. Similarly, starting with mental imagery is less threatening for most people than using art media, another backup possibility for those who are intransigent.

Yet another possibility is to ask whether they would be more comfortable using art materials in private, without you watching them. Some will agree to do so if you leave the room, and this can occasionally work as a first step. Others may be willing to make drawings or paintings if they can do so at home. They can then bring their artwork into the session and you can look at it together, as you would if it had been produced in your presence. In fact, some patients respond more positively to doing homework in art, as described in Chapter 13.

In other words, even if someone rejects your first invitation to use art materials, don't give up. You can try a less threatening place on the road to creation. Of course, there will be patients who will never agree under any conditions, since the fear of exposure, or the pain of anticipated shame, is just too inhibiting. Some will try once or a few times, and then say they've had enough. But it's certainly worth a try.

If art is offered as an option rather than an imperative, you will lose very little; and whatever happens, it's grist for the therapy mill. For those who resist creating with media, despite your efforts to help them explore their anxieties, you may find that some of the alternatives help them to take the plunge and to experiment.

Most of the ideas offered here to help patients overcome resistance assume that the underlying cause for their reluctance to use art materials is anxiety. But, you may ask, what about people who don't seem at all anxious, but who are oppositional, either passively or actively so? You may decide to explore the negativity and what it might mean, which sometimes works. Or you may try a less direct route.

I remember a stubborn adolescent boy who rejected art, but who manipulated a flexible tubular piece of metal sculpture I had on the coffee table that could be pushed and prodded to make different shapes. After he had become somewhat more comfortable with psychotherapy, I asked him what the different shapes he was making reminded him of. This he liked and enjoyed doing, while I found the sequence of his projected images useful in understanding him.

Eventually, he decided to write poetry, stimulated by some of the "wacky" ideas he had thought of about his shapes. He had found an art form that he liked better, and in which he felt more in charge, especially since he could work on his poems at home before bringing them in to read aloud to me. Although he never did decide to draw or paint, he enjoyed telling me what sort of illustrations might go with the poems he had written.

At one point he started to bring in pictures from magazines to illustrate his poetry. He was then willing to try, "just once," to make a collage using such magazine pictures. He brought the pictures in from home, but put them on colored paper and used other art materials in my office. He rather liked what he had made, and took it home to put up in his room. From that time on, I made sure that materials for collage were easily available, and he would decide whether he wanted to make one, either using the magazines in my office or pictures he had brought in.

As you can see, being patient and flexible about alternative roads to expression may lead to success. A postscript: The young man went off to college in another city, and asked for a referral to a male therapist, whom he liked. He wanted to stay in touch, however, so periodically I would receive a poem in the mail, sometimes with a letter about what was going on in his life.

What Next?

The following chapter discusses how you might behave during the art-making process. As with inviting people to create, what you do and don't do while people are working has a considerable impact on how useful it will be to include art. As you will see, it is not so difficult, since what matters most is to respond and to observe. In Chapter 5, I will focus on what you can do to facilitate reflection after the creative process is finished, describing what you might do to learn from what has occurred and the products that have been made.

Chapters 6–10 will deal in more detail—first, with the use of art in assessment; and then, in the course of the therapeutic process, with the specifics of art therapy with adults, children, families, and groups. Chapter 11 considers other art forms, such as drama, photography, and creative writing; Chapter 12 covers another area related to art—mental imagery. In Chapter 13 I describe some ways of prescribing the arts for patients to do on their own, both as homework and as therapeutic activities.

Chapter 14 offers a brief introduction to the field of art therapy, as well as a variety of ways in which you can make use of the expertise of art therapists. This includes working together, which is another way to make this book more useful to you: by learning from sharing experiences and skills.

4

During the Process

While People Work

Although you will be speaking while introducing materials or answering patients' questions about the task, once people have started working the most important thing you can do is to observe (see Figure 4.1). Naturally, if they talk spontaneously while they work, you will need to respond—but it is probably best to do so in a nondirective way, which encourages them to pursue whatever they have initiated.

If they don't talk while they work, even though there are just two of you in the room, your best bet is to be quiet. Since you are used to interacting with words, being silent for long periods of time might seem really strange, especially at first. You may feel as if you're not doing your job. However, as you will find, people's behavior with art materials is full of rich, and often subtle, observational opportunities.

The more you learn to look, the more you will see, and the more active and interesting the observational process will become. As this occurs, you will be gathering important data about patients, some of which is difficult or impossible to obtain in strictly verbal interviews. You can learn an amazing amount by simply watching how and what people create—and the more you observe people while they are making art, the easier it will become (cf. Irwin & Rubin, 1976).

Looking: How to Observe

Although many things about human beings are evident in their verbal behavior, how they respond to the invitation to use art materials often

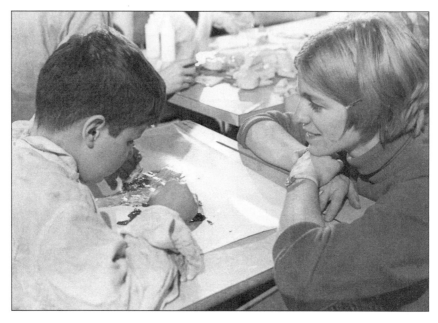

4.1 Observing Carefully

yields additional clues (DVD 4.1). Some are found in their decision-making processes, some in their interactions with you around the tasks, others in the nature of their creative behaviors, and yet others in their activities with the materials themselves (Figure 4.2).

From the first, there are useful clues, many of them nonverbal, when visual expression is added to the therapeutic mix. If someone is talking while they're working with materials, for example, there is always a relationship between what they're saying and what they're doing, even though it may not be immediately apparent (4.1A).

Taking Notes

Even though you may not do so routinely, it is a good idea to make written notes of what you're observing, paying special attention to the aspects of both process and products discussed in this chapter (4.1B). The note taking need not be elaborate, but unless you have an exceptional visual memory, you will find that recalling things like sequences within a drawing, or the temporal connection between artistic behaviors and facial expressions, is not easy.

If you don't usually take written notes during a session, one way to explain the need to do so is that it will help you remember the details of the artistic process. If you do it casually, as if you take it for granted that pa-

4.2 Observing Siblings' Drawings

tients will accept it, they are more likely to do so. If people are uneasy about your taking notes, you can also offer to let them look at your pad if they wish, which helps to allay anxiety about what you might be writing down.

Decision Making

If, as I have advised, you allow for some choice, how patients decide what to use and what to make can yield a veritable gold mine of information. If they are looking at or talking about media they might use, what is rejected is as important as what is chosen.

An individual's degree of hesitancy or decisiveness is usually evident, as is his or her way of coping with indecision. There might be an obsessive-compulsive sort of ritual, or its opposite: impulsivity. Whether the decision is about which shade of clay to use, what color marker to select, or where on the paper space to begin, patients' behavior in response to both free and specific tasks is inevitably illuminating.

Interaction with You

After you tell patients what you'd like them to do in art, you will quickly find out how cooperative or resistant they are, as well as how eager or hesitant they are to engage with materials. Whether they are fearful or trusting of you is also evident in their response to your invitation, as well as to your explanation of why it will help. In addition, in the course of the decision-making and doing processes of working with art materials, whatever the task, you will get a sense of how dependent or autonomous people are.

Seven-year-old Jim, for example, moved his chair closer and closer to me during the joint making of a city of wood blocks in which he had insisted I participate. Although he began by suggesting that we make separate buildings (Figure 4.3a), he eventually placed them together (Figure 4.3b). Making sure that his buildings were touching those already glued down by his partner, his wish for closeness and unmet dependency needs were even more apparent in his manner than in what he made or the story he told.

Reaction to Materials and Task

Here, too, there is both verbal and nonverbal information to guide you in understanding the people you see. Art materials themselves can elicit all kinds of emotional reactions, from pleasure to disgust, from happy anticipation to fear and discomfort. Many of these responses will be nonverbal, expressed in facial reactions and body movements, such as approach/avoidance behavior.

Similarly, whatever the task, whether free or specific, there will be reactions on many levels. If people are anxious, they may have difficulty understanding what you've asked them to do, even if you have tried hard to be clear. As noted in the previous chapter, it is important to invite any questions they may have about the task, and to do so in such a way that they feel comfortable asking them.

If you have asked them to choose and to do what they want, they may be pleased, or they may wish that you had given them more direction. Conversely, if you've specified a topic, they may wish they had more freedom. Of course, they may not verbalize such responses, but these are sometimes suggested in nonverbal behavior, like body movements or facial expressions.

Creativity

This area is one you have probably had less opportunity to find out about in verbal therapy, at least in the beginning. It is evident, however, from the first in how people work in art. You can observe, for example, whether they turn to stereotypes or are instead more original and imaginative. You can also see how fluent they are in their thinking, especially if you ask for associations, like inviting them to tell you all the images they can find in a scribble.

In addition, you will be able to assess how rigid or flexible they are in their approach to the task, as well as how compulsive or free they are in how

4.3a Two Buildings Separated

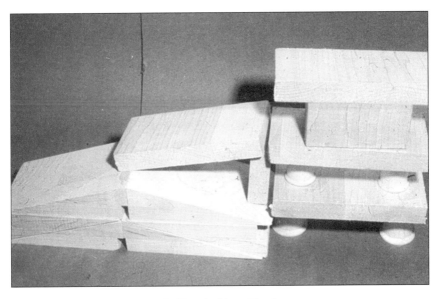

4.3b Two Buildings Touching

and what they create, regardless of the medium. Watching the process allows you to get a better sense of how constricted or open people might be as they work, which is not necessarily reflected in the end product. Many of these attributes of creativity, such as individuals' degrees of flexibility, have a direct bearing on their capacity to make changes in psychotherapy.

Activity

While people work with art materials, you can learn a great deal by watching what happens in their faces, their hands, and their bodies. For example, you can see whether they are more tense or more relaxed, as well as whether they are awkward or coordinated. You will also be able to tell whether they tend to be more deliberate or more impulsive in how they use the art materials.

You will certainly be able to observe whether they are able to focus and to become involved in creating, or whether they are more or less distractible. You will see how organized or disorganized their working processes are—a dimension that may be visible in the finished product, but not necessarily so. It is actually possible for the end product to look one way, when the process has been otherwise.

While people are using art materials, there may also be verbal and nonverbal indices of how they feel about what they are making, whether they seem to be generally pleased or rather critical. For the sake of clarity, I have described all of these dimensions as if they were polarities. However, in truth, they actually exist on a continuum, rather than being either one or the other.

Body Language

Although all art-making involves the body as well as the mind—another good reason for including art in your work—there is a great deal of variation, depending on the person, the medium, and the mood. You observe nonverbal communication during verbal therapy as well; but you have a great many more opportunities while people use art media.

In addition to noticing body orientation and tone, you will also begin to observe other behaviors, such as the amount of pressure being used with different drawing and painting materials, the tempo of the working pace, or the nature of the energy being expended. The evolution of motor behavior in the course of the session is especially revealing. Does there seem to be an increasing tightening or a gradual relaxation from the beginning to end of the hour?

Changes in the Art during the Process

There are other things you are probably not accustomed to observing, some of which are visible only during the process of making art, and rarely if at all in the end product. This is true of the sequence in which parts or items are done, as well as changes made in the course of creating (DVD 4.2).

Sequences

The order in which parts or sections of a drawing are made is especially telling. For example, if a person draws a human figure from the head down, that is different from starting with the trunk or the feet, and adding the head at the end. The former is the usual method, while the latter raises the possibility of a cognitive disorder, though it does not confirm its existence (4.2C).

On a more psychodynamic note, if someone draws a cage *before* making a wild animal inside it, that is different from doing the enclosure *after* the animal. Although the need to contain the wild animal is evident in both cases, the cage-first artist may be more fearful of things getting out of control than the one who can wait to create the cage later. Of course, such a hypothesis would need to be confirmed through other associations and behaviors.

When a person represents any group, such as the family, the order in which members are depicted is likely to be one index of their relative importance; relative size is usually another. If you are seeing the whole family and are unable to observe each person's sequence individually, you can ask individuals to write a number under each person in their picture, indicating who was drawn first, second, and so on. It is important to make the request only after the person is finished, so that self-consciousness doesn't influence the order of representation.

In addition, if more than one piece of artwork is created during a single therapy session, that sequence itself is a kind of narrative. As with the order in which a patient brings up different topics in verbal therapy, the series of artistic statements is not accidental, but instead carries meaning. And, even though you may think you will remember later, it is wise to note the date, as well as each item's place in the sequence, on the back of a paper or bottom of a sculpture. That information will facilitate your ability to review the sequence at the time, and especially at a later date.

Modifications

When someone erases repeatedly, or needs to start over, such behaviors generally reflect anxiety of some sort. Even when erasures, covering over, or redoing are moderate, it is useful to note which parts of a picture or sculpture are involved, on the assumption that they carry more emotional loading than the rest.

The artist will usually rationalize any atypical creative behavior, attributing it to the difficulty of representing a particular part or object. Nevertheless, while it may indeed be true that hands are hard to draw, the erasure of the hands is still meaningful and should be noted. Parenthetically, so is their omission or exaggeration.

Some materials, like tempera paint and oil crayons, allow the artist to literally cover over something that has been represented. Noting the sequence of what is created, therefore, gives additional information that is not always visible in the final product.

Other media, like finger paint and clay (4.2A), permit making something, erasing it, and making something else, a drama that can go on for a long time, with multiple images (4.2B). Here are three examples of how dynamic and useful observing the steps in such a process can be.

Rose: A Story in Finger Paint

A picture of "Taco, the Horse" (Figure 4.4) was only the last word in a long sentence of images and associations by 5-year-old Rose. She began by angrily banging the powder paint container, saying, "I'll show this bottle who's the boss!" Although she said she hated getting her fingers messy and really hated finger paint, she looked longingly at the moist finger-paint jars while mixing powder paint and water with a large brush. Brushing on the paint, Rose continued to express concern about cleanliness:

4.4 "Taco the Horse" by Rose (Finger Painting)

"I'll clean up every mess I make, after each little mess, not one big mess. No wonder I never get stuff cleaned up at school. All the kids mess around and piss!"

She then went and got the creamy finger paint and glossy paper, vigorously smearing huge gobs of paint on the surface, expressing her ambivalence with a combination of grins and verbal ejaculations of words like "Yuck!" and "Ick!"

Rose's series of images began with a scribble, which was followed by a bell. She then drew a heart, which was reworked several times. Next were squiggle lines called "Snakes Tangling Up," then two squiggles with faces meeting in the center, called "Two Snakes Kissing. Every day they're tangling up!"

After that, Rose tried to draw a boy into the paint, with much reworking and dissatisfaction: "I'm not an expert on this. Ooh! That's a bad boy!" He was quickly erased, and was followed by an attempt to "just make a snake," during which Rose became concerned: "I gotta find the end. He can't got a tail! It looks more like a horse."

This same animal was finally developed into "Taco," who was later described, in an interview about the picture, as "a boy horse who is goin' to eat grass. His mom is callin' him for supper right now, but he's not comin' to eat. If he's hungry, why doesn't he come to eat? His father is gonna spank him if he doesn't come. His mother will spank him too. He's not allowed to eat any more grass. He didn't hold his temper, 'cause he hit the baby horsie! He told his mom and his mom spanked him. The others are telling his mom too, 'cause he hit his baby!"

Rose's behavior with the materials, as well as her series of images and associations, provided a wealth of information, including her attraction to and intense anxiety about the messy finger paint; her anger with the materials; her kissing dyad; her difficulty drawing the boy and the snake's tail; and her image of a boy horse—without a tail—who is hungry but doesn't want his mother's food and who is bad for wanting other food, as well as for hitting his baby.

Together these suggested Rose's feelings of being excluded from the parental couple, as well from the mother-baby dyad. Her rage and hunger were both seen as bad, as was her wish to be messy like the baby. It will probably come as no surprise to discover that she was the eldest of two, and that her younger sibling was a newborn baby brother.

Ellen: A Drama in Clay

Ellen, a shy 8-year-old, placed a piece of red clay onto an electric potter's wheel, which could be made to turn by pressing a foot-pedal (Figure 4.5).

Putting her hands on either side of the clay, she called it "a little lump." She then pushed her right index finger into the center, saying she was making "a little hole." Ellen pressed the top down, trying to flatten the clay. Then she squeezed it a little and announced, "I'm makin' a barrel, one of those wooden barrels." With a grin, she commented, "This is a smooth feel, it feels so good. This one's gonna be for my mom. This'll be of beer. She loves beer!"

She then added a piece of clay, covering a hole in the side, and called it "a patch for any holes." Ellen commented that the clay felt like "mud," and said it was getting "tall." She proceeded to put one, then two, then four fingers in the center, making a larger hole, and commenting that "I made it pretty deep!" She announced, "This isn't gonna be a barrel, now it's a vase." At this point a piece of the clay broke off, and Ellen said she wanted to "start all over again. This clay stinks! It smells awful!"

Having expressed her frustration over being unable to control the clay on the wheel, Ellen announced, "I'm just gonna let it do what it wants to do. If it goes to the side, it goes to the side." As the clay started to form an amorphous shape under her hands, she said with some tension, "It looks

4.5 A Child Using an Electric Potter's Wheel

like a ghost. I don't like ghosts. I'm not gonna make it into a ghost. I was gonna make a bell. I dunno. You'll see." She then commented that the shape under her hands didn't look like a bell, but more like "a hump."

Grinning as she put more pressure on the foot-pedal, which made the wheel turn faster, Ellen said, "This is doin' a hula dance!" I asked whether it was a boy or a girl, and she said she wasn't sure, as the shape became more phallic inside her hands. Then she giggled and said "Someone's takin' a bath! This is weird! I'm gonna make it smooth!"

I commented that the clay was getting taller and taller and Ellen said, "I want it shorter and shorter." She then poured water on it and put her finger in, so that she made spiral shapes on the wheel, protesting as if she'd been chastised, "It's not babyish!"

At that point she wondered if the time was up, and when told there was more, decided to stop using the wheel and paint the vase she had made the preceding week. She spent the next few minutes doing so rather compulsively, despite a few drips along the way.

There seems to have been a shift at the moment when the clay broke off and Ellen noticed the "awful smell." It was then that she decided to "let it do what it wants to do," simultaneously denying responsibility for what might emerge, and permitting herself more leeway. It was at this point that the imagery become unbidden, first scary (the ghost), then exciting (the hula dancer, taking a bath).

Shortly after that, there was what Erik Erikson (1950) would call a "play disruption." The ideas stirred up by the series of images were probably threatening, so she abruptly stopped using the wheel and proceeded to decorate something already completed, the vase.

Knowing that her mother was an alcoholic, I heard the wish to provide beer in a barrel for her as stemming from Ellen's longing for her mother's approval. She was the least liked of the four children, the odd one in her mom's eyes, the one she just couldn't relate to. Ellen couldn't acknowledge her anger at that point, nor her fear of her mother's loss of impulse control when drunk. Like the images Ellen projected onto the clay on the potter's wheel, mother's alcoholic behavior was both exciting and frightening—for when she was drunk, she was more loving toward Ellen, yet more volatile as well.

Mrs. Lord: A Narrative in Acrylic

When the time came to say goodbye to me and Dr. Mann, her male psychiatrist, who was leaving the city, Mrs. Lord, the depressed young mother you read about in Chapter 2, denied anger or fear. Her artwork and associations to it, however, spoke otherwise (DVD 4.3).

In her penultimate art therapy session, she chose to use acrylic paints, putting them directly onto a small (9″ × 12″) canvas with a palette knife (4.3A). As she spoke of her current concerns, including sadness about termination, Mrs. Lord made a series of separate green and yellow oval shapes.

Regressing to the dependent behavior of her early sessions, she asked whether it would be "all right to mix the colors together." Reminded that she could do whatever she wished, Mrs. Lord mixed them slowly, then rapidly, smearing almost the whole surface, creating a large mass of thick, yellow-green paint. She finished by painting a solid white border surrounding the mass, effectively containing it (4.3B).

As was characteristic by then, Mrs. Lord was sure she was finished, and placed the painting on the easel (4.3C) where we both regarded it (Chapter 2, Figure 2.5). Her first thought was of the ocean, and her spontaneous title for the painting was "Sea Mist" (4.3D).

Surprised by her association, she went on to say that she didn't like the sea, that she was afraid to go in the water, and afraid of the fish, a fear she couldn't seem to conquer. "Whenever anything brushes my leg, I really, you know, go crazy! Jellyfish, shark—what is it?" Laughing nervously, she described her fear of horses, and of being bitten by a dog, recalling that she'd grown up "in a neighborhood with a lot of vicious dogs," and commenting that so many of her problems went back to her childhood.

She returned to her fear of swimming in the sea, and being bitten by a shark. When asked how she felt about the picture, she called it "a big round blob" and said—as she often did in regard to her artwork—"I don't know how it got like that. I didn't intend for it to be like that."

She thought of how her daughter Lori was sensitive and fearful, as she'd been the previous night when she'd had an image of a man crawling up a ladder to her room or her mom's. Mrs. Lord said that although she tries to protect Lori, the child tends to ruminate about her fears, something she does too. She went on, saying "I try to push it out of my mind, like I do anything that I'm afraid of."

I then wondered whether all this imagery about fear of attack (sharks, dogs, male intruders) was in any way related to the impending termination and her anxiety about being more vulnerable, less protected. Mrs. Lord agreed that, although she tended to deny anxiety, it was heightened in anticipation of the separation from her two therapists.

What was intriguing in regard to sequence within the process was the nonverbal drama: first creating a series of separate oval shapes, then energetically smearing them together, and finally containing the mass with white.

My hunch at the time was that she was expressing the anger she didn't want to feel, as well as denying the separateness implicit in the impending termination. Of course, this was my association, not hers. For that reason, as well as because this was a delicate time in a difficult termination process, I did not share these thoughts with her.

Projection Works Both Ways

This is a reminder of something you will need to remember about the projective aspects of artwork. You, as well as the patient, will inevitably have ideas about the meaning of thematic and formal elements in the person's creative products. While it is true that your associations are more likely to be relevant the better you know the person and his or her issues, it is still vital not to get your own projections mixed up with theirs, and essential not to impose your ideas.

Listening: How to Attend

Active listening, like active observing, is a skill that improves with practice, primarily because it is continually rewarded by what you learn (DVD 4.4). If patients speak spontaneously while they work, they may talk about the process or the product, or they may discuss something else, like what they dreamed last night, or their worries about a colleague (4.4A).

As with observing, your best bet is always to let them lead the way, rather than imposing your own agenda. In part, this is because they will be more comfortable. But it is also because what they say is revealing about whatever they are creating while they say it, even if it seems at first to be completely unrelated (4.4B).

This fascinating phenomenon is really quite similar to many other kinds of associated behaviors you are used to observing. You watch facial expressions and body movements while people are talking, noting that a person moves closer when saying one thing, or flinches when saying another.

What is being said while people are creating art offers a similar kind of opportunity. For example, if a boy pounds the clay hard while talking about how much he loves his baby sister, you can hypothesize that his feelings toward her are more complex, and that he's not so comfortable with the angry ones.

To Talk or Not to Talk?

Once patients have begun using art materials, it is best to let them do what is most comfortable. That means that if they want to work quietly, it is wise not to intrude. On the other hand, if they want to talk while they work, with you or with each other, that's fine, too (4.4C). What matters is to respect their spontaneous response to using art materials, and to react sensitively as well as supportively (4.4D).

Although I know of no studies of this phenomenon, after more than 40 years of doing art therapy, it is clear to me that some people can operate on more than one expressive channel with comfort, even facilitating one or both, while others cannot. It appears that this is not something people can modify, which makes me hypothesize that it is based on innate differences in neurological "wiring."

If you interrupt a single-channel artist with questions, they will stop creating in order to answer, or will continue working as if they didn't hear you. Conversely, doodling or fooling around with clay seems to dramatically loosen the tongues of others. Paradoxically, therefore, using art materials may facilitate or inhibit spontaneous verbalization during the creative process.

In any case, it is best to adopt an interested, unintrusive stance. If people talk spontaneously about what they're making while creating, it is again best to let them lead the way. This is because any question or statement on your part is likely to be heard as a value judgment. What you say can also affect the end product, so that it's not the same as what the person might have created without your commentary. While this is certainly no crime, it prevents both of you from seeing the most honest and authentic kind of artistic expression.

To Do or Not to Do?

There are, of course, facilitating interventions that can be vital to the success of inviting people to create. You need not worry that including art activities requires you to be a passive, echolalic robot. Far from it.

In fact, you have to be more physically active in order to help people get started using materials. You may also need to be active to facilitate their creative work by helping them find scissors, tape, glue, or whatever they may need at the time.

I have simply emphasized some of the riches that can be gleaned from quietly but actively listening and watching, observing the subtle and evanescent details of the working process. Even if there's a great deal of talk while people create, it's still important to try to observe things like sequences, erasures, and other data that cannot be seen in the finished product. Similarly, it would be virtually impossible to remember which statements occurred during which part of the creative process, if you did not note such connections at the time.

In general, if people can work comfortably, it is best not to use materials yourself, for several reasons. First, you can observe and listen better if you are unencumbered by your own art activity. Second, what you do and how you do it is likely to have an impact on patients, and may even modify what they do in some fashion, whether it's to imitate or to differentiate from what you're doing.

On the other hand, there are times when your own use of materials can help reduce patient anxiety, allowing them to create more freely (DVD 4.5). This may be true for some individuals (4.5A), families (4.5B), and groups (4.5C). If you do use art materials, however, it's best to stay at a very simple level, such as doodling or fooling around. Modeling the use of materials in this way can be helpful, especially at first. Indeed, it may be essential for those with cognitive impairments.

Another occasion for you to use materials is when you want to stimulate others to do so without directly requesting it. In the after-school workshop groups that I led at the Child Study Center, I became aware of what I termed the "Pied Piper effect." There was always a variety of activities available, including games; but whenever I would start to work with a new art material or process, the youngsters, in spite of their other options, would gradually begin to try it as well. This kind of modeling can be helpful with those who are inhibited about using messy materials, for example, but for whom you think it would be useful to try a medium like finger paint or clay.

Conclusion

What you do while someone is working with materials is really not so different from what you do while someone is speaking. Just as you wouldn't interrupt a patient in the middle of a sentence, so it would be intrusive to interrupt a person who is quietly working on a creative product, especially if he or she seems to be genuinely absorbed in the process. If the person initiates verbal interaction while he or she works, however, that is a completely different situation.

On the other hand, you may need to intervene verbally for any number of reasons (DVD 4.6). If you are under time pressure to gather information, for example, you might ask whether you can interview them while they work, and if they agree, you can then see how feasible it is to do so (4.6A).

Another reason you might need to interrupt artists is to let them know that they need to finish what they're working on, so that you'll have time to talk about the experience while it's still fresh. There is enough individual variation on this score that you may be able to let a person go on working while you inquire about such phenomena as what it felt like to use the medium, to do the task (4.6B), or to come to a clinic (4.6C).

As for questions about the product itself, however, it is usually best to discuss these when the artist and you can both sit back, relax, and focus on the looking and reflecting part of the process, which is the subject of the next chapter.

CHAPTER

5

After the Process

Doing and Reflecting

Although there is much that is healing about the creative process alone, doing art as part of psychotherapy always involves some kind of reflecting as well (DVD 5.1), which is an important way of extending and expanding its therapeutic potential (Figure 5.1). In the film *Art Therapy Has Many Faces* (Rubin, 2004), the section on "Facilitating Reflection" is most relevant for this chapter.

Nonverbal Reflections

The reflecting can be nonverbal, like moving or dancing in response to the artwork. If actually moving is an uncomfortable idea for you or your patients, however, you can easily ask what sort of music or movement might go with what they have created.

The reflecting can also be in the form of another image. You can suggest that they look at what they have made intently, trying not to think in words, and then create another image that seems to follow the first. Another kind of request is to make another image, not so much to *follow* what is being viewed, but rather in *response* to it—a subtle but meaningful distinction.

Verbal Reflections
A Title
Perhaps the simplest kind of verbal association, which is also easy to request, is to ask patients to give their artwork a title (5.1A). If they seem to

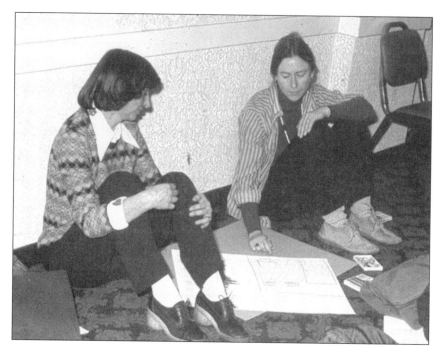

5.1 Two Women Reflect on Their Joint Drawing

be blocked in doing so, you can suggest that they look at what they have made and then write down whatever pops into their minds. It is important to stress that they need not be concerned about whether the title makes sense.

Writing

For many patients, especially in groups, writing down their thoughts and associations privately is another way to extend the creative process (5.1C). You can suggest a specific kind of writing, like a poem or a story; or you can request something more spontaneous, like whatever comes to mind. In a group, it may help to ask that people be quiet, so that everyone can concentrate on what they want to write about whatever they have created.

Interviewing

Indeed, the communicative mode you are most familiar with in therapy will probably be the most useful in helping you and your patients learn from their artwork, including figuring out what it "means." In many ways, whatever they have created can, like a dream or fantasy, easily become a spring-board for thoughts and associations. These are sometimes written, more often spoken (Figure 5.2).

What Was It Like?

It is always a good idea to begin by wondering—if they haven't already told you spontaneously—what it was like to be invited to use the materials and to do what you requested. You might also ask how they were feeling, as well as what they were thinking while they were creating. In addition to general queries, you may want to inquire about how it felt to be watched while they worked, or what it was like to use a particular medium.

It is especially important to invite patients to give you feedback about any possible negative aspects of the experience, like feeling exposed or inadequate. Not only can you be empathic, you can also let them know that it's perfectly normal to feel that way.

Framing

In order for the artist to be able to focus on the product without distraction, it may help to add a simple frame for two-dimensional work, or a base

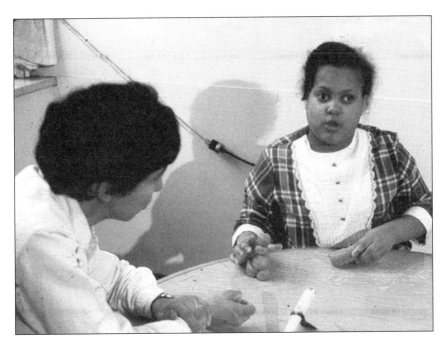

5.2 A Blind Girl Talks about Her Clay Horsie

for three-dimensional work. Construction paper is excellent for this purpose, especially when you invite patients to select the color (5.1B).

For drawings or paintings, you can put rolls of masking tape on the back of the picture and then attach it to a piece of colored construction paper of the next larger size; this becomes the frame. Even a temporary framing of this sort helps patients to focus on the image, because the boundary lessens the visual noise and distraction of everything else around it.

Similarly, if a person has made something three-dimensional, it helps to put it on some sort of attractive base. A piece of construction paper larger than the bottom of the sculpture works well, as does allowing the patient to select the color. In addition, a frame or base usually makes products look more attractive.

Looking Intently

Although it may seem obvious, this step is often neglected, despite the fact that it greatly enhances the process of reflecting on artwork. Looking without talking, even for a brief amount of time, promotes a kind of taking in which, because it is relatively rare, may be all the more useful.

Putting creations in a place where both (or all) of you can easily see them greatly facilitates joint viewing. Where you do it depends on the particular space. You can use an easel, a piece of cardboard, a table, or any other surface on which you can place artwork. Bulletin boards, doors, walls, and floors are also useful (Figure 5.3), and are even better for simultaneously viewing more than one product.

What Do You See?

Once you have placed the art where it is visible to everyone, you can begin the looking process. It is best to start by simply looking, without focusing on any specific aspect of the artwork or making any particular judgments. After a period of open-eyed looking, patients sometimes speak spontaneously.

If not, you can ask them to tell you what they see (5.1D). Then you simply follow their lead, and explore together, going wherever their thoughts take you. This approach to looking was articulated in detail by Mala Betensky, a phenomenological art therapist, in a book (1995) and in a chapter in *Approaches to Art Therapy* (Rubin, 2001a).

Open-Ended Questions

Many patients, when asked to tell you what they see, will respond concretely or minimally. For this reason, the next step is to ask open-ended questions, which invite people to respond in an unthreatening way with-

5.3 Group Members Discuss Drawings

out influencing what they say. Being open-ended in queries about art is not as easy as you may think, since you, too, will project your ideas and feelings onto the artwork.

Because of this, you may unwittingly phrase questions in such a way that you subtly suggest the response. Like observing people creating and listening to what they say while they're doing so, interviewing people about their creations gets easier with practice. No matter how much experience you may have, however, helping patients to talk about their art always involves a considerable amount of trial and error.

Although there are some general guidelines, there is no way to know in advance what will work well with any particular person or group. As with any other kind of clinical interviewing, you can be more or less nondirective, depending on your own orientation. What is true for strictly verbal interaction applies equally well to discussing artwork: It is generally best to begin with what is most comfortable for the patient. If you plunge into sensitive areas before people are ready, they will be less willing to express themselves openly, in art as in words. Asking for a description of a picture (5.1E), however, or inviting the patient to tell you about it (5.1F) is a safe way to begin.

Requesting and Extending Associations

You can ask a person of any age general questions, such as the following, that evoke genuinely personal responses, such as:

What *comes to mind* while you look at the (picture, sculpture)?
What are you *thinking about* as you regard your artwork?
Does it *remind* you of (anything, anyone, any place)?

There are many different ways to help people of all ages to project another level of meaning onto what they have created, further amplifying the dialogue. Here are some more questions you may want to ask, depending on the nature of the artwork:

- *Abstractions* (nonrepresentational artwork)
  If these shapes (lines) were people, *who* would they be?
- *Places* (or Spaces) (indoors or outside)
  If you were in the picture, *where* would you be?
- *Creatures* (people or animals)
  If they were to *talk*, what would they *say*?
  If you could read their minds, what would they be *thinking?*
  What might they be *feeling?*

A common way to help people extend their associations to their artwork is to ask them to tell you *what's happening* (5.1E). Depending on the subject matter, they may simply respond by naming objects, like "It's just a house with a tree outside." From there, however, you can ask logical, open-ended questions, such as, Who lives there? Is anyone inside right now? If so, what are they doing? and so on (5.1F).

In addition, patients of any age can be asked to *make up a story* about their artwork. When they are finished, you can ask what might have happened *before*, as well as what might happen *next* (5.1G). Another alternative is to invite them to *show* what would come next (or what happened earlier) with art materials, rather than telling it (cf. DVD 13.3A).

In the course of this kind of open-ended interviewing, in which you help patients to further extend the ideas stimulated by their art, you may well be uncertain about some of their responses. As with verbal interviews, it is reasonable to ask for clarification. It helps to say that the problem is yours (in understanding what they have said) rather than theirs (in expressing their ideas).

Creative Interviewing

There are an infinite number of ways to extend the interview process based on patient artwork, depending on your goals (5.1H). Using a trial-and-error approach can be an enjoyable challenge (5.1I). It allows you not to get too discouraged when you get minimal responses, but rather to explore another avenue (5.1J). It is somewhat like trying to find your way through a maze: when blocked, try another route. As you can see, what I am recommending is very different from following a standardized set of questions, like those in the usual *postdrawing interrogation (PDI)*.

Although the questions recommended for projective drawing tests have been thoughtfully selected, they may stifle the kinds of extended and enriched responses you can get with a more playful and creative approach, which I believe will be more useful to you in the end. Needless to say, if there are some specific questions that are part of a PDI that seem useful to your work in a particular instance, there is nothing to stop you from asking them. I think, however, that it is best to do so *after* you've explored people's associations in a more open and creative way.

What about "Why" Questions?

It is very difficult to resist the temptation to ask patients why they used a particular color or chose a particular subject. After all, why wouldn't such queries be appropriate? In my experience, alas, "why" questions are generally useless, because most people really can't tell you why they did something in art, even though they will occasionally spontaneously offer such ideas. "Why" questions coming from you, unfortunately, are also likely to put the artist on the defensive, so it is best to use alternative modes of inquiry, such as those noted earlier.

"What Does It Mean?"

If a patient asks you what his or her artwork means, you can honestly say that you cannot know by yourself, but that together you may be able to figure it out. If the question persists, then ask what he or she *imagines* you think it means.

In addition, you can ask the artist for his or her own interpretation, which gives you further information about that individual. It is my conviction that, as with all symbols, especially visual ones, there are many layers and levels of meaning in any creative product. What is important is to explore as much as you can, in a way that is comfortable for both you and your patients.

Self-Assessment

Patients will inevitably judge what they have made, and even young children can be quite self-critical. These kinds of evaluative comments usually occur spontaneously, and on rare occasions are positive and proud. More often, they're negative. As you told your patient when you made the request, creating art in therapy is not about making pretty or skillful artwork. Nevertheless, people's feelings about their products are as useful as their associations to them, and give you information about their self-esteem or lack of it, as well as the state of their narcissism.

There are many questions you can ask related to patients' assessments of their artistic products:

How did you *feel about it* while you were making it?
How does it *look to you* now that you're finished?
Which part did you like doing *best? least?*
Now that you look at it, what do you (*like, dislike*) about it?
What is your (*favorite, least favorite*) *part?*
Did it come out the way you had *intended?*
If not, how do you wish it were *different?*

If the answers to these questions are not clear, it's best to ask for clarification, inviting patients to *show* you, rather than guessing and perhaps being wrong about what they actually meant.

If, after looking at his or her artwork, a person wants to add to it, cover something over, or in any way modify what was created so that it's more pleasing to the artist, this can be very helpful. You can ask such questions as these:

If you could *change* it now, what would you do?
How would you make it look more the way you *wish?*
If you could *add* something to it, what and where would it be?
If you could *cover* something up, what would it be?

You may even want to present the possibility of doing so as analogous to making changes in their lives, something they may want to do but are fearful of. In addition to describing possible modifications, like making something darker, adding a color, or extending something, you can try actually covering any part of a picture that they don't like with a blank piece of paper until it looks better to them. In some cases, they can literally cut off the section they don't like.

Dealing with Patient Art

The Art Is the Person

It is vital to remember, as you work with people's ideas and wishes regarding their creative products, that art is really an expression of the self in concrete form. It should therefore be treated with the same degree of sen-

74

sitivity to people's narcissistic vulnerability as you would exercise in regard to their physical appearance.

For this reason, although it is extremely helpful to explore the patients' responses to their artwork, it is rarely a good idea to express your own evaluation, even if it is requested. However, it is a very good idea to reinforce the action of drawing, painting, or sculpting by letting patients know that you're pleased that they have used the art materials. You can applaud their willingness to overcome whatever inhibitions or skepticism they may have had by trying this less-familiar form of expression—and you can be equally positive about their agreeing to talk about their art.

Even if you like the artwork very much and feel like sharing your enthusiasm, you will get more clinical mileage by exploring what the patient imagines, wishes, or fears you think about it than by telling him or her how you actually feel. For one thing, you won't always like what patients produce, and you don't want to be false, which is something most people can sense.

Moreover, since your approval is usually important in people's therapy, you can track their progress best by seeing how their fantasies about your judgment evolve. Of course, there are exceptions. An occasional admiring comment doesn't do major harm, and can be reassuring to a self-conscious or insecure patient. And of course, a smile without a statement is fine.

There is one circumstance under which I do recommend you consider expressing your approval of what someone has made, and that is when he or she wants to destroy it or throw it away. Telling the person that you like it and would like to keep it—with his or her permission, of course—may eventually help them to accept other things about themselves of which they are ashamed. Nevertheless, sometimes a patient is adamant about not wanting a piece of work to be rescued.

When the art seems like an important statement, however, I confess I have occasionally picked something out of the wastebasket after the artist has left, and stored it in a secure location for my own reference and record-keeping.

Receiving Artwork Respectfully
Even when a person has produced simple stick figures or nondescript smears, these should be received with as much interest and respect as a fully elaborated drawing or painting. The verbal analogy would be that we listen to all utterances, including asides, mumbled phrases, and casual comments, with the same interest as we do to more carefully formed statements. All are expressions of the patient, so that our reception of pictures, like words, is a powerful statement of our respect for the person.

Much of this is expressed nonverbally, through your facial expressions, for example, and ways of touching and handling the products. Thus, even when you are just making sure that the artwork can be seen, especially if you are the one moving or mounting it, it is important to do so with care. Similarly, any discussion of products, even if sometimes playful, needs to be carried on in a fundamentally serious tone, which is another way of conveying respect.

Storing Patient Art

Although there will be times when a person insists on taking artwork home, it is best to explain at the outset that you will be keeping the work done in treatment so that you can refer to it later, as needed (DVD 5.2). Individual drawing pads are an easy way to store what has been created. Or, if only small drawing paper (9″ × 12″) is used, a file folder for each person will be sufficient (5.2A).

If you offer larger sizes, you will need to find another way to store artwork. School- and art-supply houses sell cardboard portfolios that can be closed, tied with a string, and stored either upright on the floor or flat on a shelf. The size you buy depends on your largest size of paper.

If you have three-dimensional materials for modeling or construction available, you can put those products on windowsills, tabletops, or shelves (5.2B) in (or out of) closets. Children, adolescents, and some adults may want very much to take certain creations home. In that event, a camera is a handy way of recording what they have made. In addition, constructions of blocks, or compositions in sand, which cannot be preserved, can be photographed for reference and record-keeping (5.2C).

Displaying Patient Art

If you are using visible surfaces to store sculptures, you're also displaying them at the same time. Although I used to worry about the possible negative effects on individuals of seeing other people's artwork, I eventually changed my mind. In fact, art that was visible turned out to be an excellent stimulus, eliciting comments that were extremely useful in the clinical work (DVD 5.3).

I first experimented with a large bulletin board in my office (Figure 5.4) inviting each patient who wished to exhibit to choose one picture for display (5.3A). Most children elected to do so, competitively wanting to show off, while most adults did not. When I ran out of private shelf-space for storing clay, I began using visible places like table surfaces and windowsills (5.3B).

Much to my surprise, there were considerable fringe benefits of displaying art. For one thing, pictures on the wall and sculptures on tables made it easier for people to express curiosity, admiration, envy, and criticism of my other patients, through making comments about their art. There were always some who didn't notice art by others, at least not until they were ready to deal with their own competitive feelings, at which point they discovered what had been there all along.

Perhaps most relevant for this book is that the visibility of the artwork, which ranged greatly in sophistication and quality, seemed to help some of the more reluctant patients to give the creative process a try, even if they chose not to display anything they made.

Naturally, depending on your patients and setting, you may decide that public display is not a good idea, especially if the anticipated problems outweigh the potential benefits. As with which art media to offer or where and when to do so, the question of exhibiting artwork has to be decided in a way which is comfortable for you (5.3C).

In an institution of any kind, the question of whether to display patient art beyond the room in which it was produced is likely to arise. In most hospitals, clinics, schools, and treatment centers, it seems to be a good idea—

5.4 Bulletin Board in My Office

as long as individuals always remain in charge of whether they want to display anything, and if so, what it would be (5.3D).

Public display can be one way to reward those who are proud of their work, further enhancing their self-esteem (DVD 5.4). If individuals want to write something (beyond a title) about what they've made, that also enhances the educational value of the exhibit. Art displays, especially with explanatory notes by you or the artists, are also a vivid way to educate other staff members. Not only does it reinforce the involvement of those served, it has a positive impact on those who visit them (5.4A), as well as brightening the setting itself. Whatever the purpose, displaying art within an institution can be useful, as long as it is optional for individuals.

For people whose self-esteem is low, it can also help to show what they have made in even more public settings. Exhibiting art in banks, libraries, galleries, and other such places is a wonderful way to educate the general public about the creative capacities of people with mental or physical disabilities.

Creative Growth, a program for developmentally disabled adults in Oakland, California, has an art gallery next door (5.4B). It exists primarily to sell the work of its artists, some of whom—like Dwight Mackintosh (5.4C; MacGregor, 1992) and Judith Scott (5.4D; MacGregor, 1999; DVD 5.6)—have become rather famous.

The Living Museum at Creedmoor State Hospital in Queens, New York, often has exhibits for its artists, who come from their homes to work in the studios provided by the hospital (5.4E).

"Outsider Art"

Art by those with various kinds of emotional disorders—in particular, chronic mental illness—has had a powerful appeal for art collectors in recent years, and has become a source of income for a number of artists.

Known as *outsider art*, it is usually created independently by the artist, often at home, though sometimes in an institution, a workshop, or some other sort of outpatient program, like the one run by Hospital Audiences in New York City.

Sometimes outsider art has been the result of an invitation by a teacher or therapist to draw or paint (Cardinal, 1972; Hall & Metcalfe, 1994). Lest you expect to find a budding Leonardo in every sketchbook, however, it is important to know that such discoveries are rare. But they do happen, and not only when working with artists, art teachers, or art therapists. For example, a psychiatrist named Joseph Berke encouraged his patient, Mary Barnes, to paint as part of her therapy during a severe regression. Mary's discovery of painting as therapy (Figure 5.5) led to a career as a painter long

5.5 Mary Barnes Painting

after she had recovered from her psychotic illness (Barnes & Berke, 1971; Barnes & Scott, 1989).

Discovering Art as Therapy

People with a wide variety of problems that bring them to therapy may, if offered art, discover that drawing or painting can be soothing, as well as satisfying. They may even end up pursuing art activities on their own, both during and after treatment. While most rarely go beyond being amateurs, there is no question that discovering an activity that is creative, absorbing, and fulfilling is inherently therapeutic (cf. Chapter 13).

Sharing Patient Art
With Family

In addition to displaying artwork in the office, institution, or community, there are other ways in which sharing people's products can help you to help them. In group or family therapy this happens automatically, and indeed, looking at and responding to other people's work is sometimes even more useful than looking at one's own creations (DVD 5.5).

Even in individual therapy, you can often help a child or one member of a couple by getting his or her permission to show a particularly eloquent piece of artwork to a parent or partner (5.5A). This can be done with the artist present or not, as you and the patient decide.

A drawing of an anorexic girl's self-image (Figure 5.6) for example, was immensely useful to her parents, who until then had been unable to grasp what she was struggling with. A boy's powerful sculptures of angry monsters enabled his parents to understand how much unconscious rage was behind his pervasive and sometimes crippling anxieties (5.5B). And a compulsive child's volcanoes (Figure 5.7) helped his parents to grasp the fears behind his obsessional behaviors. Seeing what he was trying to put a lid on helped them understand just how much pressure he was under.

With Professionals

There may also be times, especially when you are part of a treatment team, when you will want to share a person's creative products and thoughts about them with other professionals (5.5C). As with showing them to parents or spouses, you will need the patient's permission; but you may not be able to invite the artist to be present at, for example, a team meeting or a case conference (5.5D).

In most institutions with a team approach, it makes sense to get individuals' permission to share anything about their treatment (including art) with others at the outset. Because pictures and poems are so very personal and concrete, however, it also makes sense to have patients sign a specific release form regarding their creative products, which can be more or less formal, as you wish (5.5E).

One of the nice things about sharing artistic creations is that they often reveal not only people's conflicts, but also their capacities. Nevertheless, if a patient makes it clear that some particular piece must remain private, you would need to make an equally good case (e.g., danger to self or others) for going against his or her wishes.

It is never a good idea to do so secretly, since other staff members may well let it slip, and the therapeutic alliance you worked so hard to build will be destroyed. Besides, if you really respect the artist's right to be in charge of their work, you won't be tempted to disregard their wishes.

The same principles apply to exhibiting the work in an educational setting, whether it is a class lecture or a conference presentation, even if it is far away from where it was produced. The person's permission is still necessary, whether the drawing is to be shown in the original, in slide form, or as an illustration in an article or a book.

Blanket permissions to share art for educational purposes are generally adequate legally, but if you have any concerns at all about an individual's

5.6 Anorexic Girl's Self-Portrait

possible reaction to your use of any particular product, it is always best to check it out with the person directly. Although you may have to give up on sharing some work you wanted to show, it is more important to respect the individual's right *not* to be seen, as much as his or her right *to* be seen (i.e., shown to others, displayed, etc.).

5.7 Compulsive Boy's Painting of a Volcano

Ownership and Disposition of Patient Art

Many clinicians I have known, including some of my own supervisors from other disciplines, feel that anything the patient makes in the course of therapy, especially in the therapy space, belongs to the therapist or institution as part of the patient record. Art therapists, since we are also artists, are not so comfortable with that idea, and instead generally feel that the creator owns the art. I have already suggested that if someone wants to take a creation home, it can be photocopied or photographed for your records—unless you need to keep it until the next session for some reason, like sharing or scoring it. Of course, you will need to get the artist's permission to do so.

Reviewing drawings that have been made, during the course of therapy as well as at termination, is an excellent way to look back at the process and to evaluate it together. This, in my opinion, is the most compelling argument for keeping people's products in the therapy space.

At the end of treatment, however, it seems only ethical to me to allow patients to take home whatever they wish. If you want to photograph any take-home product for your own records or those of the institution, most patients will agree, as long as they are assured that such records will remain confidential.

Conclusion

Although some might think that the invitation to create and the involvement in a creative process are the most important aspects of using art in therapy, what happens after the doing is over is equally important. Try not to be discouraged if looking at and talking about art is difficult or disappointing at first. Interviewing about artwork takes practice, but as you do it repeatedly, you will find it not only enjoyable, but also extremely enlightening.

CHAPTER

6

Using Art in Assessment

Projective Techniques

Chances are you have not only heard of using images in assessment, but have already done so yourself. Although projective techniques are more of an art than a science, they continue to be used by clinicians, largely because they are quick and richly informative.

My interest in them, and the reason for including them in this book, is that understanding patients is certainly a necessary condition for helping them. I am not as convinced as some are that you can read a great deal from what you find out through visual assessments, even when there are rating scales, reliability studies, and a vast literature of presumed connections between responses and conditions.

I am persuaded, however, that such ways of getting to know people are immensely useful, not only because they are efficient (an excellent reason for using them), but also because I do believe that patients can tell you a great deal about themselves in this way that they may not want or be able to put into words.

So whether you are screening for possible organicity (one of the areas where drawings have been found to contribute useful information) or simply want to get to know someone better, visual images can be extremely helpful. In some approaches, you invite responses to visual stimuli; in others, you ask people to create something.

The assumption in all such techniques is that people reveal important information about themselves about which they are not usually conscious. They cannot tell you because they don't know it, but they can tell you indirectly, through responding to and creating images. Because people project their internal worlds when they interpret or make visual symbols, pictures seen in Rorschach inkblots, stories told about Thematic Apperception Test (TAT) cards, and drawings of the human figure or the family do, in fact, convey potentially useful information.

One good reason for using image- and art-based projectives, regardless of whether they require creating or responding, is that they can be quite enjoyable. This is especially important during the assessment phase, since entering therapy is generally stressful.

Fortunately, the more experience you have with any particular technique, the more useful it will become for you. As you repeatedly collect data in a particular way, your personal frame of reference will grow. No book, course, or manual can match the cumulative experience of hearing numerous Rorschach responses, or of collecting and studying a great many human figure drawings.

Responding to Visual Stimuli

Fortunately, projecting ideas onto images comes as naturally as making marks. The desire to give meaning to ambiguous stimuli is part of being human, whether we are finding pictures in the clouds or trying to figure out what is going on between people. We have a need to make sense of the otherwise confusing stimuli that surround us. For that reason, to be asked what a shape looks like, or what is happening in a picture, is inherently intriguing.

As is true when inviting people to talk about their artwork, it is best to request responses to images in a similarly playful, open-ended fashion. Patients are reassured to hear that, as with their own creations, there is no right way to respond. You can honestly say that in both situations you will work together on the possible meanings of their projected ideas, based on their own associations.

Although you are always free to use standardized tools like the Rorschach or the TAT, I suggest that you also experiment with a more personal approach. It is actually not hard to create your own collection of visual stimuli. You can use photographs, art reproductions, and other images that appeal to you from books, magazines, newspapers, and postcards. There is really no limit to the potential sources for such projective visual stimuli— including the Internet (DVD 6.1).

Just remember that the more ambiguous the image, the more possibilities there are for projection—that is, the more people will be able to see in it. There are many ways to request responses, which will allow patients to tell you about themselves in an enjoyable yet revealing fashion. These include selecting, arranging, and attributing meaning to whatever images you have chosen to present to them (6.1A).

Selecting

If you want to engage patients actively in the process of looking at visual stimuli, you can ask them to select photographs from magazines or art reproductions from a set (6.1B). You can specify the number they can select or the time they can spend, or you can leave either completely open. After they have chosen one or more images, with or without any specified criteria for selection, you can then use their choices as stimuli for telling whatever ideas or stories come to mind. As with interviews about their own art, it is best to start with open-ended questions—like, "What comes to mind as you look at these (or this)?"—before going on to more specific ones, which are usually suggested by their responses to the first.

The principles for this kind of interviewing are identical to those for asking about things they've created. That means that, for the most part, questions that don't suggest the answer are best, that you need to follow the patient's lead whenever possible, and that trial and error is the way to proceed. By all means use your creativity, but be careful not to let your projections get in the way of helping patients explore and elaborate their own ideas.

There are an infinite number of possible criteria you can specify which can foster different kinds of selections. One nonthreatening way to begin is to invite patients to *choose* one or more items from among any number of images:

- Those they like *best*
- Those they *dislike*
- Those that remind them of *themselves*
- Those *that remind them* of any appropriate category, such as: a significant other, an experience, a dream, a place, and so on
- Those they think *go together*

Such selections will lead to further associations, as you pursue whatever they can tell you about their choices. Since you have told them what to look for in choosing, they may even describe why they chose what they did. As with their own artwork, however, "why" questions from you can be threatening, although their reasons for selecting may be more accessible to them than those behind creating.

Arranging

When you use a number of pictures containing more-or-less related subject matter, you can ask patients to put them into some sort of *order* or *arrangement*. You can then inquire about the order or arrangement they have created, asking them to describe it to you. Whatever it is, you will learn more about the person making the decisions (cf. DVD 7.8C).

After patients have put the images in some sort of order, you can ask them to make up *stories* about the sequences they have created. You can then follow with open-ended questions, which help them further extend their projected narratives. Another alternative is to request that they put several (4 to 8) selected pictures into an order that *tells a story*.

Giving Meaning

If you present people with *abstract* stimuli, such as blurred photographs or ambiguous shapes, you can ask,

- What does this *look like?*
- What does this *remind you of?*

If you show people *representational* images you can ask,

- What do you think or imagine is *happening?*
- What might happen *next?*
- What may have happened just *before?*
- Is there a *story* about this picture?
- What sort of *feeling* does it give you?
- Does it *look like* or *remind* you of anything in particular?
- As you look at it, what *comes to mind?*

Depending on the content of the image, there are an endless number of ways to ask people to imagine things that help them to relate to it. The following are a few examples.

- Places
  Where would you be if you were in that picture?
  What *sort* of place is this?
  What might *happen* there?
  Who might *live* (or go) there?
- People
  How *old* do you think that person is?

87

What *kind of* person could that be?
(If gender is not evident) Is that a *boy or a girl* (a man or a woman)?
What do you imagine that person is *thinking* (*feeling, wishing*)?
If that person were to *speak*, what would (he or she) *say?*
- Art reproductions
What *sort of person* do you think created this?
Why do you suppose the artist created it?
What might the artist be trying to *say?*
What do you think the artist wanted you to *feel?*
What do you imagine the artist wanted you to *think?*
If you had to give that artwork a *grade*, what would it be?
What do you *like* about that work of art?
What do you *dislike?*

Although it isn't always easy for inhibited patients to find meaning in images, it can be fun when you ease the way with unthreatening and evocative questions. The challenge is to invite their ideas without suggesting or influencing their responses. All of the questions just noted are examples of the kinds of inquiries that are designed to help people project meaning onto images so you can get to know them better. No doubt you will think of many others.

Magazine Photo Collage

Although you may not want to conduct the entire protocol, a technique invented by art therapist Helen Landgarten, which she called *Magazine Photo Collage* (1993), may be of interest to you. You might find it useful in suggesting ideas for using preselected images—pictures cut or torn from magazines—as stimuli for projection. Landgarten developed the protocol for use with clients from diverse cultures, since many projectives present images of only one kind of person (DVD 6.2).

The idea is to offer collections of pictures of individuals from different ethnic backgrounds, so that all clients can find images of people with whom they can identify. The person is first asked to select images, to paste the pictures on paper, and is then given a choice of telling or writing what comes to mind. The procedure can be done with individuals or groups. I am noting Landgarten's suggestions, which you are free to use, or to modify as you wish (6.2A).

Given a box of people pictures and one of miscellaneous items, the client is asked to do the following:

1. Select pictures that catch your attention, paste them on paper, and write or tell what comes to mind.
2. Pick out 4 to 6 pictures of people, paste them on another paper, and write or tell what you imagine each person is thinking and saying.
3. Pick out 4 to 6 pictures that stand for something good and something bad, paste them down, and tell what they mean.
4. Pick out one picture from the people box, paste it down, and write or tell what is happening to that person. Do you think the situation will change? If the answer is yes, find a picture illustrating the change or tell what will make it change (6.2B).

Finding and Creating Projective Stimuli

You may want to invite patients to look for photographs or art reproductions themselves, and to bring them in for your joint perusal. This is one of many ways in which you can extend what happens in the session as homework, even if people are in a residential setting (DVD 6.3). There are always magazines to be looked through and pictures to be found.

You also involve people even more actively, by suggesting that they create their own stimuli. One method is to make ink or paint blots by folding a paper in half while the liquid is still wet, and then pressing down before opening it up. Most people are familiar with this exercise, since it is frequently used by primary-school teachers.

Another technique is to use glossy paper (like finger-paint paper or shelving), put a drop of ink on it, and ask the person to blow it using a straw, but not touching the paper (Figure 6.1). You hold the straw an inch or so above the paper, and then blow hard enough to make the ink move. The designs are delicate, varied, and useful as stimuli for projection.

After the blot or blow-painting is done, you can ask what the shapes remind the patient of, and what might be happening in the picture. As with a scribble drawing, it may help to turn the paper so that it can be looked at from all possible angles. And, as with anything you look at together, you can go on exploring as long as the responses are fruitful.

Projective Drawings

Despite numerous research studies, in which the most common assumptions about the meanings of specific drawing signs have not been validated (Kaplan, 2003), projective drawings have remained extremely popular among clinicians. This is probably because they are easy to administer and elicit a wealth of data in a very short period of time. Since global ratings

6.1 *Two Women Blow Ink Using Straws*

have been found to be more reliable, some useful hypotheses about patients can also be generated quite rapidly.

As noted in the last chapter, you can learn a great deal by observing patients' behaviors with you, with the materials, and in response to creative tasks. When you add what can be gleaned from interviews about the artwork, it is clear that—even if drawings alone cannot provide an accurate diagnosis or a complete map of a patient's internal world—the entire process can give you a substantial amount of information about the individuals who create them.

Standardized procedures for using drawing tasks with patients go back 100 years. During that time, clinicians have developed many different ways of using drawings in assessment. Some have stressed cognitive functioning, while others have focused on emotional issues.

Central to all projective drawing tests is the assumption that formal elements—like line quality, placement, and shading—are as significant as subject matter. Although there are copying and completion tasks, the most common involve representing specific themes.

The topics that have been suggested and used are no doubt popular with therapists because they provide information that is useful in various kinds of clinical decision-making, such as provisional diagnostic classification, assessing the need for hospitalization, developing treatment goals and procedures, and evaluating the effectiveness of such interventions as administering medication (DVD 6.4).

Themes
A Person

By far the most popular topic is the drawing of a *person*, which has been used since the 1920s by clinical psychologists. The topic was chosen initially to measure intellectual development, as in the procedure designed by Goodenough in 1926 and modified by Harris (1963), Draw a Man (or DAM); as well as in the one developed by Koppitz (1968), Human Figure Drawing (or HFD). There is sufficient lawfulness in drawing development that assessing cognitive functioning is actually one of the more successful uses of drawings, especially in individuals with atypical language development, for whom verbal tests are less valid (6.4A).

People drawings have also been used to look at emotional issues, as in the tests designed by Machover (1949)—Draw a Person (or DAP)—and Buck (1948, 1992)—House-Tree-Person (or H-T-P). In the latter, the house and the tree are assumed to be self-representations as well. Hammer (1958) suggested adding three crayon drawings to the pencil pictures of the original test. Burns (1987) later suggested that all three be represented in a single drawing, which is thought to show how people see themselves in the environment (6.4B).

Along with the hypothesis that an individual projects core personality traits in drawing behavior (Hammer, 1958, 1997), there is the related assumption of an internal schema, the *body image*. This idea, originated by Paul Schilder (1950), is no doubt one reason for the continuing popularity of person drawings. Another is the belief that human figure drawings, even when not explicitly self-portraits, are essentially self-representations.

A Family

Similarly popular, because it elicits a quick glimpse of the patient's interpersonal situation, is a drawing of the *family* (6.4C), first described in 1931 by psychiatrist Kenneth Appel. He suggested drawing each family member separately, but also asked that they be doing something (DVD 6.5).

This idea was popularized in 1970 by Burns and Kaufman in the widely used Kinetic Family Drawing (KFD): "Draw a picture of everyone in your family, including you, doing something" (6.5B). A pediatrician and a psychiatrist suggested asking for a KFD at some specified time in the future, adding yet another dimension (Kymissis & Khanna, 1992).

Burns (1990) later proposed drawing the following pictures of family

91

6.2 Mother-and-Child Drawing

members, each one inside a circle or mandala: father, mother, and self; and self and parents. One variation on the family theme is a *Mother-and-Child Drawing* (Gillespie, 1994; Figure 6.2), while another is an *Animal Family* (Hammer, 1958) or an *Abstract Family Portrait* (Kwiatkowska, 1978; cf. DVD 10.1B).

The family of origin can be represented in a *genogram* (McGoldrick & Gerson, 1985), and the usual diagrammatic method can be greatly enlivened by asking the person to use his or her own shapes and colors for different family members (Riley, 2003, pp. 392–393).

Although the family is the first and most dynamically significant group in anyone's life, others become increasingly important in the course of development. In the 1940s, psychiatrist Joseph Moreno, inventor of psychodrama, suggested making pictorial diagrams of interpersonal relationships, the most popular of which he called a *sociogram*. The sociogram can be modified by adding colors, as suggested by psychologist and art therapist Mala Betensky in her assessment protocol for adolescents (1995). It is also used by art therapist Charles Anderson.

Some recent variations include asking the patient to draw the following:

- A group (Hare & Hare, 1956)
- A kinetic school drawing (Prout & Phillips, 1974)
- A classroom (Klepsch & Logie, 1982)
- A teacher and child (Prout & Phillips, 1974)

Standardization in Drawing Tasks

Most projective drawing tasks require standardized materials—usually, $8^{1}/_{2}'' \times 11''$ white paper; a no. 2 pencil; and, when chromatic, specific colors and types of crayons. The instructions are also clearly specified, as are the guidelines for any postdrawing interrogation (PDI).

While a number of projective drawing tests have been shown to be *reliable* (stable), whether they measure what they are supposed to (i.e., whether they are *valid*) is a heavily debated issue. It is the source of most of the criticisms leveled at all projective techniques, especially drawings.

Most art therapists question cookbook approaches to the interpretation of any kind of artwork. That is probably because, having worked with people in the creation of art, we have seen considerable variability. Nevertheless, we still find that creating art, including drawings, is extremely helpful in the getting-to-know-you process sometimes called *assessment*.

Enriching Projective Drawings

Unless you need to use a scoring manual based on drawings collected under standardized conditions, as is true if you are doing research, you will get much more information—and your patients will have more fun—if you can request common topics in a more flexible fashion. The areas that make a difference are materials, surfaces, and the wording of the instructions for the tasks.

Even if you're collecting DAPs or KFDs for a study, something as minor as using drawing paper rather than printer paper will provide patients with a sturdier surface on which to create. It will also allow them to press hard and to erase frequently without tearing the paper. If, in addition, you provide a soft drawing pencil (like an Ebony pencil) and a large gum eraser, people will be able to make a greater range of strokes, as well as more types of shading.

Moreover, if you can do without using standardized materials, you will be free to offer a much greater range of media and drawing surfaces for any topic, including those you are used to requesting. Being able to choose among papers of different sizes, as well as from a range of colorful and inviting drawing materials, can make a big difference.

You will still get the information you are familiar with, along with the additional data provided by the media themselves. You may be surprised to see how much markers, chalk, or Craypas can add to what is expressed in an H-T-P or a KFD, and how much more people can tell you when the paper space they choose is twice as large.

More and better art materials actually elicit a potentially wider range of responses, thereby allowing you to obtain more information. For all of these reasons, I hope that you will consider exploring new ways to request projective drawings.

In addition to your offering a greater range of choices in media and paper sizes, I also suggest that you word your invitations in such a way that they allow the maximum degree of freedom in the representation of the topic. You can still ask patients to represent your favorite themes, but you don't need to be as specific about the wording if you're not scoring the drawings. This not only allows you to see a greater range of possible outcomes, it may even reduce the anxiety stimulated by asking someone, for example, to "make the very best person that you can" (Harris, 1963, p. 240).

As for obtaining a greater amount of clinical data, just think about the possible significance of a person's omitting him- or herself, a parent, a sibling, or a child from a drawing of the family. Eight-year-old Jack, for example, drew the family as consisting only of the baby, shown as displacing him from his bedroom (Figure 6.3).

His older sister, very unhappy about being involved, expressed her opposition in a creative fashion, making a portrait of a person with a characteristic from each family member. Such clues, whatever they turn out to mean for that particular individual, can never be available if the instructions for a family drawing specify that everyone, including the artists themselves, must be represented.

6.3 Jack's Drawing of "The Family"

In other words, the projective drawing tasks that have been most widely used probably do provide useful information about the people you are seeing for assessment and/or treatment. But I believe they can tell you even more if you expand the range of what people can represent, by making the instructions less restrictive and by offering more options of materials and drawing surfaces.

Expanding Projective Drawings

While it is true that the topics already noted are indeed the most widely used, there is no reason you shouldn't consider requesting others as well. In fact, there have been many other drawing themes proposed by clinicians from all disciplines. Here are just a few, beginning with some popular topics not attributed to anyone in particular:

- A self-portrait
- An abstract self-symbol
- Myself as an animal
- Myself in the future
- A teacher
- A doctor
- A monster
- A wish
- A bridge (Hays & Lyons, 1981)
- A rosebush (Allan, 1988)
- A road (Hanes, 1997)
- A person in the rain (Hammer, 1958)
- A Person Picking an Apple from a Tree (PPAT; Gantt & Tabone, 2003)
- The most unpleasant thing imaginable (Harrower, 1958)
- A favorite kind of day (Manning, 1987)

Like the human figure or the family, such topics are not chosen at random, but rather because they are assumed to symbolically tap significant issues. A *bridge*, for example, was proposed by art therapists Ron Hays and Sherry Lyons (1981), because the symbol represents connections as well as transitions. The instructions—to indicate the direction of travel by an arrow, and to show where the artist might be with a dot—further amplify the information elicited.

Sometimes drawing themes evolve from clinical observation. For example, art therapist Trudy Manning (1987) noticed that the abused children she was seeing often drew inclement weather. She then theorized that drawing *a favorite kind of day* would reflect how a child viewed his or her interpersonal environment. She went on to design and to validate rating scales, using measures of weather, size, and movement. Because it has been useful in screening, the topic is often requested by art therapists assessing children for possible abuse, along with other creative tasks.

In truth, you can request anything you wish. This can range from something free (no topic) to one of the subjects listed earlier—and, of course, you can ask someone to represent any other theme you have heard about or thought of that seems applicable to the person or group you want to understand. The possibilities are limited only by your own imagination. If you haven't already done so, I am certain you will find that thinking up meaningful drawing tasks in assessment is as creative as thinking of facilitating questions to ask in an interview.

Conclusion

As you can see, there are many ways you can understand the people you serve by inviting them to respond to images and to make drawings. You don't need to give up the Rorschach, but you might try extending that kind of inquiry by adding other kinds of images or shapes, whether presented by you or created by the patients themselves.

If you're already asking for projective drawings, you can try giving choices of paper sizes and things to draw with. You will still get all of the data you're used to, and probably even more, by using sturdier and more varied materials. If you can also modify the instructions to allow more leeway, I believe that you can obtain more and richer information.

I hope to have offered you some new ideas that appeal to you enough to try them out, as you are getting to know the people you're assessing. Be aware, however, that the language of color and form is, like poetry, very difficult to quantify. Even if that could ever be accomplished, the whole is still greater, deeper, and more meaningful than the sum of its graphic parts.

Messages contained in artwork are best understood in the context of all associative behaviors—before, during, after, and in response to the images themselves. So when you use standardized drawing tasks, like the H-T-P or the DAP, be aware that generalizations about the meanings of various drawing signs are hypotheses, at best.

It is also important to recall that projection is a very personal matter, and that it works both ways. In addition, studies have found that the variable of artistic talent affects judgments of pathology and normality in art productions by people of all ages. Most projective drawings are generally used along with other diagnostic data (interviews, questionnaires, tests,

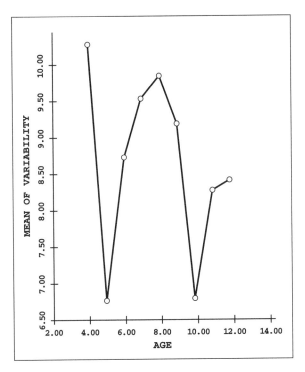

6.4 Intra-individual Variability by Age

etc.) as part of an initial assessment. Experienced clinicians agree that one art product—like one act or thought—cannot possibly be a valid sample of anyone's behavior, whether the focus is on a person's potential, problems, or both, including warning signs (DVD 6.5).

One reason that a single drawing can be misleading is that people are variable in their drawing behavior, as in other areas of functioning. What they draw at any particular moment depends on many factors, like how rested they are, how comfortable they feel, what is going on in their lives, and so on.

As it turns out, even variability itself seems to be variable. In a study I conducted with two child psychiatrists, we collected human figure drawings from 20 children (10 boys and 10 girls) at each age level from 4 to 12 on a Monday, Tuesday, Thursday, and Friday in the same week. Made at the same time of day, and with the same instructions and materials, the drawings were then coded and randomized, and a group of judges scored them for developmental level (roughly equivalent to IQ) using the Goodenough-Harris scale (Harris, 1963).

We had expected that intra-individual variability in scores (measured

6.5a *First Monday (Day 1), "A Nut"*

6.5b *First Tuesday (Day 2), "A Martian"*

6.5c *Second Monday (Day 7), "My Cousin"*

6.5d *Second Tuesday (Day 8), "My Friend"*

6.5 *Four Person-Drawings in Eight Days by Same Child*

by the standard deviation among the four drawing scores for each child) would gradually decrease from ages 4 to 12 (DVD 6.5). Much to our surprise, we found not simply an overall decrease, but instead, a cyclical pattern, with high variability at specific age levels (4 and 8) and low variability at others (5 and 10; see Figure 6.4; DVD 6.6A, B, C, and D). Moreover, when we decided to score the sets of drawings for content and visual variability, we found the same pattern as with scores (Figure 6.5a–6.5d; DVD 6.8B–E; Rubin, Schachter, & Ragins, 1983).

In the next chapter, I will briefly describe some of the assessments that have been developed by art therapists. As with the Magazine Photo Collage described earlier, you may find ideas you can adapt for your own work, even if you don't wish to use the entire protocols as originally designed.

CHAPTER

7

Art Therapy Assessments

Introduction

There is no standardized or commonly accepted approach to using art in assessment, any more than there is a universally accepted way of using art in therapy. A great many different methods have been proposed. You are free to adopt any part of those I will describe. Most of all, I hope that you will consider getting to know your patients in some new ways using art.

Unstructured and Semistructured Interviews

Free Choice

The approach that I have personally found most useful with both adults and children is quite simple: a free choice of media and topics (DVD 7.1). It involves asking the patient to choose what to use and what to make from among a variety of materials (Rubin, 1973, 2005). While I offer a wide range of materials with which to draw, paint, model, and construct, the assessment can also be conducted with a more limited selection.

The basic idea of an unstructured art interview is that the way the individual organizes the time reveals his or her general style of being in the world. The person's behavior with the therapist, with the art materials, during the process, and in relationship to the products are all diagnostic data. As you may recall from Chapter 4, there is a great deal that can be usefully observed. If you are willing and have the space, I suggest that you offer the following options:

1. Drawing surfaces (white and colored paper, 9″ × 12″ and 12″ × 18″)
2. Something to draw with (markers, oil crayons, colored pencils)
3. Something to paint with (watercolors, tempera paints)
4. Something to model with (plasticine, earth clay)
5. Something to make a collage with (magazines, scissors, glue)

The exact selection of materials you provide is up to you. But you will probably be surprised at how having even a limited choice—like thin and thick markers, or markers and colored pencils—will enrich what you learn. While this interview can be done in as little as a half hour, 45 to 60 minutes is preferable.

Although some individuals (7.1A) work on one product (7.1B) for most of the time (7.1C), the majority end up creating more than one in the course of a session. The changes in their behavior and in their art over that time span provide additional diagnostic data (7.1D). Since I believe that behavior is lawful, and that there is meaning in the sequence itself, the way it unfolds is very instructive (7.1E).

This, of course, happens in a verbal interview as well. The difference is that you have added a good deal of information to whatever transpires between you in words. There are components available only in an unstructured art interview, like selecting the medium and the topic, as well as those aspects noted in Chapter 5—the sequence of actions within each product, the nonverbal behavior in relation to the activity with the media, verbal behavior in relation to the product, and a great deal more.

Three Media

Edith Kramer's *art assessment* also allows considerable choice of topic and sequence (DVD 7.2). However, because she feels that each medium reveals different things about the artist, this interview requires the making of, first, a pencil drawing; then a tempera painting; and finally a clay sculpture (Kramer & Schehr, 2000). Although this format was originally designed for children, it can be used with adults as well. The patient chooses not only the subject matter of each piece, but also the order in which the painting and modeling are done (7.2A).

In Ellen Horovitz's *cognitive art therapy assessment*, the individual is similarly required to do a drawing, a painting, and a clay sculpture (Horovitz-Darby, 1988). In this format, the patient decides on the order in which he or she will use the materials (7.2B).

Visual Starters

One of the problems with free-choice procedures is that, except for young children and gifted others, they can be quite threatening to the non-artist and can cause considerable blocking and anxiety. For that reason, art therapists have developed a number of ways of helping people to overcome their fear of the blank page, using what I have called *visual starters* (DVD 7.3).

Although most were not specifically designed for the purpose of assessment, they are especially helpful in the early stages of your work, which is generally when you are getting to know people. In fact, the scribble drawing is included in many art therapy assessment batteries. For that reason, I have decided to describe them here, although they are also extremely helpful in the course of treatment as well.

The artists who created prehistoric cave paintings as many as 25,000 years ago used a technique similar to the scribble drawing by painting or drawing animals where the rock naturally shaped itself like the body of an animal, like a bison or a horse (7.3A).

About 500 years ago, the Renaissance painter Leonardo da Vinci made a similar suggestion. He recommended looking at the ambiguous marks on stained walls as a way of generating ideas for a composition:

> I cannot forbear to mention a new device for STUDY which, although it may seem trivial and almost ludicrous, is nevertheless extremely useful in arousing the mind to various inventions. And this is, when you look at a WALL SPOTTED WITH STAINS. . . .
>
> You may discover a resemblance to landscapes, beautified with mountains, rivers, rocks, trees, or again you may see battles and figures in action, or strange faces and costumes and an endless variety of objects which you could reduce to complete and well drawn forms.
>
> And these appear on such walls confusedly, like the sound of bells in whose jangle you may find any name or word you choose to imagine. (Richter, 1970, p. 254)

Dots, Lines, and Shapes

Something already on the paper, something for the artist to elaborate and complete, is helpful to adolescents and adults, and to inhibited children as well. It can be quite simple, like a dot, a line, or a shape—or several dots, lines, or shapes. You can invite patients to make the starter themselves, and you can give them the option of doing it with their eyes closed, which is usually less threatening. If people are uncomfortable making their own starters, feel free to do it for them.

Since this is a game-like approach, you may want to make one yourself as well, to model how to do it. At this point, patients are encouraged to find as many images as they can in the starter, which is itself informative. Then, using the dot(s), line(s), or shape(s) as a beginning, they are asked to make a drawing or painting of whatever is suggested to them.

There are several procedures developed by therapists in which the clinician draws something as a stimulus and the patient is invited to complete it. Walter Brown (1967), for example, *drew out* schizophrenic patients by placing a dot on the paper, and Ron Hays (1979) proposed a dot-to-dot exercise with children too young to respond to a scribble.

Psychiatrist Mardi Horowitz also invited patients to do a series of (six) drawings, beginning each time by staring at a dot he had placed in the middle of the page until they saw an image. He called it the *dot-image-sequence* (1983).

Similarly, you can draw a line or a shape on a piece of paper and suggest that the patient develop an image from it. There are many other visual starters that can be developed by you or by the patient, such as the kinds of blots described in Chapter 6. Of course, patients can be invited to make their own dots, lines, or shapes if they prefer.

Egg and Cave Drawings

One inventive method in which the therapist creates something for the patient to complete is to be found in two assessment tasks developed by therapists in Japan (Tanaka, Kakuyama, & Urhausen, 2003). They incorporate the interactive aspects of Winnicott's (1971b, 1989) *squiggle game*, as well as universal themes with resonance on many levels. Although designed for children, adults find them intriguing as well. In both procedures the therapist first draws a shape (an egg or a cave), and the patient is then invited to fill it in imaginatively.

Squiggles and Scribbles

By far the most popular such procedure among art therapists is known as the *scribble drawing*, an easy and unthreatening way to start out. It is also remarkably rich as a stimulus for material that is not likely to surface spontaneously in either words or images. The scribble drawing, like a dot, line, or shape, is another kind of visual starter, upon which patients can project their own personal imagery.

It has an interesting history, having been invented independently by two highly creative individuals during the 1940s (which was also a period of early excitement about projective techniques). One was a playful British psychoanalyst and pediatrician named Donald W. Winnicott; the other was an inspired American art teacher named Florence Cane. Each came up with the notion of developing a picture from a self-made scribble. Although their ideas were similar, their ways of carrying them out were quite different.

The Squiggle Game (Winnicott)

For Winnicott (1971b, 1989), what he called the *squiggle game* was a rapid way to get to know a child he was assessing (7.3B). He often conducted consultations with youngsters brought from a distance, who he might see only once. It was therefore vital to find ways to get to know what was on each child's mind as quickly as possible.

His approach was an interactive one in which he and the child took turns making squiggles for the other to complete and to name, using a pencil on writing paper. There were typically several exchanges of images, leading to a narrative.

The technique itself can be used with adults as well as with children. However, because it involves the therapist's projections as well as the patient's, it should be done only by experienced clinicians with a good deal of self-knowledge. Although game-like, it is a very powerful interaction, and it is important to monitor your responses so that they are in the patient's interest, always following his or her lead.

The Scribble Drawing (Cane)

Cane (1983), unlike Winnicott, was an artist who was teaching gifted children. Her primary goal was to stimulate spontaneity in their creative expression. Because she was also a dancer, her *scribble* technique included preparatory breathing and movement exercises, and was done at an easel on large drawing paper with soft pastels (7.3C).

Later taught by her sister, art therapy pioneer Margaret Naumburg (1950, 1953, 1966), the scribble is extremely popular among art therapists. It is most helpful in overcoming anxiety and resistance, which, though rare among children, are common with adolescents and adults.

The scribble drawing is, in fact, part of the first assessment batteries created by art therapists: the *Ulman Personality Assessment Procedure (UPAP)* designed by Elinor Ulman (1975) in 1965 (7.3D) and the *Family Art Evaluation (FAE)* developed by Hanna Kwiatkowska (1978) in 1967 (7.3E).

Requesting a Scribble Drawing

Although Florence Cane used easels, large paper, and chalks, you will probably be most comfortable asking people to work on a table or a pad. I suggest that you use 9″ × 12″ white drawing paper; and that you invite patients to develop an image found in the scribble. Offering a choice of drawing materials (markers, oil crayons, pastels, or colored pencils) and paper sizes (12″ × 18″ as an option, if you have the space) allows individuals to select what they're most comfortable with.

I usually demonstrate the process by first making a scribble of my own, and then inviting people to see what it reminds them of, before they do it themselves. Naturally, whatever they project onto my scribble provides valuable diagnostic data as well. The instructions are to let the hand move freely, without trying to draw anything in particular; to make a continuous line, not lifting the hand from the paper; to stop before the line gets too complicated; and to use a relatively light color. I also tell people that they can make the scribble with their eyes open or closed, whichever is more comfortable for them (7.3E).

After making the scribble, patients are asked to turn the paper all four possible ways, and to say what images come to mind from each point of view. They are asked not to fill in the shapes, but to find a picture. They are then invited to develop one or more of the images they have seen, omitting any lines that don't belong and adding any lines, shapes, and colors that are necessary in order to help others to see what they found. One man found "A Woman Waking Up in the Morning" in his scribble (see Figure 7.1), a title that greatly distressed his wife. In addition, Linda Gantt suggests a three-dimensional variation taught by Kwiatkowska, the "clay scribble."

Stimulus Drawings

Art therapist Rawley Silver (1978, 2001, 2002) worked for many decades on an approach to assessment that began in her work with deaf children, but has since been conducted with patients of all ages and a variety of conditions.

The three tasks in the *Silver Drawing Test (SDT)* focus on cognitive abilities: predictive drawing assesses the ability to sequence; drawing from observation, the ability to represent spatial relationships; and drawing from imagination, the ability to deal with abstract concepts, as well as creativity and the projection of emotions (DVD 7.4).

For the third task, and for the *Draw a Story Test*, she uses another kind of visual starter, the *Stimulus Drawing* cards created by Silver herself (7.4A)— 50 line drawings of people, places, and objects (7.4B). In the SDT and the Draw a Story Test, people are invited to select two images from a group of 15 cards. They are then asked to combine them in a new picture that tells a story. In the *Stimulus Drawing Assessment*, all 50 cards are used.

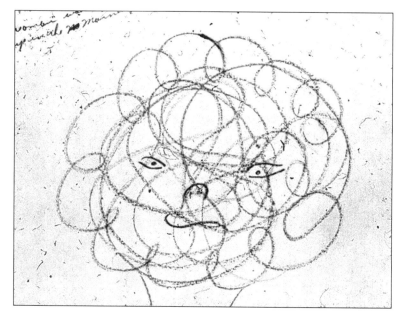

7.1 *Woman Waking Up in the Morning*

In addition to conducting the tests as described in Silver's (2002) manual (7.4C), you can also use the Stimulus Drawing cards independently, in treatment as well as in assessment. These visual stimuli, which are in fact very evocative, are yet another way of giving people ideas for pictures.

Some Individual Assessments

Many creative ideas have been proposed for assessment through art, and there is not sufficient space to tell you about all of them. Although there are many individual assessments that have been developed by art therapists, I shall just describe a few: several single-drawing assessments that require no art experience, and that can be done using materials that don't make a mess.

Brief Art Therapy Screening Evaluation

Like many creative ideas, this procedure is one that grew out of external pressures: in this instance, to gather diagnostic data as rapidly as possible. The assessment takes 30 minutes, and is so efficient and rich that, soon after it was developed, it was used routinely for screenings at Friends Hospital in Philadelphia. Created by art therapist Nancy Gerber (1996) it is called the *Brief Art Therapy Screening Evaluation* (BATSE; DVD 7.5).

The patient is asked to draw a picture in 5 minutes, thus reducing some of the anxiety about creating the product. The topic is *a picture of two people doing something in a place*, and is done on a small sheet of white drawing paper, using eight fine-tip colored markers. The only request is that the artist not make stick figures.

As with many projective drawing tasks, Gerber specifies the questions to ask after the drawing is complete, during the post-drawing interrogation (PDI). She has also developed a manual (Gerber, 1996), which details the instructions and the PDI, as well as some guidelines about what to look for in both the drawing and the interview.

A Person Picking an Apple from a Tree

For almost 30 years, art therapist Linda Gantt has been working to correlate elements in art products with psychiatric diagnoses. In her ongoing research, she and collaborator Carmello Tabone have been collecting drawings of *A Person Picking an Apple from a Tree* (*PPAT*; Gantt & Tabone, 2003).

The topic was first introduced by a therapeutic art educator named Viktor Lowenfeld (1957), because it helped children identify with the activity. For a variety of reasons, it has turned out to be a wise selection.

Gantt and Tabone have been systematically securing PPAT drawings at intake and at discharge, as well as before and after such events as ECT and changes in medication. Because the patients' diagnoses are arrived at independently by a team of other professionals, they have been able to look at their relationship to variables in the drawings (DVD 7.6A, B, C, and D).

In order to do so, the researchers have developed and refined what they have named the *Formal Elements Art Therapy Scale (FEATS)*. The scale, which has high interrater reliability, is spelled out in a detailed rating manual (Gantt & Tabone, 1998; 7.6E).

Because any assessment of artwork has to include both content and form, the scale contains categories in both areas. The scale itself is a useful reminder of some of the things one can look at in patient artwork. It relies exclusively on global ratings, which have been found in projective drawing research to be the most valid and reliable measures.

Life Line

Like all art activities, this topic is relatively quick and, like many, yields a considerable amount of data in a short time. In addition, because it is possible to represent multiple people, places, and events in a single pictorial space, it conveys information in a unique fashion. This is impossible with words, which have to be spoken sequentially over time, and cannot therefore be grasped in the same way.

A *life line*, while no substitute for a verbal history, adds another dimension to the story of anyone's life. I recommend a choice of drawing materials. The task can be done on a piece of paper as small as 12″ × 18″, although a larger piece or a roll of paper is useful if you want to provide more space.

You ask the patient to show the story of his or her life using shapes, colors, and images in a linear fashion, like a road or a river. It may help to request that the person identify significant periods and events, perhaps using particular symbols and colors at those points in the line. The life line often amplifies and enriches the picture you are able to obtain of someone's past from other sources. Sometimes one is created spontaneously (DVD 7.7).

Past, Present, and Future

In her assessment protocol for adolescents, psychologist and art therapist Mala Betensky included a task that she called *adolescent window triptych*. The patient is asked to create three drawings: one of the past, one of the present, and one of the future (Betensky, 1995). This or some variation on it is yet another way to elicit visual reflections about time, although unlike the life line, in which people sometimes include the future, this approach explicitly requests it.

Life Space

If you want information about a person's social situation, you can request a picture or a diagram to show that visually. This idea is conceptually related to Moreno's sociogram and social atom. I have also invited patients to make what I call a *life space picture* (Figure 7.2) showing the people, places, and activities that are most important in their lives at the present time.

If you have space for a large (18″ × 24″) piece of paper, that is ideal; but if not, it can be done on a smaller size, such as 12″ × 18″. It is helpful if you can give a choice of paper color as well as size, since the color itself can represent how someone sees his or her life space at that moment in time. Finally, as with other tasks, I recommend a selection of different drawing media.

Art Assessment Batteries

There are numerous assessment batteries, designed by art therapists for individuals, that specify multiple products. Because they are fairly extensive and usually require large paper and pastels, I shall not describe them here, but refer the reader to Chapter 7 in *Art Therapy: An Introduction* (Rubin, 1999) for an overview and (DVD 7.8) for a glimpse (cf. also Brooke, 2004).

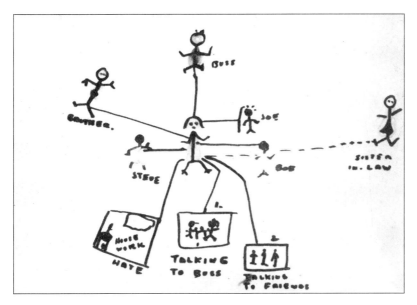

7.2 A Life-Space Drawing by a Woman

Both the UPAP (Ulman, 1965; 7.8A) and the *Diagnostic Drawing Series* (*DDS*; Cohen, Hammer, & Singer, 1988; Mills, 2003; 7.8B), as well as the MARI Card Test (Cox, 2003; Kellogg, 2002; 7.8C) have been in use for some time now. Like any other projective procedure, each of these batteries is especially helpful to those who have repeated them with different clients.

Another typical series, the *Levick Cognitive and Emotional Art Therapy Assessment (LECATA)*, was published by Myra Levick (2001). Though originally designed for children, it can be used with adults as well. There are six tasks to be done on 12″ × 18″ white drawing paper with 16 oil crayons, as follows: (1) free drawing, (2) self-portrait, (3) scribble, (4) developed scribble, (5) a place, and (6) a family (cf. Bush, 1997; 7.8D).

Various specialized protocols have been published, such as that developed by Marcia Sue Cohen-Liebman (2003) for use in the forensic assessment of children for possible abuse, or the one by Judy Wald (2003) for the assessment of cognitive functioning and emotional state in elderly stroke patients. As you might imagine, Wald includes a wide variety of both structured and unstructured tasks, including copying a geometric shape, drawing a clock, choosing colors to represent how one is feeling, and a free painting, as well as the Silver Drawing Test.

One lesson to be learned from both research and clinical experience is that, if you decide to use drawings or other art products in assessment, you would be wise to ask for more than one.

Family Photographs and Videotapes

Although you might wonder about this category, *phototherapy* has become a part of art therapy, perhaps because it is also visual and can be similarly expressive as well as responsive. Asking patients to bring in family photos or albums (Akeret, 1973; Weiser, 1993) requires no special materials. It simply involves inviting them to take their personal photographs to the therapy session, and then to show and tell about what they have brought in to share (cf. DVD 11.4).

Like a life line, it's another way of getting a history, and a vivid one at that. Like a life space picture, it's another way of exploring interpersonal relationships. As part of getting to know patients, it is an extremely useful adjunct. Home videos, too, are another useful source of diagnostic information.

Understanding Kitty via Video

I once saw a little girl named Kitty whose hand-flapping, disinterest in other children, and other bizarre behaviors led me to wonder whether I was seeing early infantile autism, pervasive developmental disorder, Asperger's disorder, or something else. Although I referred her to a child psychologist for diagnostic testing, she was so oppositional that the findings were inconclusive.

In addition, her parents' memories of Kitty's early years were not only inconsistent, but also vague. So I asked whether they had videotaped her when she was little. They had, and were willing for me to view their home videos. The tapes revealed the intrusiveness of her mother, who was the main videographer. Her narration, as well as her interaction with Kitty while she was filming, introduced another possible motive for the girl's symptoms.

Although the child was a fine artist (Figure 7.3; DVD 7.8B), her therapy had really started to progress when she began to involve me in her previously solitary dramas. She loved to shut me *out* of the playroom space (adjacent to my larger therapy room), and would gleefully control when and how she would let me *in*. Sometimes she would shut me *in*, being equally bossy about how and when she would let me *out*.

At first I thought she was telling me—by making me feel left out—that she was feeling excluded from the closeness between her younger brother and her mother. While that was true, it was not the most important message she was trying to communicate through her repetitive drama.

After viewing the videotapes of her early years, I realized that her primary need was to create a *boundary* between us. Her withdrawal from me

110

7.3 Kitty's Picture of Wonder Woman

and from other children was not simply an avoidance of people. It was also a way of separating from her loving but anxiously overinvolved mother, who had a difficult time differentiating Kitty's needs from her own.

The information contained in the videos also helped Kitty's mother's therapist to help her to separate, thus giving Kitty the space she needed to grow autonomously. As Kitty worked through her problems in art and drama therapy, she became more sociable at home and at preschool. Much to my surprise, she was even able to handle public school (with good supports), which I could not have imagined when I first met her.

What Can You Learn from Art?

Art and Psychopathology

Although all diagnostic inferences from art need to be approached with caution, drawings can sometimes help in *screening* for problems. They are especially useful when trying to pick up possible signs of serious emotional disturbance, organicity, and of acting-out (particularly suicide or homicide; cf. DVD 6.5).

However, while there are some ways in which art products can help in differential diagnosis, it is hardly simple, as experienced clinicians have found. So far, research attempts to validate *drawing signs*—like shading as an indication of anxiety—have found them to be less successful than *global ratings* (Kaplan, 2003).

Judging Psychopathology from Art

Reflecting both the skepticism and the enthusiasm surrounding the use of art in projective techniques, two art-therapist/psychologist teams designed similar studies in the late 1960s independent of one another. Each asked the simple question of whether people could judge psychopathology from spontaneous art expressions. Could they tell which picture was done by a patient and which by a nonpatient?

The judges in the study using adult paintings (Ulman & Levy, 1968) were more successful than those in the study using child drawings and paintings (Rubin & Schachter, 1972). Although neither found that success was related to years of clinical experience, a subsequent investigation showed that training art therapists in how to look at paintings did increase their accuracy in identifying adult psychiatric inpatients (Levy & Ulman, 1974).

Phenomenological Understanding

Art therapist researchers have questioned many generalizations about patient art, largely because of the experience of helping people with different diagnoses to create. Harriet Wadeson designed a series of studies at the National Institutes of Mental Health (NIMH) to identify the characteristics of artwork by people with various psychiatric disorders (Wadeson, 1980).

Many of her findings remain valid, like the fact that clinically depressed patients tend to use less color and to make weaker lines. Nevertheless, art therapists in acute inpatient settings have also noted that depressed patients often make defensively cheerful drawings and paintings, full of rainbows and bright colors.

In her drawing studies, Wadeson also sought to obtain a phenomenological understanding of the patient's experience. She asked for drawings on such topics as what it feels like to be depressed, to have delusions or hallucinations, or to be in seclusion. Without assuming anything, Wadeson discovered a great deal about people's subjective experiences of mental illness and hospitalization, which had eluded verbal description.

If you request such topics, you will be pleasantly surprised that asking a patient to represent what it feels like to be anxious, or to be an immigrant, or any other topic that is germane, usually elicits information that cannot be easily put into words.

Creating Reveals Capacities

One advantage of using art activities as part of an assessment is that they very often reveal people's strengths and abilities, as well as their problems and weaknesses. This is largely because, in order to use art materials to successfully perform a creative task, a patient has to call on many cognitive and emotional capacities.

Unlike answering a questionnaire or responding to a structured diagnostic interview, an art assignment calls on the individual to plan, to organize, to manipulate materials and tools, and to create something that fulfills the therapist's request, whatever that is.

It is true that there are no right answers in projective techniques, and there is certainly no right or wrong in art—another reason it is useful in therapy. In order to use art materials constructively and creatively, patients, no matter how disabled they may be, have to make use of what is *right* with them, rather than what is *wrong* with them.

Thus, even if we can't translate drawing signs or ratings into neat diagnostic classifications or predictive certainty, there is much to be gained by adding art to the assessment of patients of all ages. Although it would be wonderful if we could actually read people's minds by looking at their art, it is a very complex business. Nevertheless, there is a great deal you can find out about those you serve through art, which will help you to help them. And that is wonderful.

CHAPTER

8

Art in Adult Therapy

Introduction

The last two chapters described some of the ways in which looking at and creating images can enhance the assessment process. If you see mainly adults or adolescents and have already used projective techniques, chances are that you have done so primarily during the diagnostic phase. But art is also extremely useful during therapy with people of all ages, not just children. This chapter will focus on ways of using art during the treatment of older adolescents and adults, whose verbal skills are so well developed that therapists are usually not motivated to add visual expression.

Unless you see young children, you are unlikely to want to offer art during every therapy session. Like relaxation, hypnosis, or any other optional technique, drawing, painting, or modeling can be introduced any time it seems potentially useful. You can also leave some art materials accessible for patients to use as they wish. It is not necessary to make art a regular part of therapy, unless you find that it is clearly facilitating progress. It can easily be introduced intermittently, and can be useful even when done only occasionally.

Experimenting with when and how to suggest art will allow you to find the most comfortable way of incorporating it into your work. Don't be afraid to try. Trial and error works as well here as it does with questions about products. After all, patients can always refuse, just as they can always be silent. If you do it in a nonthreatening and tactful way, however, you will find that art in therapy can be exceptionally helpful, especially with certain kinds of people and problems. Art is not only immensely versatile, it

114

is also remarkably rich, as you will discover when you add even a pad of paper and a set of markers to what you offer.

Inviting Patients to Make Art

Regardless of your theoretical bent, you do best to begin, as described in Chapter 3, in the section "Introducing Art to Patients." As noted there, it generally helps to acknowledge peoples' anxieties and to invite them to talk about them. It also helps if you explain some of your reasons for adding *art as a second language*, and if you stress the benefits for them in particular. In that regard, I believe you have an advantage over art therapists, because you can honestly say that you yourself are not an artist any more than your patients are.

Even so, you can also say that you know that adding visual communication to the therapeutic interchange can help in many ways. Although many reasons have been noted in Chapters 2 and 4, let me remind you of some of the more persuasive arguments for getting patients to consider trying art. One is finding out new things about themselves—not just what's causing their problems, but also their strengths. Another is speeding up the process of therapy by offering an alternative way to think about things.

Many therapists, and quite a few patients, too, are convinced of the power of the unconscious to affect people's lives. If so, you can tell clients that creating art will enable them to gain access to memories, ideas, and feelings they can't get to in other ways, no matter how much effort they expend.

Whatever the task, whether free or specific, it is important to make it as clear and as easy as possible, so that patients can perform it willingly and successfully. Since you don't care if what they do is aesthetically pleasing, you can say that, too (although people will still react positively, negatively, or ambivalently to what they have created). Of course, such reactions provide grist for the therapeutic mill, along with anything else that comes up in the process of creating art (DVD 8.1).

Free Expression

Regardless of your preferred theoretical orientation, you may want people to express themselves as freely as possible. However, if a piece of blank paper and an open invitation to make anything they wish causes blocking, there are also many less-threatening ways to help patients create. Some ways of beginning were noted in Chapter 3 as well as in Chapter 7. They included doodling or fooling around with media; using a visual starter like a dot, line, scribble, or blot; and building a picture or collage around images cut from magazines. People can also get ideas about what to draw by closing their eyes, seeing what images come to mind, describing them to you, and then choosing which to represent.

If you are analytically oriented, you might want to ask patients to draw images without thinking about what they will draw, *thinking with their hands* as spontaneously as possible; and then to follow with one or more images, each stimulating the next, a visual kind of *free association* (cf. DVD 12.5). The possible ways of getting started are, as noted before, limited only by your imagination.

Analytically oriented therapists aren't the only ones who value free expression. In fact, this way of working is compatible with all kinds of psychotherapy, and is often preferred by humanistic, transpersonal, and developmental therapists who use art in their work. Free drawing, painting, and modeling is even compatible with behavioral and cognitive approaches, and can also be used in systemic approaches with individuals, families, or groups.

Topics and Themes

Depending on many clinical variables, however, and also compatible with any orientation, you may want people to draw something specific: a theme or a topic. Janie Rhyne, for example, translated personal construct theory into a drawing task, asking patients to make simple abstract line drawings of eight primary emotions: fear, anger, joy, sadness, disgust, acceptance, anticipation, and surprise (Rhyne, 2001).

You may want to request the representation of such internal experiences, which can be psychological like longing or physical like a migraine headache (Figures 8.1a and 8.1b). Or you may want to invite patients to represent something external, like a happy or painful memory, or something they wish for.

There are numerous tasks that can give you a sense of a person's life over time as well as at present, like the life line and life space pictures described in the previous chapter. Similarly, the request for a family drawing can include temporal aspects, whether in the past, like the *family of origin*; or in the future, like the *prospective kinetic family drawing,* suggested by a pediatrician and a psychologist (Kymissis & Khanna, 1992).

A *family drawing* is easier for some people to do if they have the option of making it *abstract*, using a shape and color for each member (Kwiatkowska, 1978). Another variation that sometimes appeals to patients is to represent each person by a *symbol*. Yet another is to use specific imagery, like

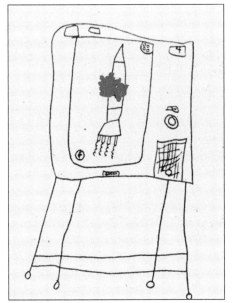

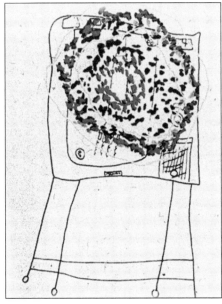

8.1a A Migraine Headache: Before   8.1b A Migraine Headache: During

animals or fruits, to represent family members. The possibilities are end-less, and I hope you will use your own imagination to think of others.

Traumatic Memories

In the case of repressed or dissociated traumatic memories, like those of physical, sexual, or psychological abuse, the image is often a gateway to what was largely a nonverbal event, especially if it occurred before the person had words. You can suggest drawing people, places, or events related to the trauma, as a way of helping people to reach beyond repression or dissociation for what they need to remember and to reintegrate. The memory may be vivid, but may have been locked up due to the feared consequences of disclosure.

Sometimes therapists are afraid to ask people to represent a trauma, yet such a request is often just what is needed in order for a patient of any age to feel safe exposing what had been kept secret. In fact, recent work in short-term trauma resolution suggests that in order to objectify dissociated memories so that people can recall, rework, and reframe them, drawing is an excellent modality.

A less forbidden form of telling than talking, drawing is often a step in that direction (Cohen & Cox, 1995). Rather than a free choice, what is

117

needed here is something much more structured, specific to the traumatic event itself (Steele, 2003).

In addition, the common posttraumatic stress symptom of intrusive mental imagery can be sometimes alleviated by drawing and discussing the unbidden images, a persuasive reason for a patient to try doing so. Psychiatrist Mardi Horowitz (1983) has described using this method with good results.

In fact, if you are a behavioral or cognitive therapist working on modifying specific behaviors or maladaptive thoughts, you are likely to be inviting mental imagery, which is known to be helpful in such procedures as desensitization, flooding, and implosion. By adding art imagery to your armamentarium, you give patients yet another way to imagine, to practice, to think about, and to visualize specific ideas or behaviors the two of you are working on. For that reason, asking for a drawing of a mental image, whether spontaneous or suggested, adds another dimension to the work.

As noted earlier, many cultures long ago discovered the magical power of the image in practices like voodoo, sand painting, and probably the cave paintings as well. I am convinced that this is one of the reasons that making art is intrinsically therapeutic—that representing the feared object is a way of bringing it under one's own symbolic control. The incorporation of drawing into modern, focused cognitive-behavioral approaches to anxiety and other disorders is yet another way of working on the problems at hand, and may well be related to "image magic" (Kris, 1952).

Drawing on the Dialogue

Another rich source of drawing ideas is the verbal interaction between you and your patient (DVD 8.2). For example, after someone has described a dream, it may enhance your mutual ability to learn from it if you invite them to draw it. If someone is having difficulty putting something into words, it often helps to ask the person to try to draw it, as a way of clarifying the feeling or event for both of you (DVD 8.2A).

Even when patients have articulated something beautifully, it sometimes feels like they have found the words, but not the music, for what they're trying to express. This is especially true for people who use intellectualization and rationalization defensively. For such patients, drawing something can help them get in touch with feelings, and to do so at a deeper level (8.2B).

In solution-focused and narrative approaches to therapy, drawing things like the problems identified by patients, as well as possible solutions to them, is a vivid way to explore and envision changes a person, a couple, or a family might make. In such work, it is often useful to identify and to draw obstacles in the way of problem resolution—as in Shirley Riley's metaphor of a mountain—as well as to draw wishful, imagined miracle solutions (Riley & Malchiodi, 2003).

Whether the topics raised in the interview arise completely spontaneously or in response to specific questions by the therapist, they are an excellent basis for requesting a drawing. What is important is that representing something, even after discussing it for some time, adds a new level of awareness, meaning, and in most cases, feeling. As you practice using this approach, you will find that it gets easier to identify and select themes over time.

Different Approaches to Using Art

The idea for this book occurred to me while I was revising a book entitled *Approaches to Art Therapy: Theory and Technique* (Rubin, 2001a). In that volume, art therapists who have studied different orientations to psychotherapy describe how they have applied the thinking therein to their work. These orientations include psychodynamic ones (Freudian and Jungian) and humanistic ones (person-centered, phenomenological, Gestalt, and spiritual or transpersonal), as well as those that are behavioral, cognitive, developmental, systemic, and eclectic. If you wish to further examine those that are closest to your way of doing therapy, Appendix B contains brief descriptions of what is contained in each chapter of that book.

My assumption is that, as a therapist whose main interest is helping people to master problems that are psychologically based, you have already found certain approaches to be useful and compatible with your way of conducting treatment. Since art is a tool, not a theory, its use in therapy can be adapted to any theoretical orientation.

In order to give you a sense of the links between psychological theory and technique, I will now note some ways of dealing with patient art that are compatible with primarily verbal approaches, some of which are likely to have relevance for you.

General Issues

What you do with art and your patients is, of course, up to you. This, like the timing and nature of your inclusion of art, will vary in part as a function of your general orientation and consequent way of doing therapy. Here are some examples of how different theoretical orientations might be translated into technical procedures when using art with patients. Since they are extremely brief, they are far from exhaustive, and do not in any way reflect all of the many ways in which any particular theory can inform the technique of inviting and learning from patient art.

Although each of the following sections is identified by a particular way of thinking about and doing psychotherapy, I hope that you will read all of them, as any might contain ideas you may want to adopt or adapt. If you are like most clinicians, even though you may have a preferred way of understanding human psychology and the process of change, you are also pragmatic and flexible about the specific techniques you use.

Psychodynamic/Analytic

As an analytically oriented therapist, you will no doubt be drawn to ways of evoking internal imagery in the art your patients produce, perhaps using some of the stimulating techniques noted earlier (DVD 8.3). You are likely to be especially attracted to ways of fostering free expression in as spontaneous a way as possible. If you are a Freudian, you will also invite associations to the art as freely as possible, before being more directed in your interviewing (Rubin, 1983, 2001b; 8.3A).

As in verbal therapy, you will try to get the patient to follow the analytic rule: to suspend logic and judgment, and to go wherever their thoughts may lead. As anyone who has been in analysis knows, this is so difficult that being able to do it is one sign of readiness for termination. A person who takes off from a drawing and lets associations flow more or less freely will usually end up far afield from where he or she started. The assumption is that such a meandering flow will lead to what is pressing for expression in the patient at that moment in time—the focal problem or conflict (Luborsky, 1984).

In addition to encouraging a freely associative process in any interviewing about the art, you will see the product and hear the associations in terms of the patient's developmental level (including fixation points and regressions), relationships with others (object relations), and internalized conflicts (Freud, Nagera, & Freud, 1965).

You will also be looking at the person's capacity for symbolization, sublimation, introspection, and self-observation. In addition, you will be attuned to transference manifestations: in the creation of the art, in the product itself, and in the associations to it. Finally, you will be monitoring your own countertransference reactions to both the person and the artwork. If your focus is on ego psychology, especially the symbolizing and synthetic function of the ego, you will be more likely to value well-sublimated art productions, like art therapist Edith Kramer (8.3B). There are others who believe in art *as* therapy whose orientation is not psychoanalytic, but whose position is to support the creative process, to help the individual to gain control, and to neutralize toxic feelings and impulses (DVD 8.4).

If your focus is on symbolization, you will interview and listen in the metaphor, like Laurie Wilson (8.3C).

If you are a Self psychologist, chances are that you will be especially attuned to the narcissistic aspects of making art, exposing the self, and showing the product. You may look for a way to acknowledge what the patient has created, offering some kind of affirmation, perhaps nonverbally. You will try to be empathic with whatever has been expressed, and you will be particularly concerned about how the patient feels about the product: scared, proud, ashamed, shy, and so on (Lachman-Chapin, 2001; 8.3D).

If your focus is on object relations, you will be looking for symbolic reflections of the patient's internalized world (8.3E) of self and others (Irwin 2001; Robbins, 2001, 2002). These are especially evident in self-portraits (Figure 8.2), though they are also apparent in other representations. How you respond to the person and his or her art will depend largely on your perception of where the individual is developmentally, and what he or she needs from you in order to grow and develop further.

If you are a Jungian, you may not talk *about* the image as much as learn from it. You will therefore want to help your patient focus on and then respond to what he or she has created, using the technique of *active imagination* (Edwards, 2001; Wallace, 2001). This usually includes prolonged

8.2 Woman Drawing a Self-Portrait

looking at and getting to know the image, which can then reveal its valuable secrets to its maker. To this end, you might suggest that the person engage in a dialogue with the image, which can be silent, audible, written, or drawn, as desired.

You may also encourage your patient to move in response to the image (8.7B), as a way of further understanding what has been presented (8.7C) as in the work of expressive arts therapist Carolyn Grant Fay, using *active imagination* (8.7D).

As you look at the product together, you will be trying to assess where that person is in the *individuation* process, and which *archetypes* are being expressed. You will also be attuned to the degree of *introversion* or *extraversion*, and whether the person is dominated more by feeling or thinking, sensation or intuition.

Humanistic/Transpersonal

If you are a *humanistic* therapist, you will be likely to favor free expression, though you might also be interested in tasks that promote self-actualization and self-definition more explicitly (DVD 8.4). Your interest in patient art will probably be primarily in the development of self-awareness, a feeling of competence, and increased self-esteem.

If you have a *holistic* bent, you may work on your patients' sense of themselves in the community and the world, and, if you are *transpersonal*, in the universe (Garai, 2001). These areas of emphasis will no doubt determine the tasks you choose to present, as well as how you deal with what people make. You will probably encourage your patients to find their own meaning and direction in their art, and to do the same in life.

If you are person-centered (formerly client-centered), you might, like Carl Rogers' (1951, 1961) daughter Natalie (2001), invite patients to draw about whatever comes up in a verbal interview, offering options of drawing materials. When Natalie Rogers interviews people about their art, it is in a highly respectful fashion, continually reflecting what has been said, and checking with clients to be sure that they have been heard and understood (8.4A).

If you are a Gestalt therapist, you will probably use multimodal techniques (8.8D) like sound, movement, and drama to help people get in touch with their feelings, focusing on the here and now (Rhyne, 1995, 2001). You will do everything you can to assist them in developing their own visual language. You are also likely to help people take responsibility for their artwork, as well as for their lives (8.4B).

If, like Fritz Perls (1969), you believe that every element in the dream represents the dreamer, you may apply that assumption to drawings and paintings as well. Inviting a patient to be and to speak for whatever is represented, including shapes and lines, is a way of dramatizing and thereby further understanding what has been expressed. If you are convinced of the *isomorphism* of drawings, you will view structural aspects of the pictures as reflecting the person (Rhyne, 2001).

If you are an Ericksonian, you might invite patients to draw either during or after hypnosis. Milton Erickson asked a woman suffering from Obsessive-Compulsive Disorder to engage in *automatic drawing*, which was most helpful in her treatment (Erickson & Kubie, 1940). This technique is especially powerful for getting at repressed traumatic material. Like Erickson, you are also likely to focus on metaphors, including those found in drawings (8.8J; Mills & Crowley, 1986; cf. DVD 12.6D).

If you are a phenomenologist, you will probably inquire about patients' subjective experience of the creative process (Betensky, 1995, 2001). Unlike the Jungian, who wants to know what the image is *saying* to the maker, the phenomenologist is more interested in what the maker can *see* in the image. They are similar in emphasizing a silent kind of nonjudgmental looking, but different in terms of the goal. For this reason, a phenomenologist is most likely to pursue the question "What do you see?" as thoroughly as possible, before asking whether anything seen in the art is related to the artist's own life (8.4C).

If you are existential, you will want to be present *to* and *with* your patients as they explore their experiences in art. You will also, like other humanistic therapists, honor and support each person's ability to chart his or her own course in creative work as well as in relationships with others and with the world (Moon, 1995; 8.4D).

If your transpersonal orientation is also a spiritual one, you may encourage patients to engage in some sort of meditation or relaxation (8.8N) prior to creating with materials (cf. Farrelly-Hansen, 2001; Franklin, 2001). Pat Allen's approach to art therapy requires that people in an open studio work in a mindful and intentional way. She also suggests that they refrain from commenting about their art, and focus instead on making, looking, and learning from it through silent *witness writing* (8.8P) that is then shared with the group—also without comment or analysis (Allen, 1995, 2001, 2005; cf. DVD 5.1C).

Developmental

If you think psychoanalytically, you are likely to be familiar with studies and theories of normal and atypical development, from infancy through adulthood, which guide your work (Colarusso, 1992; Tyson & Tyson, 1990). Even though you might subscribe to another frame of reference about human psychology and change, your orientation could also be developmental (DVD 8.5). This is most likely to be the case if you are working with children, or adults with cognitive disabilities. For all aspects of growth—intellectual, emotional, social, and physical (8.5A)—art interventions can be designed to support, and sometimes to further, higher levels of functioning (8.5B).

Even when people are suffering from degenerative diseases, such as Alzheimer's, it is often true that expressing themselves graphically may help them to be more organized or articulate in what they are able to "say" (Figure 8.3).

Of course, in order to use a developmental approach effectively, you would need to become familiar with normal cognitive and artistic development, in order to help patients move to increasingly advanced levels (cf.

8.3 Alzheimer's Patient Doing a Drawing

Aach-Feldman & Kunkle-Miller, 2001; Anderson, 1992; Malchiodi, Kim, & Choi, 2003; Piaget, 1952; Piaget & Inhelder, 1971; Silver, 1978, 2002).

Cognitive-Behavioral

If you are a cognitive and/or behavioral therapist, you are more likely to use directives for artwork in order to pursue specified goals (DVD 8.6). You might therefore employ modeling or shaping, helping patients to progress in their art to a higher developmental level or a more adaptive stance. Ellen Roth was able to apply this kind of thinking to art therapy with emotionally disturbed, mentally retarded children, with considerable success (Roth, 2001).

You could suggest specific topics designed to help individuals identify maladaptive thought patterns, which can then be represented visually as well as verbally. Selected themes are also likely to be helpful when dealing with phobias or other anxieties, whether you use desensitization, flooding, implosion, or some other treatment method. Ann Sayre Wiseman uses a technique for helping adults to "map" their dreams, and to think about having them turn out differently. It is based on her work with children's nightmares (8.6A), and is quite inventive. If you begin by requesting mental imagery before it is represented, you may also use some kind of relaxation technique (Benson, 1975) to facilitate that part of the process (Epstein, 1981; Rozum & Malchiodi, 2003).

Art therapist James Consoli (1991) used a combination of hypnosis, mental imagery, and drawing to help patients overcome symptoms of post-traumatic stress. He called it *psychimagery*, and found that putting patients into a light hypnotic trance helped them gain access to traumatic memories, which they were then asked to draw, and discuss, in order to assimilate them, so that they could go on with their lives (cf. DVD 12.3).

Psychiatrist Louis Tinnin and art therapist Linda Gantt engage patients' cognitive abilities as a way to gain control over the aftereffects of traumatic events. Working with patients suffering from PTSD and dissociation, they first help them to unearth and then to draw fragments of memory as these arise. With the goal of creating a coherent narrative of the trauma, the pictures are then put in order and re-presented to the patient. This is a screative way of concretizing, and eventually mastering, otherwise overwhelming and mostly preverbal traumas (8.6B).

Systemic/Solution-Focused/Narrative

If you have a systemic frame of reference, you are likely to be thinking in terms of *family*, even with only one patient in the room (DVD 8.7).

Drawing-tasks that relate to the family of origin, like a genogram, or to the current family, like the problem (8.7A), are therefore likely to be relevant. This would also be true for such tasks as a sociogram, or the drawing of a group (Hare & Hare, 1956), showing how early relationships are played out in current interpersonal relationships.

If you are attracted to recent developments in family therapy, such as solution-focused and narrative approaches, you are likely to work with patients to develop explicit strategies for change. In these models, tasks, while specific, may well grow out of the particular situation of the couple, family (8.7B), or individual in whose growth you are collaborating (Riley & Malchiodi, 1994, 2003; 8.7C).

Eclectic/Integrative

If you are eclectic, which is probably true for most therapists at least some (if not all) of the time, your use of art will vary like other interventions, according to what you feel a particular patient, family, or group needs at any clinical moment. Since art is so versatile, this is not at all difficult to do (Ulman, 2001; Wadeson, 2001).

The Role of Art over Time

Stages in Psychotherapy

Although there are many different ways to conceptualize stages in the treatment process, these are usually dependent, at least in part, on the particular theoretical constructs underlying your work. Thus, a Freudian analyst looks for the development, working through, and resolution of the transference neurosis. A Jungian looks for the achievement of individuation. A cognitive-behavioral therapist looks for the elimination of maladaptive thoughts and behaviors, and the development of more adaptive ones, and so on.

Nevertheless, there are some universal characteristics of any treatment process that are, in a sense, theory free. I'm referring to the early need for therapist and client to get to know each other and to form some sort of collaborative partnership, often known as a *working alliance*. No matter what your orientation, you want the patient to feel safe and to develop trust. You expect that there will be some testing of you and of the limits, and you look forward to a time when the communications are more open.

During the middle phase of therapy, you hope that the two of you are working together on whatever task is appropriate to your form of treatment—in other words, that the person in analytic therapy is expressing, facing, and accepting what has been hidden; or that the person in cognitive therapy is developing more successful ways of coping. You hope the patient is either *working through*, learning, or in some way growing as a result of increased awareness, understanding, and a new experience of interpersonal relatedness with you.

During the ending phase, you hope that individuals have accomplished their goals, whether to resolve the internal conflicts underlying the symptoms or to feel more the master of their fate, in charting their way in an existentially uncertain world.

You also hope that patients will be able to say goodbye, and to learn from what is experienced during the process of termination. It seems to me that such an evolution in therapeutic work is present, regardless of orientation, and regardless of whether the therapy is long term, time limited, individual, or with others. There are specific advantages to the use of art at each of these stages.

How Art Helps at Different Stages
Beginning Phase

In the beginning, using media can be a way for people to relax and to relieve tension, the usual motive for doodling in everyday life. Art can also be a way for you to get to know the person above and beyond—and, some would say, beneath—what he or she is able or willing to tell you at that point. It is also another way to obtain a history as well as a sense of the individual's situation and concerns at the time of the intervention.

Middle Phase

During the middle phase, art can be helpful in achieving your goals in different ways, depending on your approach. If you are psychodynamic, your patients' images and associations can help to make the unconscious conscious by raising ideas and impulses through the act of representing them. There is considerable evidence that this kind of nonverbal symbolization facilitates the eventual goal of conscious awareness (Wilson, 1999, 2001).

If you are humanistic, creating art can be a way for patients to get in touch with and to define their authentic selves, as well as to explore their place in the world. It can also be a way of imagining new possibilities as they take charge of life energies that may have been previously unavailable in their striving for self-actualization. And, if you are holistic or transpersonal, the experience of focused creating can be a way for your patients to get in touch with, and to feel a part of, forces beyond themselves.

If you are behavioral, making art can be a safe way for patients to imaginatively and symbolically practice new kinds of behaviors. If you are cog-

127

nitive, the visual thinking involved in drawing, like the thinking with the hands involved in modeling, can be another way for patients to look at and understand how they see the world, as well as to explore new possibilities without risk or consequence (Arnheim, 1969).

If you keep drawings in a place where they can be easily accessed, they provide extremely useful reference points at all stages of treatment (DVD 8.8). If you decide to look back at one or more items (8.8A), earlier artwork can help to jog memory or to stimulate almost-ripe insights (8.8B). Art is especially useful at various points (8.8C) as a way of re-viewing what has taken place in the course of treatment (8.8D). Art also functions as a transitional object for separations during the course of therapy, and especially at the time of final parting (8.8E).

Ending Phase

The ending phase of therapy is therefore a time when your inclusion of art is extremely helpful. Images are a vivid and concrete way to review what has occurred over the course of treatment. Anything a patient has created and you have stored can be looked at in the order in which it was made— a powerful way of reliving what has gone on (Chapter 5).

You can put the products in a pile and look at one drawing after another, or you can spread them out on a table, floor, or wall to get an overview. Such a review is helpful at the end of a session, at any juncture in treatment, and at termination.

Another way that products created during therapy and kept in your space can help in termination is by becoming the property of the patient, to the extent that he or she wishes. I usually invite patients to choose what they want to take, and offer to store the rest. Even if you don't have storage space for everything, it is still useful to ask patients which products they want to keep for themselves, and which they would like you to have.

For Elaine, who had struggled with a lifelong depression due to abuse throughout her childhood, art therapy became a way of finding out what was inside, in a place that felt increasingly secure over time. Knowing of Winnicott's work, she called it a "holding environment," and gave that title to one of her sculptures. In it, a person (Elaine) holding an infant (her small, victimized self) leans against a well-rooted tree, her favorite symbol for support (see Figure 8.4a).

Four years after that sculpture was made, I retired from full-time practice. It was extremely difficult for Elaine to say goodbye, even though she had made an excellent attachment to another therapist in the course of a long transition period. She took most of her artwork home, but left a good deal with me, too.

8.4a "Holding Environment" by Elaine

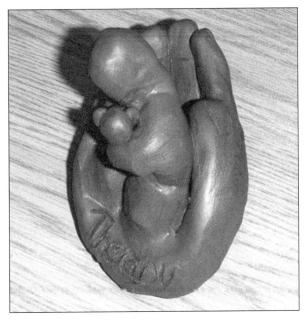

8.4b "Therapy" by Elaine, Done in the Last Art Session

In her last art session, Elaine made a sculpture that reminded me of the one she had done earlier, which she had decided to take home (8.12I). The tree had not been in her work for a while, perhaps because she felt more grounded herself. In its place was a hand, cradling a person who is holding a baby (Figure 8.4b). Although she traced the title, "Therapy," into the wet clay, she called later and asked me to smooth it out, feeling that the sculpture alone said it even more eloquently (8.8F).

Whatever he or she chooses to keep, the patient takes a piece of you and your joint work, a true "transitional object" (Winnicott, 1971a) that is as helpful in separating from therapy as a blanket is in parting from mother. Any products taken home are mementos of your shared journey—reminders of you, the person with or for whom they were created.

These products of their own imaginings, no matter how humble, do help people, especially those who are having a hard time with termination, to say goodbye. Leaving artwork with you is like giving you a piece of themselves, deposited as a form of concrete insurance that its creator will not be forgotten. I never cease to be amazed at the potency of art in this regard, which becomes dramatically evident when someone returns for further therapy many years later and refers to the art he or she made during our earlier work together.

Conclusion

This chapter has noted some ways of using art in your work with adults and older adolescents. I have included a brief discussion of ways that adding what Janie Rhyne called "visual languaging" to your patients' communicative options can help them to work on their goals, regardless of your theoretical orientation.

There are many more, and in the DVD accompanying this book, you will get a glimpse of them, including some examples by clinicians who are not art therapists. I hope that this volume and the live examples on the DVD, along with your own personal and clinical explorations, will lead you to join their number.

CHAPTER

9

Art in Child Therapy

Introduction

Because art is a natural part of child therapy, and because children respond differently than adolescents and adults to the idea of using art materials, this chapter is addressed specifically to those who work with children. Since their verbal abilities are more limited, and they are already comfortable with art media, youngsters stand to benefit considerably if you broaden your offerings of materials and ways of using them.

I have decided therefore to begin with an overview of the kinds of art supplies which will enhance your work in child therapy, since they will be so crucial to your success. I will then make some additional suggestions specific to work with children and adolescents, who, though generally more willing than adults to use art materials, still need help to maximize their effectiveness. I will also describe and discuss some of the developmental variables you need to be aware of when looking at children's artistic products, whether in assessment or therapy.

Art Supplies for Child Therapy

Although you might think children wouldn't care or notice, sturdy art supplies are even more critical in child therapy. That is because children are likely to be much harder on materials than older adolescents or adults, and they, too, will have a more satisfying creative experience with good-quality supplies. Appendix A contains additional details about art materials, as well as information about resources (cf. also DVD 3.1).

Papers

Whatever medium children choose, sturdy paper is essential, since they are likely to work vigorously. Because newsprint is thin and tears easily, I recommend 60- to 80-lb. white drawing paper. It is a good idea to have more than one color of paper and several choices of sizes. Some youngsters work small, and some work large, so you will need white drawing paper and assorted colors of construction paper in the following sizes: 9″ × 12″, 12″ × 18″, and 18″ × 24″.

For groups or families you may want to get 24″ × 36″ paper as well (white for sure, assorted colors if you wish). This larger size requires that you have a big enough surface to accommodate it, whether on a table or taped to the wall. For finger paint, you will need a package of 11″ × 16″ glossy paper, and cafeteria-style plastic trays to contain the mess—and the children's anxieties about it. It is most economical to buy white drawing paper by the ream (500 sheets), while construction and finger-paint paper are sold in smaller packages of 50 or 100 sheets.

Things to Draw With

Pencils

A soft *drawing pencil*, like an Ebony pencil, is best for most children, along with a good large eraser. For older children, it is nice to have several drawing pencils of varying degrees of hardness, like a No. 2, a No. 4, and a No. 6. A set of 8 to 12 *colored pencils* is also recommended, the kind that can be used wet as well as dry. For older children and adolescents, *charcoal pencils* are also manageable.

Crayons

Wax crayons are very appealing to youngsters, and sets of many colors (48 to 64) are both exciting and stimulating. The standard size is fine for most, although little fingers sometimes do better with the larger crayons. *Payons*, which can paint on wet paper or when dipped in water, are also attractive.

Oil crayons (like Craypas) are more grown-up looking, and are therefore more appealing to older children and adolescents. In addition, they can be blended more easily. The thin ones are fine for the majority of youngsters, although the thick ones are a little more manageable for some young children. Sets of 16 colors are adequate, though more are stimulating.

Chalk and Pastels

Children like both thin *pastels* and thick *poster chalks* of moderate quality in sets of 12 to 24. You will also want to buy a spray can of *fixative* or hair spray to set the chalk particles so they won't smear easily when a drawing is finished. If you want to involve youngsters in using the spray, you will need to open a window. There are also *pastel pencils* for finer work.

Markers

Children need to have both fine and broad *felt-tip markers* available. Washable *watercolor markers* are best, although you may also want to have a few permanent *ink* or *paint markers* on hand, in case a child wants to draw or write on plastic or metal. Those that are especially appealing to older children and adolescents are the metallic ones in silver and gold, as well as a variety of colors. Because they are difficult to wash off hands, clothing, and furniture, it makes sense not to offer them to the very young.

Things to Paint With

While optional for work with adolescents and adults, paint is essential for child therapy. There are three main kinds: tempera, watercolor, and finger paint. All are water soluble, and can therefore be washed off easily.

Tempera

Tempera can be purchased in small sets of colors, and can be used directly from the jars, as long as a cup of water is available to clean the brush before using a new color. These sets are easily portable, and work well when painting on a table.

Since children use large quantities of paint, you may prefer to buy tempera in 8- or 16-oz. containers, and to pour it into muffin tins or plastic cups. I recommend a jar of each of the most commonly used colors: red, yellow, blue, green, purple, orange, black, brown, white, and flesh. Children can mix additional colors in cups, tins, foil trays, or paper plates.

Tempera markers (the names vary according to the brand) are essential for children, though optional for adults. They can be used to make lines or dots, or to fill in broad areas. They are especially nice when there is concern about mess.

Water Colors

Water colors are difficult for young children to use, though children over age 10 can usually manage them successfully. A decent brand is important, and it is more stimulating if you buy a set with 16 as opposed to 8 colors. Although water colors also come in tubes, these are more difficult for little ones to manage than those in tins, especially ovals.

Finger Paints

Finger paints are useful for youngsters who have problems with their impulses, whether they are inhibited or out of control. A good-quality set of 8 to 12 assorted colors is best. One of the easiest ways to finger paint is to use shallow plastic trays, like those in cafeterias with or without paper (Figure 9.1). You can also finger paint directly onto a water-resistant table.

If the child works directly on a tray or table, you can make a *monoprint* of the image at any point by pressing a piece of paper onto whatever has been drawn and carefully lifting it up. While optional for adults, finger paints are highly recommended in child therapy.

Brushes

Brushes come in many sizes and shapes, and vary in quality. You will need to buy some pointed and some flat brushes of moderate quality from an art supply catalog or store, not the drugstore. Children need both thick and thin brushes, with at least three different sizes of each. Even if you have an easel, short-handled brushes are easiest to manage.

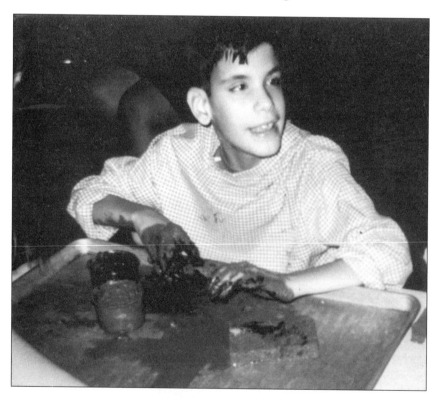

9.1 Boy Finger Painting Inside a Tray

Things to Model With

Plasticine

Plasticine (oil-based clay) comes in different colors that children like; they also like the fact that it doesn't dry out, which is useful for some purposes. Since it is stimulating and is less threatening than earth clay for those who fear loss of control, you need to buy some in assorted colors. Colored plasticine and clay are both essential for child therapy.

Earth Clay

Clay that forms in the earth is easiest for youngsters to work with, and can be used with or without water. You will need string or thin wire to cut out chunks of clay from a larger piece (it is usually sold in 10- to 25-lb. bags). I recommend the smooth kind used in schools, ideally one bag of red or brown and one of gray or white. You don't need to have a kiln (a special oven for firing clay at a high temperature to make ceramics), since clay can air dry, and can be painted and varnished or shellacked as well.

Synthetic Modeling Media

Synthetic modeling media are also available in many varieties. Some air dry like clay that has been fired, and some, like *Sculpey* or *Fima*, can be baked in an ordinary oven. Another synthetic material that is even "cleaner" than plasticine (which is oil based) and is very appealing to young children is *Model Magic*. Most of these alternative clays come in a neutral tone as well as in a variety of colors, and some can also be painted.

Modeling Dough

Dough, either homemade or commercial (like Play-Doh) is used by many child therapists. While this is a very pliable medium, it does not hold its shape well or have a smooth surface when it hardens. With homemade dough, however, the mixing process itself can be therapeutic, and involves adding color (food color or powdered tempera paint) to a flour, salt, and water combination. Dough is fine to use, but it is no substitute for clay or plasticine when it comes to modeling.

Papier Mâché

Papier mâché enables children to make lightweight puppet heads and other kinds of sculpture. It involves dipping strips of newspaper into a glue-and-water mixture, then placing them on a shaped base of clay or some other material, such as a balloon, aluminum foil, or crumpled newspaper.

Pariscraft, another material that serves the same purpose, is gauze impregnated with plaster of paris, like what is used to make casts. It comes in

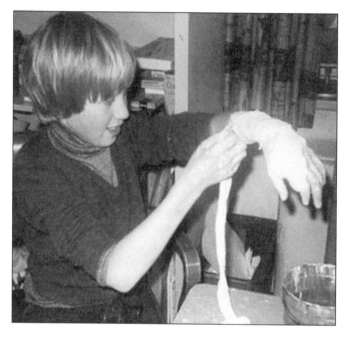

9.2 Making a Cast with Pariscraft

a roll, which can be cut into strips and dipped in water before being placed on a base (Figure 9.2).

Tools and Bases

Tools for modeling are many and varied. Children usually use their hands, but if they are anxious about mess or for some purposes (like making holes or lines), they will need other tools. Tongue depressors, craft sticks, and orange sticks are fine; but a set of wooden or plastic clay tools, some with wire loops and serrated edges, is a nice addition.

Bases for modeling include paper, paper plates, cardboard, and Masonite (which can be used under any modeling material). Older children often like using a small plastic turntable (available in hardware stores) so that they can easily see what they're making from different angles. For Pariscraft and papier mâché, as well as for earth clay used with water, a tray helps to contain the mess.

Things to Construct With
Two-Dimensional

Assorted colors of construction paper (all sizes, especially 12" × 18") are important in collage. For variety, you may also want to buy other kinds of paper, especially those that are visually attractive, like glossy and metallic papers, tissue paper in assorted colors, or rolls of cellophane.

You can also collect pictures from magazines and other sources, as well as a box of scrap materials, like wrapping paper, yarn, and ribbons. In addition, children of all ages enjoy tearing or cutting pictures out of magazines themselves. You will need to get some child-size scissors (round and pointed), including some for those who are left-handed.

Three-Dimensional

Children can use colored pipe cleaners, soft soldering wire, toothpicks, craft sticks, and tongue depressors, as well as any scrap material that is safe for them to manipulate, such as wood scraps without splinters. For both two- and three-dimensional construction, children will need small bottles of white liquid glue, glue sticks, tape, and staplers. For three-dimensional work, bases can be made of styrofoam, clay, plasticine, or wood; and a plastic turntable is useful here, too.

Working Surfaces
Tables

If you work with children, you probably already have a *table* with sufficient work space for art activities. If you are buying one, be sure that the top is made of an easily washable material, and that it is sturdy. Adjustable legs are nice, but cushions or phone books for a child to sit on work well, too. If you plan to use art with groups or families, a larger table might be needed, so you may want to look for an expandable one, as with a drop leaf.

Easels

Easels are especially appealing to disorganized children, and it seems as if they do help some to focus on the art activity. If you don't have space for a floor easel, a wall or table easel is an option that can be stored in a closet when not used. You don't need an expensive one, but it is important that easels, like tables, not be wobbly. If you can find one with a blackboard surface, children can also draw (and erase) with chalk, an appealing option for some youngsters at some moments (Figure 9.3).

As for surfaces (DVD 9.1), options help (9.1A). Children can work comfortably on the floor (9.1B), at a chalkboard (9.1C), a table easel (9.1D), on the wall (9.1E), seated (9.1F), or standing (9.1G), and on erasable drawing boards (9.1H).

9.3 Boy Drawing on a Chalkboard

Cleanup Issues
Smocks

Although most adults don't require one, some sort of *smock* is essential for children who use art materials in therapy (DVD 9.2). Old shirts worn backward (9.2A) work well for people of all ages, and you can also purchase smocks designed for young children (9.2B).

Sinks

Little ones require either a *sink* in the room or one that is easily accessible. For messy materials, you may want to have some soap and water in the playroom (in a bucket or plastic container), as well as paper towels and packaged wipes.

Setting Things Up

If you have enough space, you may want to have some or all of the art supplies visible all the time. If you don't have enough space to leave them out, you can organize them so they are visible on closet shelves, or on a rolling cart in a corner. Such arrangements enhance the likelihood that children will be able to use the art materials spontaneously and independently.

On the other hand, if you would prefer that children not make art whenever they wish, it makes more sense to store materials in a closet or cupboard that is opened only when you decide. Plastic carrying containers, like those sold in hardware stores, are very helpful for organizing and transporting art supplies. Whether some, all, or none of the materials are visible at all times, organization and consistency in how and where art supplies are kept are especially important for work with children and adolescents.

Introducing Art to Children

Inviting Participation

Although most children will naturally pick up and use art materials if they are visible, some may require a specific request to do so (DVD 9.3). Younger children usually have little trouble getting started, especially if they are invited to choose anything they wish and to do whatever they want (9.3A).

However, if they balk or say they don't know what to do, which can happen with older or insecure children, one approach is to narrow the choice for them as you might for a reluctant adolescent or adult: "Well, would you like to start by drawing, painting, or modeling?" Once the category is selected, you can give further help: "Would you prefer tempera, watercolors, or finger paint?" They will eventually make the choice, with your supportive assistance.

If you are requesting that they use a particular material or that they make a specific topic, you will need to state the task in terms appropriate to the child's age level and cognitive ability. Although most children will begin without needing much (if any) assistance, there are some who feel inadequate, who tell you that they can't draw (or paint or sculpt) or make a _____ (whatever you've requested).

If a child expresses concern about not being able to do what you've asked, it is helpful to reassure him or her that skill in art doesn't matter. You can explain that art in therapy is more like playing. It's mostly for fun   not like art class at school, where you have to do things well according to the teacher. With children who can understand, you can use some of the same arguments for the usefulness of art that are appropriate for adolescents or adults, but in terms appropriate to their age.

Once they get used to it, most youngsters are quite comfortable with the idea that coming to therapy can help them with their worries or their troubles. So if you explain that drawing, painting, or modeling can help the two of you to figure things out better, that may be sufficient to overcome whatever is behind their hesitancy.

Older children and teens may, like adults, be worried that you will see something in their art that they won't know about, some sort of secret that you will find out against their will. As advised with older patients, you can tell them that any meanings in their art are something the two of you will have to figure out together, because they are, in fact, the experts on their own creations (cf. DVD 3.3C).

Reluctant Children

Even with your very best efforts to make the introduction of art media nonthreatening, however, you may run into some youngsters who reject the option. It makes sense to first inquire what it is they're concerned about. They may say that they're not worried; they just don't like art or don't want to do it. The simplest solution to this problem is to leave the art materials out where they are visible, and to suggest that whenever they feel like trying them they can do so.

Another option is to ask if they mind if *you* use materials, which they usually don't. You can then use art media yourself in a casual way, such as doodling with a marker, squeezing some clay, putting dabs of paint on wet paper, or some such unthreatening and playful practice.

While I can't guarantee that this will work, it usually does, especially if you're patient about it. In children's therapy groups, seeing, their peers enjoying work with art materials usually helps anxious or oppositional youngsters to overcome their inhibitions. In individual therapy you may need to be the model, but it is best not to pressure them to join you.

Adolescents

Young teens and sometimes even younger preadolescents may find any kind of art activity to be babyish. A different route to creating, might be using one of the many kinds of construction toys available (9.3B). As with media, it is less threatening to ask whether they want to fool around with a set (9.3C), rather than asking them to make anything (9.3D). Here, too, you may want to do the same. Although teenagers usually are extremely self-conscious about their performance, they are also very interested in themselves, their primary developmental task being identity formation.

It is also relevant to remember that they are going through a developmental phase when both narcissism and exhibitionism are heightened. This is evident in such behaviors as coloring their hair, piercing tender body parts, and getting tattoos. For these reasons, being able to create something uniquely their own has tremendous appeal, as long as their performance anxiety can be overcome. After all, this is the age when even non-musicians are into dancing and playing guitars.

For adolescents, however, having more age-appropriate art materials is absolutely critical. Drawing with the same kinds of crayons they used in kindergarten is much too threatening, since they are already fighting a normal regressive pull as they struggle to move toward young adulthood, which is both appealing and terrifying (Blos, 1962).

It therefore helps if you offer them more adult drawing materials, such as pen and ink, charcoal, or artist's pastels. If adolescents find watercolor or tempera too childish, you might buy sets of gouache or acrylic paints in tubes or tins. Both are water soluble and can be used on paper or cardboard (9.3E).

If they want to sculpt, some of the newer clays that can be baked in regular ovens might be most appealing. Some of these are water based and some, like Sculpey or Fimo, are oil based and come in different colors. Teenagers also respond positively to making collages, particularly those in which they can express their interests, using a combination of pictures from magazines (especially those aimed at adolescents) and a variety of papers, as well as different art materials.

This is also a period when many spontaneously take up writing journals, diaries, and often poetry, to deal with the overwhelming and confusing changes they are going through. The hormones are racing and the temptations to achieve altered states of consciousness through drugs and alcohol are tremendous, so the fact that the arts provide a natural high is especially relevant (cf. DVD 11.6B).

Adolescents are one of the groups for whom multiple modalities really make sense. Music and dance are generally central in their lives, and something as simple as having a CD player available can make a substantial difference in their attitude toward psychotherapy (9.3F).

With this age group, it is important to remember that they are normally ambivalent about getting close to adults. After all, they are engaged in trying to separate from their parents and to become more independent.

For adolescents, perhaps even more than other age groups, having an art product as the third party in the room helps to modulate the inevitable intimacy of psychotherapy. In many ways, therefore, the very nature of adolescence makes incorporating art and other modalities into treatment a good idea, as long as their probable reluctance can be overcome.

The Importance of Choice

Choices are as important for children and adolescents as they are for adults, perhaps even more so (DVD 9.4). This true because in other sectors of their lives, they are usually not allowed to be in charge, whether at home, at work, or (for teens) at school. Authority figures are often seen as the enemy, because teens may feel unfairly controlled by the adults in their lives.

If it is common for parents and school personnel to see the child as the one with the problem, it is equally common for young people to see the problem as the parents or the teachers (9.4A).

It therefore helps youngsters of all ages to be able to select what they want to use—whether it is the size or color of paper or clay, the specific drawing or painting material, or the brushes or clay tools (9.4B). If you have an easel and a table, they can choose their working surface as well. Options in both media and task enable children and teens to be in charge in a way that isn't usually possible elsewhere (9.4C).

In addition to being able to be the boss not only of themselves, but of what they use and what they make, youngsters, like adults, benefit from being allowed to choose what is most appealing to them. Something as minor as being able to select the paper size can make a big difference in a child's comfort with drawing or painting.

Special Considerations for Work with Children

I have noted some ideas about what you might do with reluctant children or adolescents to help them create. I have also spent some time on the value for all children of having choices. In regard to the areas dealt with in preceding chapters, including deciding what to do and how to do it, the considerations for work with young people are essentially the same as those for work with adults.

For example, there are hardly any tasks or themes that are appropriate solely for children and adolescents. The exception would be those peculiar to their life circumstances, such as drawings of their school or teachers, or a theme like "what I want to be when I grow up" (9.4D). Otherwise, human beings of all ages can draw people and families, wishes and fears, whatever topics might appeal to you as relevant to your work with them.

Certain attributes that are valuable in your work with adolescents and adults are even more critical when using art with children. For example, being flexible is vital, as is being playful. By this I do not mean becoming another child, which would be frightening, but rather being able to receive and to respond to what they make and what they do with it in a creative, as well as an empathic, way. However, there are some issues specific to child therapy that deserve to be noted, such as the setting of limits and being aware of developmental variables in their artwork.

Freedom and Limits
Art media, much more than blocks or board games, can sometimes stimulate regression and acting-out, especially in children whose controls are

9.4 Making a Pictorial Target

weak. You may feel uneasy about inviting such youngsters to use clay or fin-ger paint, for fear that they might become disorganized in some fashion (DVD 9.5).

My experience, however, is that, when given choices, even psychotic children tend to protect themselves, to find materials and ways of working that allow them to stay in control. Fortunately, there is a good deal of per-missible regression (9.5A, B) and aggression that can be constructively con-tained in the creative process—one of the many reasons to make art avail-able to clients of all ages (9.5C).

Nevertheless, if things do get out of hand with art materials, as in any kind of play, you need to set limits firmly, kindly, and empathically. You may even be able to redirect the activity to a more acceptable way of using me-dia, which allows the children to safely discharge their energy within some sort of structure.

For example, on one occasion, the boys in a group of 8-year-olds started throwing clay at each other, which of course had to be stopped. After a group discussion of what had happened, they were invited to make large pa-per targets of cartoon or fantasy characters (for greater disguise) at which they could then safely lob small clay "bullets," one at a time, from behind a clearly defined line of masking tape (Figure 9.4).

On another occasion, an 11-year-old began to use a hammer, not to pound nails into the wood she had been working with, but to attack the table, making dents in the surface. She was offered a large chunk of gray clay, and invited to use the same hammer and action. Not only was she able to discharge the aggression safely by hitting the clay; she eventually ended up making a powerful sculpture of a monster, molding it with considerable care (cf. DVD 9.5D, E).

The answer, in my opinion, is usually not limiting the art activity or the materials you offer. Rather, it is being clear about what is and is not permitted, and being creative, if possible, about suggesting alternative activities that can meet similar needs. Of course, there are exceptions to every rule, and there certainly have been times when I have suggested a more contained (smaller) space, or a more controllable medium (like drawing vs. painting) to help children regain self-control.

Looking at Children's Art Developmentally

Because how you perceive what children are producing, even if you never say a word about it, will affect your response and probably their sense of your reaction, it is important to touch on some of the developmental aspects of children's art. If you work with youngsters, you are probably well versed in child development. It is also important to have some familiarity with normal stages in art, so that you know where children are, and how their art relates to their chronological ages. This is especially true if you are working with patients at any age level who have developmental delays.

Although a few have looked at developmental levels in painting and modeling (Golomb, 1974, 1992, 2002), the literature on normal stages in children's drawings is by far the most extensive (Gardner, 1980). And while many workers have studied drawing development, the framework that remains most popular among art therapists is one first proposed in 1947 by Viktor Lowenfeld (1957). The stages are described in considerable detail in *Creative and Mental Growth*, which is now in its seventh edition (Lowenfeld & Brittain, 1982). The most relevant edition for therapists, however, is the third (Lowenfeld, 1957), which includes an extensive chapter on "Therapeutic Aspects of Art Education" (omitted from later editions after Lowenfeld's death).

Others have also proposed ways of organizing developmental levels (cf. Rubin, 2005, and Malchiodi, 1998b). Only when you know where someone is developmentally will you be able to foster progression (cf. Aach-Feldman & Kunkle-Miller, 2001; Roth, 2001; Silver, 1978, 2002).

As you might imagine, there are many different ways of doing so. It is interesting to note, for example, that when body parts were dictated by the adult, preschool children drew human figures at a higher developmental level than when they were simply asked to draw a person (Golomb, 1974, pp. 152–163); or, that human figures by neurologically handicapped youngsters done with white crayon on black paper were at a higher level than those drawn with black on white (Uhlin, 1972, pp. 87–94).

The main reason for most child therapists to know normal drawing development is so that you don't misinterpret something as pathological when it is actually age appropriate (DVD 9.6). For example, neither color nor size are realistic when a child is in what Lowenfeld called the "pre-schematic" stage (roughly 4 to 7 years).

Thus, a purple cow or a pink tree is perfectly normal. Relative sizes are also unrealistic, but unlike color—which tends to be fanciful—can also be an index of the relative importance of objects in the child's world. This is evident in Becca's drawing of the Wizard of Oz (Figure 9.5), where the yellow brick road and the house landing on the wicked witch dwarf both the tree and the rainbow, yet more realistic two years later (9.5A)

Similarly, x-ray drawings, in which things inside are shown as if a body or a house were transparent (see Figure 9.6), are quite normal during this period (9.5B). They are, usually, however, signs of either retardation or psychosis in adults, and a cause for concern in older children.

9.5 The Wizard of Oz—Age 6

9.6 X-Ray Drawing of a Baby inside a Mommy

There is also a kind of logic in some of the drawings done by young children, which, though they look odd, make very good sense. For example, a child might represent people seated at a table so that you can see everyone from the same point of view, which allows you to get the picture (9.5C). Similarly, the catching and throwing arms of ball players might be represented, while the inactive arms are omitted (Figure 9.7). It is important to know that this is probably not a sign of body-image confusion or of castration anxiety, but is more likely to be an example of this peculiar but sensible logic (9.5D).

Similarly, if you are familiar with the normal repetition of symbols at the schematic stage, you'll be as accepting of it as you are of the need for preschoolers to repeat experiences in dramatic play. In both, the repetition is part of active mastery, not a sign of being fixated, or of the perseveration that characterizes the play and art of autistic and neurologically impaired children.

In addition, the self-consciousness and self-criticism that begin at around age 10 for most children (earlier for bright ones) are also indices of

9.7 Playing Catch Requires Only
One Arm

a developmental need—to try to represent the world realistically—and not a sign of low self-esteem. You may also be surprised to learn that it is normal for adults and adolescents to plateau at about a 10- to 12-year-old level without further art instruction.

Temporary Regression

It is normal for people of all ages to regress at times of stress. When you know where a child usually functions in art, a sudden change is an index that something is disturbing the youngster. Lisa's painting in her preschool classroom (9.5E) was so much less organized and so much muddier than her usual work (9.5F) that it alerted her observant teacher. She was not surprised to discover that Lisa's mother had gone to the hospital that morning, to deliver yet another younger sibling.

A 5-year-old boy who was paralyzed from the waist down, when asked to draw a person, produced a rather advanced picture of a clown (9.5G). Asked to draw himself on the other side of the paper, he made a very early human figure—a crude enclosure with rough indications of limbs and features (9.5H). About his self-portrait, he explained: "The legs got lost in the grass." Because we know how bright he was from his clown drawing, we can hypothesize that the massive regression in the self-portrait indicated not only what he *knew,* but also how he *felt* about his damaged body.

Conclusion

This chapter has sketched out some of the areas relevant for work with children that are not covered elsewhere in this volume, including details about materials, limit setting, and developmental issues. However, if you are interested in learning more about the use of art in child therapy, you may also want to consult the third edition of *Child Art Therapy: Understanding and Helping Children Grow through Art* (Rubin, 2005).

Other useful resources are the books by Edith Kramer (1958, 1971, 1979), Mala Betensky (1973, 1995), John Allan (1988), and Violet Oaklander (1969), as well as the first one on art therapy by Margaret Naumburg (1973). In addition, there is a volume edited by Caroline Case and Tessa Dalley (1990), as well as recent books by Gussie Klorer (2000) and Cathy Malchiodi (1997, 1998b, 1999b).

If you are interested in using art with children who have disabilities, you can consult the books by Frances Anderson (1992), Janet Bush (1997), David Henley (1992), Rawley Silver (1978, 2002), and Don Uhlin (1972). In addition, for work with adolescents you may consult those by Helen Landgarten (1981, 1987), Debby Linesch (1988), and Shirley Riley (1999).

10

Art in Family and Group Therapy

Introduction

So far I've been talking in a general way about how therapists of widely differing theoretical orientations can incorporate simple art materials and techniques into their work, using whatever media they are comfortable with. In addition to using art in your work with individuals of all ages, you will also find it very helpful with couples, families, and groups. As with individuals, it doesn't have to be elaborate. In fact, I believe that you can greatly enhance treatment by adding just a stack of paper and some markers to what you offer your patients.

As noted earlier, one of the major advantages of art with any group of two or more is that everyone can "talk" at once. In that regard, it is remarkably efficient. This is equally true of what has been created, which can be seen simultaneously by all participants.

Family Art Evaluation

There are numerous art assessment batteries for use with families. All of them involve some combination of individual and joint creative activity, and all include one or more representations of the family itself (DVD 10.1).

Kwiatkowska

The pioneer in this area was Hanna Kwiatkowska (1978), the first art therapist at NIMH beginning in the 1950s (10.1A). Her *Family Art Evaluation (FAE)*, designed in the 1960s, provided so much information in such a short period of time, that it was soon used routinely as part of the intake procedure. Kwiatkowska's evaluation involved six drawing tasks in the following order:

1. Free Picture
2. Picture of Your Family
3. Abstract Family Portrait
4. Scribble Drawing
5. Joint Family Scribble
6. Free Picture

One that she included routinely, and that she felt was rather difficult, was the *Abstract Family Portrait* (10.1B). Although it is true that some are uncomfortable with the ambiguity of the task, I have found it to be a useful option for adults who are especially anxious about drawing human beings.

Her group task, the *Joint Family Scribble*, was easily done in her setup, with easels in a semicircle. Kwiatkowska saw families of adolescent inpatients, so that the youngsters were usually old enough to project an image onto a scribble. Each family member first makes a scribble independently. The group then looks at all of them, in order to choose one to develop as a family. After it is selected, they work together to develop the image they have agreed on (10.1C).

Rubin and Magnussen

Other art therapists, inspired by Kwiatkowska, developed a variety of modifications for different settings. In 1970 a clinical psychologist and I designed a three-task procedure at the Pittsburgh Child Guidance Center (Rubin & Magnussen, 1974; see Figure 10.1), which we taught to interested colleagues in psychiatry, social work, and psychology. Since it was fairly easy for others to learn and to use, I will describe it here.

Scribble Drawings

The first task is to develop an image from a scribble on 9″ × 12″ white drawing paper, using one of the media in the middle of the table (crayons, markers, colored pencils). The family sits around the table and each person creates a scribble drawing (10.1D), using the instructions described earlier (Chapter 7, p. 105; DVD 7.3E).

Younger children, for whom developing an image from a scribble isn't possible, and those in the family who finish early are invited to make a *free drawing* (10.1E). When done, they are asked to give the drawing a *title*, whatever comes to mind. Afterward, they take turns describing their pic-

10.1 Family Art Evaluation at PCGC

tures, one at a time, and being questioned by other family members (see DVD 7.3[2]).

Family Representations

Each person is asked to represent the family (10.1F), using a medium and surface of his or her choice (crayons, markers, chalk, or colored pencils on 9″ × 12″ or 12″ × 18″ white drawing paper; or plasticine clay in different colors). You can offer the option of doing it either realistically or abstractly (using a different color and shape for each individual).

Although I prefer to leave it up to individuals, you can also ask that every family member be included in each picture and, if you wish, that they all be doing something (as in the KFD, discussed in Chapter 6)—all are revealing. Afterward, each person describes his or her representation and responds to questions by the others (10.1G). If it is possible to display all of the family representations at once (10.1H), that provides a useful stimulus for spontaneous comparisons.

Family Mural

The family is asked first to discuss (10.1I), and then to execute, a joint picture on a shared surface (10.1J), which can be either placed on a table or taped on the wall. They use thick poster chalks or thick markers on large white (or neutral) drawing paper (24″ × 36″ or a roll; 10.1K). Afterward, they are asked to look at the mural and to talk about both the decision making and the execution (10.1L; cf. also 10.1M, 10.1N).

These three tasks work best if you have 1½ to 2 hours available. If time is limited, however, you can modify the tasks in any way you wish, as dictated by clinical needs and circumstances. In addition to the information in the artwork itself, such a session provides a valuable opportunity to observe the family in action, in both the doing and discussion portions of the activities. The interactions are usually more spontaneous than in verbal meetings.

The discussions, in which you invite members to react and to comment on others' artwork (especially their representations of the family), are also extremely revealing. After the third task it is useful to ask the family whether their process in deciding and executing the mural was representative of how they usually function as a group. In regard to the entire session, you can ask how typical or atypical members' behavior was, compared to how things generally are at home.

Modifications by Study Group Members

The Family Art Study Group at the Child Guidance Center (Chapter 1, p. 4) was attended by professionals from all disciplines. Two of them, a child psychiatrist and a social worker, were co-therapists for a parents' group. After a month of weekly 90- minute meetings, the couples were told that each family was to come in for an art session that would be videotaped and then reviewed by the study group.

Because the leaders planned to show the unedited tapes during the group sessions, the entire procedure had to take no more than one hour. They used a small space, so that the stationary video camera could record all family members most of the time. The therapists decided to present only the second and third tasks, and to present a more limited and quickly usable selection of two-dimensional media.

The leaders proceeded to review the tapes and artwork with the study group, allotting two weeks for each family. The members discussed the art sessions in detail, learning from other families as well as from their own. The therapists were so pleased with the success of their innovative approach that they later wrote and presented a paper describing it (Henderson & Lowe, 1972).

A former psychology intern went to her first job at a California clinic. She wanted to elicit the rich diagnostic data available in a family art evaluation, but due to time pressures had to rethink what was possible. She chose a 5-minute version of the group mural, as part of a brief family evaluation procedure (Goldstein, Deeton, & Barasch, 1975).

Landgarten

Helen Landgarten's (1987) *family evaluation* uses two procedures requiring family members to work *without talking*. The first is the *nonverbal team art task,* in which a family (of four or more) is asked to divide into *two teams,* immediately revealing alliances within the family.

Like Bing (1970), who asked members to work together on a family portrait, Landgarten also suggested a kind of *color coding.* Each person is asked to "select one color marker that is different from the others and is to be used for the entire session" (Landgarten, 1987, p. 14).

Each team is then asked to work together silently on a single piece of paper, without writing or signaling to one another while doing the joint task. Landgarten notes that the task could also be to make something together in the same silent fashion using other media, like colored plasticine or colored paper, and that the same differentiation of people by colors would be observed.

The second procedure is a *nonverbal family art task,* in which the *entire family* is to work silently on the same paper. The third is a *verbal family art task,* in which the group is asked to make a single piece of artwork, this time with discussion permitted.

By requiring the family to *work together in different ways* in the course of one session, the therapist has multiple opportunities to observe their interactions. The color coding allows each person's contribution to be easily identifiable in the finished products, and can be used with couples or group members as well (cf. Figs. 10.6 and 10.7).

Art Therapy with Couples

Wadeson

Harriet Wadeson (1972), working at NIMH, suggested two tasks to be used with couples as part of an assessment (DVD 10.2). Both are useful with other family groupings, as well as for group members who aren't related. Like Landgarten's nonverbal team or joint drawings, the first one helps both participants and observers to focus on the nonverbal communication involved in using art media.

Nonverbal Joint Drawing

The instructions are to "make a well-integrated picture together without talking" (10.2A). Afterward, the couple discuss their feelings about the interaction (10.2B). If your goal is to see whether they can work together constructively, then asking them to collaborate on a finished picture is likely to give you that kind of information.

However, I have found that asking two or more people to work together without talking is most informative if no instructions are given except to share the space and to agree on the medium. They may or may not make a "well-integrated picture together," for example; may or may not tune in to one another; may divide the space, rather than sharing it; and so on.

Abstract of the Marital Relationship

Each member of the couple is asked to make an abstract picture of the marital relationship. Afterward, they describe and discuss together what each has made. This task was inspired by the one in Hanna Kwiatkowska's FAE to make an abstract portrait of the family.

Self-Portrait Given to Spouse

The third task is the most original. Each person is invited to draw a self-portrait (10.2C), which is then given to the partner. At that point, the spouse is invited to modify his or her mate's picture in any way he or she wishes (10.2D)—a rare opportunity, to say the least. The sequence of activities provides the couple with an opportunity not available in real life: to change the other person however they would like to—and then to discuss the sequence of events (10.2E).

Although it was originally designed for couples, I have found that the activity is also useful with any two family members, such as siblings, or parent and child. It can also be used with dyads in a therapy group, especially after the members have gotten to know one another. A variation on this task is to reverse it—to have each partner *make a picture of the other*, then to exchange those drawings, and have the opportunity to modify them (10.2F).

I have described the specific tasks in each of these evaluations so that you can select any that seem most clinically appropriate for those you are assessing. The paper size and materials can be optional or specified, as you wish. Another possibility is to invite the couple to draw the problem (10.2G).

Occasional Family Art Sessions

Art sessions with two or more family members are extremely useful in the course of individual therapy. If you have been meeting with both the children and the parents prior to such sessions, they are likely not only to be willing to have one, but to be relatively relaxed and natural during it. The possible subgroups who can work side by side or jointly using art are many (DVD 10.3).

Two or more siblings (Chapter 4, Figure 4.2; DVD 10.3A), a mother and child (Figure 10.2; DVD 10.3B), a father and child (10.3C), both parents and a child, parent(s) and child(ren), and both parents as a couple—all can be seen and helped using art. As in verbal therapy, you would probably

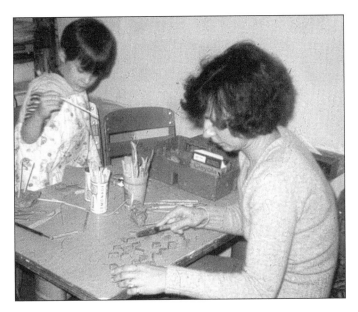

10.2 A Boy and His Mother in a Joint Session

suggest such sessions when you wanted to focus on something specific in the relationship.

The addition of art is helpful on many levels. They may have fun, even if they are normally embattled. They may be able to hear each other better by doing and seeing something concrete. And for children and parents, such occasional sessions provide opportunities for communication in a language each is able to speak with equal fluency.

Designing Family Art Activities

You can invite participants simply to do what they want, which will yield useful diagnostic information about how they interact in an unstructured situation. You can ask them to use the same material, but to make whatever they wish. You can ask them to represent the same topic, which can be general (happiness) or more specific to family issues (the ideal family).

You can also ask them to work together in any of a number of ways. You can request that they first plan, then execute a picture (sculpture, collage, construction) together (Figure 10.3). You can specify the medium, or let them decide which materials they want to use. You can request that they represent something general, like "getting along," that they make a picture of a shared family event, or that they decide together on what they want to make.

155

10.3 Mother and Son Do a Joint Picture

You can also specify the way they are to work together, of which there are many possible variations. One is to work silently (without specifying how that will play out) on a shared space. Another is to make a nonverbal drawing by taking turns, having a conversation with each other via the crayons, and so on.

Another way of working together is for one person to tell the other what to use and what to make, then switching roles so that the master becomes the servant and vice versa. Again, this is only one example of ways in which inviting interaction between family or group members using art materials can be diagnostically informative as well as therapeutically helpful.

Indeed, the possible tasks are infinite, and choosing them is an enjoyable creative challenge. Two art therapists who understand family therapy very well, and have written books on such work, were also very good at designing activities to meet emergent clinical needs. One is Helen Landgarten (*Family Art Psychotherapy*, 1987) and the other is Shirley Riley (*Integrative Approaches to Family Art Therapy*, Riley & Malchiodi, 2004).

If you want to read more on how you might go about selecting or designing tasks in the context of facilitating constructive change in the family system, their writings are excellent resources. Although you may be interested in using or modifying some of their techniques, what you will learn the most from is their rationale for choosing activities to meet specific diagnostic or therapeutic goals (Landgarten, 1987; Riley, 2003; Riley & Malchiodi, 2004).

As noted previously, the exercise developed by Harriet Wadeson—of exchanging and modifying each others' drawings—is useful not only with couples, but also with any dyad within the family, whether it consists of two siblings or a parent and child. The following are a few examples from my own experience.

During Assessment
Billy and His Mother

I found a variation on Wadeson's second task to be helpful during the evaluation of a depressed 14-year-old boy and his recently widowed mother, who together spent their first joint session doing a nonverbal dyadic drawing of their "house" (10.3D). Although they had agreed on the topic, they had also ended up dividing the paper surface, each doing his or her own very different version.

At the second session, reversing Wadeson's procedure, I asked each to draw a portrait of the other on opposite sides of a table easel (10.3E). They then corrected the drawings. Billy felt that his mother had portrayed him as bigger than he really was (10.3F), sensing her covert wish to have him replace his father as "the man of the house" while at the same time complaining resentfully that he acted as if he were the adult, instead of the kid.

His mother thought that the mouth and eyes in Billy's drawing of her (10.3G) were too large, and while modifying the features, added a "more attractive" hairstyle and earrings, which made the portrait much more seductive.

This ambivalent message was confusing to Billy, because it echoed his own romantic wishes, which were in conflict with his equally normal need to separate. Mother described Billy as "putting up a wall" between them, while Billy felt that his mom was "holding me on a leash." Their mutual ambivalence became clearer to me and to them, through the drawings and discussions.

During Therapy
Chip and His Mother

Joint art sessions held in the course of individual, group, or family therapy can be approached in an open-ended fashion or with some direction by the therapist. Deciding how to proceed here, as elsewhere, is a function of the goals of the session. Usually such meetings are planned, but occasionally they happen spontaneously, as in the following instance.

Ten-year-old Chip was having a hard time saying good-bye after almost 2 years of art therapy. During one of his last sessions, after looking at the animated films he had made, he wanted me to invite his mother—whose therapist was away that week—to join us. He asked whether they could work with art materials, as they had done months earlier. I agreed that it was fine for her to come in for the remaining half hour, if she was agreeable.

Although I had imagined that Chip wanted to make something together, he did not ask her to do so. Instead, each of them chose clay, and ended up sitting at either end of a long horizontal table, about as far apart as they could get (10.3H). Chip made a container, similar to the "secret message box" he had created during his first art therapy session. That box had been tightly closed, with no way to get in or to open it. This container, in contrast, was wide open.

While he was making his box, his mother was modeling "a woman about to have a baby," lying flat on her back, her arms outstretched (10.3I). Although they sat far apart, each seemed warmer, and more open to the other, than during previous joint sessions. I wondered to myself whether his mother was symbolically expressing her wish that Chip had been reborn through his therapy. In fact, she commented that she thought that coming to the clinic had enabled each of them to like themselves and the other more than they had before treatment.

Laura and Her Family

As you can see, there are many possible ways of working on intrafamilial problems through art therapy. Just as periodic joint parent-child art sessions can be useful, so it also happens that an occasional session with all family members can provide information or facilitate communication, in the course of other forms of treatment.

Eleven-year-old Laura was seen in individual art therapy; while her mother was seen both individually and, for 6 months, in a single parents' group led by the same male therapist. In addition to several mother-child meetings, there were times that I decided to invite the whole family to come in.

In the session to be described, I hoped to help mother see how she had isolated herself, withdrawing from her four young children and their needs, which she experienced as incessant demands. Laura, the eldest, was further burdened by her younger siblings, which exacerbated her persistent depression.

I therefore suggested a game all could play, which I hoped would enhance mother's awareness of the situation. Each family member was first asked to make a small self-representation, using colored plasticine. They were then invited to move these around silently on a shared territory—a large piece of paper—until they found a spot where they wanted to settle (10.3J).

158

When that was done, they were told to define their chosen space using felt-tip markers, still without talking to each other. Although the children were quite young, they all became intensely involved in the movement-drama. Even though mother had placed herself in the center, her territory was closed in by clearly drawn boundaries, with little indication that the space was reachable by the others. The children also isolated themselves, settling in the corners, providing themselves with symbolic protection by drawing a large house, a big fence, or a powerful pet.

After the drawing and movement process, they were invited to discuss what had happened and to reflect on it. The children were able to say how they felt they had to fend for themselves, and how uncertain they were about support from each other or their mother. She, responding with un-characteristic empathy, revised the original description of her space by say-ing that the paths she had drawn were not meant to lead *out* as she had first stated. Instead, they were meant to lead *in*.

This overburdened single mother went on to say that although it was hard, she really wanted to be available to all of the children. The session did not solve the problem, but the exercise served to get it out in the open, where it could be dealt with more easily by the family.

Bringing Art to Mother

Sometimes a youngster brings a picture to show their mother after an individual art therapy session, like Sloane (10.3K) or Andy (10.3L). The joint discussion is inevitably revealing, providing additional therapeutic benefits.

Family Art Therapy

The same reasoning about art and different theories of personality and psychotherapy, which was noted in relation to individual therapy with ado-lescents and adults, applies as well to the various approaches to family ther-apy. Art can be incorporated into psychodynamic, systemic, structural, nar-rative, solution-focused, paradoxical, postmodern, and many other ways of working (cf. Riley, 2001, 2003; Sobol & Williams, 2001).

A major asset noted earlier, especially if the family includes young chil-dren, is that art is a language that all members can speak, regardless of their ages. This is more useful than you might imagine, since this modality en-ables you to include even very little children in conjoint family therapy in a meaningful way. Laura's siblings were 4, 6, and 9 years old, yet they par-ticipated fully in the session described earlier.

Occasional Art Sessions in Family Therapy

In ongoing family therapy, as in work with individuals, drawing and other art tasks can be free or thematic (DVD 10.4). Themes can be any that are focal in the work at the time, such as "the major problem in the family" (10.4A) or "how I wish things were" (10.4B). In addition, interactive tasks can play a key role, as in the group mural of the family art evaluation or a nonverbal silent drawing. Having members draw can not only illuminate family issues, it can also be a way of actively working on them (10.4C).

For example, taking turns being the authority figure in the "master-servant game" described earlier—telling someone else what to use, and what and how to draw—can sensitize parents or spouses to the feelings of other family members who may feel controlled. Similarly, asking two warring family members to *fight it out on paper* can help to defuse persistent tensions, and to understand more about their roots. Additionally, asking two or more family members to make a picture together, both silently and with planning, are ways to experiment with working cooperatively.

Occasional Art Sessions in Couple Therapy

I once saw a couple for 2 years in weekly therapy, while their blind daughter was seen by a child psychiatrist I supervised. Art had been used during an initial family evaluation, and became especially helpful in dealing with the most sensitive and difficult areas of their relationship when they emerged as significant factors in the girl's problems.

During one session, after veiled expressions of resentment from each of the adults about disappointment in his or her partner, I wondered whether they could draw each other, working on opposite sides of an easel. Although I didn't invite them to modify the pictures, which would have been too loaded at the time, their images became reference points for the remainder of the treatment. Mr. T. represented his wife as "The Rock of Gibraltar," a tower of strength and stability in the shifting currents of life (10.4D).

At first he said that was how she *really* was. Then, responding to her hurt and anger at such unrealistic expectations, he acknowledged that he *wished* she would never show vulnerability, but that she had often let him down. Meanwhile, Mrs. T. was in tears about how impossible it was to please her husband, how hard it was to get his sympathy and concern when she was needy, and how deprived and lonely she felt.

She represented him as all wrapped up in his own activities and hobbies, with no time left for his family (10.4E). While initially defensive, Mr. T. finally agreed that she had a point, and remembered how he had placed himself far away from the others in his family drawing a year earlier. Six months later, a good deal of therapeutic work was accomplished by asking them to draw together silently for several weeks in a row. Since both of them tended to intellectualize, often and well, art was extremely useful for helping them get in touch with their feelings.

Multifamily Art Therapy

Another possible format is for several families to meet together, usually with a shared concern, like the group on the Pediatric Oncology Unit at Walter Reed Hospital (10.4F).

Seeing More Clearly through Art

One of the reasons art is so helpful in therapy is that you can bypass unconscious defenses more easily with images than with words. Highly motivated, verbally fluent couples and families often welcome the opportunity to accelerate their work through art, as in the following instance.

In family art therapy, initiated because of the persistence of 6-year-old Tim's stuttering, my co-therapist and I became frustrated by how effectively the adults could rationalize, and how hard it was for mother to see what was going on.

So one day we suggested that they try to draw on the same sheet of paper, but without talking (DVD 10.5). They drew silently for a surprising 45 minutes, each using different amounts of space, mother moving around and eventually drawing in everyone else's area. She thought she was being helpful, and was completely unaware of any resentment in the others.

Tim began by drawing a house in the center, but soon gave up, feeling squeezed out, and left to work alone with clay at another table (10.5A). His father joined him briefly (10.5B), but soon returned to work on the picture with his wife and Tim's 4-year-old sister, who was as assertive as her mom (10.5C). Later, when everyone was seated discussing the picture, Tim got up and added some more details to his house (10.5D).

During the discussion time, Tim, his father, and his sister told his mother that they didn't appreciate how she had moved into what each felt was his or her own space. Though hurt, she was finally able to hear what they had been trying, unsuccessfully, to tell her for months. Because of the impact of this event on mother's awareness of her intrusiveness, the family asked that we put the drawing on the wall for the next several meetings.

Even months later, this picture and its insight-provoking process became a frequent reference point for all of us—a dramatic reminder of some of the interaction patterns that were stressing the family system. Because they were so open to learning from experience, this family made significant changes in family art therapy, and went on to eventual success, both as individuals and, for the parents, as a couple.

Art in Group Therapy

Art can also be used in groups; and, as with individuals and families, art is compatible with groups conducted according to any theory of group dynamics or group therapy. As in those other forms of treatment, you can use art activities regularly or occasionally, as you wish (cf. Riley, 2001; Sobol & Williams, 2001; Waller, 1993).

Warming Up

If a group is just starting, or there is considerable tension in the room, you may want to begin with some kind of warm-up (DVD 10.6). With children, it can be game-like, and might involve making a construction, either individually or together. With any age level, you can ask people to *respond to* photographs or art reproductions, to choose those they like or dislike, as described in Chapter 6. If you have reason to believe that the group is easily threatened, this is quite a safe way to begin.

Creative warm-up activities don't have to use art materials. One such exercise grew out of a course I was teaching on creativity, and is easy and fun to do. The materials are simple and readily available: about four or more paper clips and a piece of paper. The paper can be letter or legal size, and the number of paper clips doesn't have to be restricted; having more increases the challenge.

The task is to "make something out of these materials" individually, using no tools but the hands, allowing any kind of manipulation of clips or paper, as desired by the artist. As with any other creation, you can ask what it's meant to be or what it reminds people of (Rubin, 1980).

A simple warm-up activity with art media that works well with groups is to let each participant choose his or her preferred color of plasticine, asking them to play around with it and see what happens. Like the paper clips and paper, the clay permits doing and undoing, changing one's mind, exploring various options, and responding to what the material itself does as part of the process.

Because its pliable nature permits some discharge of tension, using plasticine in this way can help members of a group to relax during an initial discussion. This is true for the paper-clip-and-paper activity as well, and both of these, while they stimulate competition, also end up with a great variety of attractive and interesting creations, each one unique.

A different sort of warm-up is some kind of *round-robin* creation game.

This can involve passing a drawing around the group, each person adding to the picture, which is then passed to the next person. The same can be done with clay (10.6A).

Passing just one drawing or piece of clay around provides for a very different kind of group experience than passing two in opposite directions, or having each person start something and then all pass them on at the same time.

The first creates an immediate feeling of cohesion, with everyone watching the sculpture or picture as it evolves and takes shape. Because most people are staring at the product rather than the artist, it evokes less self-consciousness than you might imagine. It can, however, be uncomfortable for whoever is being observed.

The second method (passing two items in opposite directions) is much less likely to stimulate self-consciousness, especially if everyone works at once, but there is also less feeling of group cohesion. In both, the resultant product is the group's, not the individual's, which also reduces discomfort.

Another art warm-up for adult groups is to invite everyone to draw on a shared surface (Figure 10.4), but without talking (10.6B). In a study of group art and group dynamics (Rubin & Rosenblum, 1977), when par-

10.4 Group Warm-Up: Drawing Silently on Shared Space

163

ticipants made two group pictures—one with discussion and one without—they reported feeling much more comfortable with the nonverbal task, perhaps because there is less feeling of responsibility as well as less opportunity for disagreement. It also tends to be more playful.

In fact, any group-made product, with or without words, is a good way to reduce anxiety about the outcome in the early stages of using art in group therapy (10.6C). There are many possibilities, including having individuals take turns adding to a drawing or painting (10.6D). Another is to have each member make or choose a two-dimensional shape or image, and then place it (either simultaneously or in turn) on a large, shared piece of paper or other surface. Janie Rhyne used sound and movement to help her adult groups to warm up (10.6E).

Introductions

At the first session of a group, even if you have previously met the members individually, they will need to meet each other (DVD 10.7). This can be done with art materials as well as with words. People can be invited to literally introduce themselves to the group with a drawing, perhaps using their own initials as a starter for images (10.7A). They can also make something with clay to tell others about themselves (10.7B).

Similarly, you can ask members to show, using whatever materials they wish or you decide, what they hope to get out of the group (Figure 10.5). In either case, they will know a lot more about each other than they did before the exercise.

Art during Group Therapy
Art Activities

In the course of treatment, the way in which you incorporate art activities (DVD 10.8) will depend on the setting (10.8A) and on your orientation (cf. Riley, 2001; Sobol & Williams, 2001; Waller, 1993). Art, like talk, is more likely to be unstructured in analytic and some kinds of humanistic groups, whereas other therapeutic approaches often lead to more specific tasks (Liebmann, 1986).

This is especially true of homogeneous and theme-centered groups, regardless of the leader's theoretical orientation (10.8B). For example, Diane Safran (2002) asks people with Attention Deficit Disorder in her psychoeducational groups to draw specifically how it feels to have the disorder, in topics like, "How has ADHD affected you at school?" (10.8A) or "the impact of ADHD on your relationship." Marie Wilson (2003) suggests a similarly focused series of activities for an addictions group.

In groups, as in families, creative tasks can be done by individuals, by

10.5 Sharing with Other Group Members

the whole group, or by subgroups, depending on your judgment of what needs to be dealt with at the time. By repeating certain tasks at intervals over the course of time—such as representing the group or the leader, or working on a joint project—group members can literally *see* where they have been, and what they have accomplished. An early art therapy book about a weekly group in a day hospital, *Murals of the Mind*, looked at joint murals over the course of a year, a vivid way to study group process (Harris & Joseph, 1973).

One of the most enjoyable parts of using art in group therapy is to decide, on the basis of what happened the preceding week, what you might want to do the next. Even in a short-term group, it is best in my opinion to be flexible about the sequence and specifics of art assignments, in order to meet the needs of the particular participants.

As when deciding what to do with families, you can ask people in groups to work either individually or together using art. It can be completely free, with everyone choosing what they want and making what they wish (10.8C); or there can be some commonality in either the medium, the topic, or the way of working (10.8D).

For example, everyone can be invited to use clay to make anything they

165

want, to model with their eyes closed, or to make a clay animal. Everyone can be asked to make an animal, but with a choice of clay, paint, or drawing materials. And so on.

Whatever the activity, group art sessions usually begin with some informal, spontaneous interaction, among the members, followed by the introduction of the task by the leader (10.8E). It is especially important to check with group members about their understanding of what you've asked them to do. The working time follows, during which the verbal interaction is, as in families, typically more spontaneous (10.8F).

While group members are creating, it is the same as in family or individual therapy using art. It is best to observe how people approach the task, how they interact with you and with each other in the course of working, and so on, depending on the activity. As in family therapy, there is usually more informal interaction with you and with each other during art activities than during the introductory or discussion phases of the session (10.8G).

Then, as in individual and family therapy using art, there is a time for the group to stop, to clean up, and to look at whatever has been created (10.8H). Here, too, there are numerous options. You can look at one picture at a time, either placed on an easel or held up by the artist; or you can have all of the pictures placed on the wall or a bulletin board so that they are simultaneously visible.

As in individual and family therapy using art, the discussion can be completely unstructured, or can be conducted in any number of ways. Members can interview each other (10.8I), the leader can interview each artist, or there can be some combination of the two, which is probably the most common (10.8J).

One of the assets of using art with groups is that people learn not only from their own products and associations, but also from what they *see* in the artwork of others. Because people are so sensitive about how others respond to what they have created, it is often a good idea in groups to prohibit negative judgments of other people's art. If you feel that members can handle some criticism, it is then important to explore how people feel about such comments.

As for people attributing meaning to others' creations, the notion that the creator is the expert on the meaning of his or her own art is useful here. It also helps to explain to patients that what they see in someone else's product says something about them, not about the artist. As in individual or family therapy using art, you can focus in the discussion on the process, the products, or both. According to your preferred model of group therapy,

166

you can be more or less active, more or less in charge during the discussion portion of the session.

Pictures of the Group

In addition to reflecting verbally on what has been made, it is also useful to ask group members to reflect pictorially on the group experience, especially if they have worked together in some way. Individual pictures of the group, which can be done abstractly, can be executed with drawing materials or with colored paper and tape.

I have also found that cellophane works well for this purpose, since it not only permits the creation of all kinds of two- and three-dimensional shapes, but also makes it possible for overlapping to occur because of its transparency. In this way, group members are able to represent fusion, intimacy, domination, or smothering. Conversely, clearly separated forms can represent isolation or interpersonal distancing.

If the group is small enough (three to five members), you can suggest color coding, where each person chooses a different color of marker or paper, and all members represent the small group using individual colors as agreed. This then makes the eventual comparison among the individual pictures of the group that much clearer and more vivid.

It is ideal if people can work on their group pictures in such a way that they don't see each others' until they come together to discuss them. If this is not physically possible, it still helps to suggest that they'll get more out of doing this exercise if they try not to look at what others are doing. The same is true in family therapy when individuals are representing the family.

Conclusion

As you have seen, there are many different ways to assess couple and family interaction using art. There are also many ways to incorporate family art sessions into ongoing individual, couple, or family therapy. Similarly, there are many different ways to use art in groups. And, as in individual treatment, since art is a tool and not a theory, it can be adapted for use in family or group therapy conducted according to a wide variety of orientations.

11

Using Other Art Forms

Why Other Art Forms?

Most individuals have preferred expressive modalities; some are more comfortable with music, some with dance, some with art, some with drama, some with writing. Whether such preferences are due to nature, nurture, or both, it makes sense that you might want to add more than art supplies to your therapy space in order to provide additional channels of communication for your patients.

Moreover, it appears that individuals sometimes shift from one modality to another, because a particular art form is better suited to expressing certain issues. For example, when drama therapist Ellie Irwin and I looked systematically at the products from same-day individual art and drama interviews, we found that aggressive themes were significantly more common in drama, while longings and anxieties were expressed more often in art (Rubin & Irwin, 1975).

In fact, it seems unfair and unnatural to restrict patients of any age to any single expressive modality, including words, since it is normal and natural for people to express themselves in a multimodal fashion (DVD 11.1). Because I am untrained and unskilled in facilitating expression in any modality other than art, I will share with you some of the ways I have found to incorporate other creative activities into my work, in the hope that they might inspire you to do so, too.

Mixing Modalities in Treatment

My experience with other expressive arts therapists began in a study group. Organized by a child psychiatrist, it included a drama and a dance therapist, as well as psychologists and social workers interested in the arts. The first summer, we worked side by side with the same children in a therapeutic day camp. Later, we worked jointly in *art-drama* groups for children and adolescents (Irwin, Rubin, & Shapiro, 1975) and *parent play* groups for adults (Rubin, Irwin, & Bernstein, 1975).

The more multimodal work I did, the more convinced I was of its value. In such a stimulating milieu, it was natural for us to want to learn from one another. As a result, I added dramatic play equipment like puppets, dolls, and props to the art materials in my playroom. My drama-therapist colleague added art materials to hers (DVD 11.2).

Very soon, we both added phonographs, tape and CD players, simple musical instruments, and keyboards. I discovered that the children would spontaneously use the puppets, the toys, the keyboards, and the instruments without needing help or instruction. Seeing the equipment for listening, adolescents would bring in recordings by their favorite musicians, playing selected pieces so I could better understand them.

I began using a camera to record impermanent creations, like block constructions (11.2A), scenes in the sand (11.2B), or art that someone wanted to take home (11.2C). I experimented with using a super-8mm movie camera for simple animation (11.2D), a way to tell a story with art (see Figures 11.1a and 11.1b; DVD 11.2E). When it became affordable, a video camera was wonderful for capturing all kinds of stories in motion, both live and animated.

Within a fairly short period of time, I had discovered that it was artificial to restrict patients to visual expression when music, movement, drama, writing, or photography would be more appropriate. These other art forms are the natural siblings of the visual arts, and are generally included in multimodal approaches (11.2F), which are sometimes called *expressive arts therapy* (cf. Levine & Levine, 1999; Malchiodi, 2003b; McNiff, 2001; Rogers, 1993).

Since you may be more comfortable with music, dance, poetry, photography, or drama, there is even more reason to include these other modalities in your work. Of course, the best reason to do so is that any of them might be appealing to a patient, meeting a need for expression at a particular clinical moment.

Carla's Story: Expressive Arts Therapy

The oldest of four little girls, 8-year-old Carla had been a pretty happy child. Shortly after the birth of the latest baby, however, she began to have nightmares almost every night, often wetting the bed as well. Her exhausted mother brought her to a clinic, and she was referred to me for

11.1a Doing Animation: Setting Up

11.1b Doing Animation: Filming

weekly individual art therapy (DVD 11.3). For many months she refused to talk about or to draw her scary dreams, but instead painted beautifully colored *bars* behind which the monsters were hidden (11.3A).

One day when she couldn't decide what to make, I suggested a scribble drawing. Carla must have been ready to find and to represent her "Nightmare Monster," for that is what she made, telling the story as she drew (11.3B). The monster caught first one little girl, then another, then Carla, too. After showing all three girls in the monster's clutches, she drew one yelling "Help!" Picking up a red tempera marker, she pounded vigorously on the paper, calling the blotches "soldiers," who she hoped would be able to rescue the children. Throughout most of the drama, Carla was uncertain about the outcome. At the very end, however, she declared with relief that the soldiers would win and the monster would be killed.

For months Carla drew monsters of all shapes and sizes (11.3C), using a variety of media (Figure 11.2). For a while, she cut out the monster drawings and placed them inside cut-paper cages she had carefully constructed—and for 2 weeks, she insisted that the caged monsters be locked in my desk drawers.

As Carla became more familiar and comfortable with these images, it was possible for her to extend the fantasy in dramatic play. One week, she spontaneously used soap crayons and painted my face as the nightmare monster, asking me to pretend to attack her. The following week, she reversed roles and became the monster, attacking me as the fearful child (11.3D). It was during this period that the nightmares stopped. *Art* allowed Carla to *see* the scary-mad monster, while *drama* allowed her to safely *feel* her anger.

Over the course of another year of art therapy (11.3E), she was able to become comfortable with her jealous and hostile feelings—to integrate them, eventually representing mothers and babies, like a bird on a nest waiting for her eggs to hatch (11.3F), or a mother and baby turtle (11.3G). She often shifted from art to drama, as her expressive needs required (11.3H).

When the time came for her therapy to end, however, Carla was sad. For her last project, she decided that she would make an 8mm film about monsters, suggesting that I show it to other children with fears like hers. She cut out monster heads that moved (magically) around the walls, finally scaring a little girl (her sister) at the sink.

The girl then came to see me, we returned to look at the heads together, and presto! They had disappeared! (11.3I) The film was a creative way for Carla to review the main problem for which she had been in therapy, re-

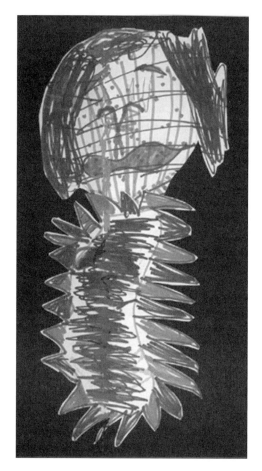

11.2 One of Carla's Monsters

minding herself of what she had learned. It was also a way to deal with her envy of future patients (siblings) by transforming her jealousy into generosity, via the defense of reaction formation.

Variations on the Visual Arts

Sandplay Therapy

People of all ages make sculptures in the sand (DVD 11.4). Since I always had a sand table in my playroom (11.4A), the idea of creating miniature worlds in a tray of sand seemed natural (cf. Kalff, 1980; Lowenfeld, 1979). The technique itself can be used by any practitioner, and the equipment can be as simple or elaborate as you wish (11.4B).

You can start by getting one or two deep plastic trays, putting dry sand in one and wet sand in the other, and asking people to make a scene in the sand-tray using miniature creatures, scenery, and other props. You can try it out with small figures and scenery from a variety or drug store.

If you decide to pursue the technique in earnest (11.4C), a national association and training are available, as well as a great deal of specially designed equipment (cf. Bradway & McCoard, 1997; Bradway, Signell, Spare, Stewart, Stewart, & Thompson, 1990; Carey, 1999; Labovitz & Goodwin, 2000; McNally, 2001; Mitchell & Friedman, 1994).

Phototherapy

In addition to asking to see family albums for assessment, you can assign specific tasks related to whatever is being dealt with in therapy (DVD 11.5). For example, if a patient is trying to understand a conflicted relationship with a significant other, asking the person to bring in photographs of him- or herself with that individual can be extremely useful. If a patient is trying to reconstruct something in the past, early photos can be very helpful in both stimulating and clarifying memories (11.5A; Akeret, 1973; Weiser, 1993).

As for taking photographs during therapy, today's user-friendly technology allows you to add this modality quite easily. Devices that permit instant feedback, like Polaroid and digital cameras, are especially useful in treatment (11.5B). Not only can the images be looked at right away, they can also be fed into a computer, where they can be arranged on the screen or printed. The ways in which photographs can be invited and used are limited only by your imagination.

Amy: Panic and Polaroids

Amy's panic attacks in elevators were creating severe bouts of anxiety, since a doctor she had to visit for allergy shots was on the top floor of a very tall building. Amy herself requested a series of instant photos, which made it possible for my fumbling attempt at desensitization to be an eventual success. We had begun by riding together on the clinic elevator, adding one floor at a time. These trips made that elevator less scary, but had no impact on her doctor visits.

However, when Amy asked if I could take pictures of her with my Polaroid camera, they turned out to be remarkably helpful. She was very specific, requesting a photograph of her getting on the elevator, riding in it, and getting out. She requested this for every trip, and asked that I write on the picture how many floors she had traveled that time.

Amy took the photographs home each week in an envelope on which she had drawn a picture of herself in the elevator. In less than a month, she was able to ride all elevators without having a panic attack, carrying the pictures with her when she went to the doctor's office. Whatever the mechanism, the photos added a dimension to the behavioral experience that I had not anticipated.

Some Other Uses of Photography in Therapy

My patients have sometimes asked to use the instant camera themselves. Taking a picture of me or the office was common prior to any interruptions in therapy, creating a literal transitional object. Another way to use instant photos is to have patients cut out pictures of themselves and/or the therapist (11.5C), to be incorporated into drawings (Wolf, 1976).

If group members take pictures of each other, they can then use them in self-portrait collages, as in the *photo-art therapy* (11.5D) developed by Jerry Fryrear and Irene Corbit (1992).

Ellen Speert worked with a client who had been raped, and who began her treatment by making "safe places" with found materials. In the course of her therapy, she slowly recalled and dealt with the event, which had left her with severe PTSD.

Eventually, since she was a photographer, she decided to create a series of staged photographs in which she pictured exactly what had happened to her. While painful, the process was more than cathartic; it helped her to assimilate and work through the trauma, and to go on with her life (11.5E).

There is something about the concreteness of a photograph that, like the physical presence of a drawing, allows a kind of integration not possible with verbal recollection alone. In the book by Judy Weiser (1993) and those by Jerry Fryrear and his collaborators (Fryrear & Corbit, 1992; Krauss & Fryrear, 1983) you will find many ideas about ways to use photographs in therapy. Simply being receptive can help (11.5F).

Film and Video Therapy

Since the clinic I worked in had videotape equipment, we often recorded individual, family and group therapy. We then played the sessions back for participants the following week—either in their entirety or in an edited version—for what was always an intense and fruitful reaction session. This process was useful in individual, group, and family therapy.

It was frequently necessary to schedule two or more follow-up sessions with the video equipment in order to help patients fully digest and utilize the awareness made possible by viewing themselves on videotape (cf. Fryrear & Fleshman, 1981).

If you want to re-view a session in this fashion, it need not be very complicated, especially since video camcorders are much more user friendly than in the past. You simply set the camcorder on a tripod and aim it at the therapy scene, and you will create a record that, when replayed, can be exceptionally useful.

Of course, you need to use your clinical judgment to assess the readiness of your patients to tolerate and learn from such feedback. As with looking at the artwork they have created, viewing both still and moving photographs is another way to gain aesthetic, as well as psychological, distance (DVD 11.6).

In the art-drama therapy groups we co-led at our outpatient clinic, Ellie Irwin and I often used slides and films taken by the leaders or the members as a way to review and reconsider what had happened during previous sessions. Looked at and discussed like their art, film was especially useful for recording dramas (11.6A). In fact, a film we made about an adolescent group, *The Green Creature Within*, was composed mostly of such photographic records, many of them taken by the youngsters themselves (11.6B).

Psychiatrist Irene Jakab and I once conducted video-art therapy with a family. They first came in for two art therapy sessions, which included many individual and family tasks, and which were taped. The following week, they viewed and responded to an edited tape of the first two meetings. Their reflections on the artwork and interactions from the first two sessions were amplified as they reviewed the video, which included both doing and discussion portions (11.6C).

Video played a key role in the therapy of Elaine, a woman in her 40s who suffered from Dissociative Identity Disorder. Thanks to psychiatrist Lou Tinnin's creative ideas, she was finally able to meet her other parts (or *alters*) that, despite hard work by both of us, had until then eluded co-consciousness.

Specializing in the treatment of clients with severe PTSD, Tinnin was using videotape feedback with considerable success. Because the process was so powerful, he advised hospitalizing Elaine for the procedure. She first had a videotaped session during which she was able to access her alters, each in a separate, split-off state of consciousness, as in my office. The next day, she watched the video of that session, for the first time meeting her parts in a fully conscious state, and was filmed while doing so. The following day, she watched and discussed the second tape (of her watching the first one), allowing her to more fully process getting to know the most important members of her interior "family," some of whom had been tormenting her for many years.

Like photography, video can also be an expressive tool. Inviting people to bring in tapes they have taken can be as helpful as seeing personal photographs, as in my work with Kitty (Chapter 7). You can also request that patients film any topic germane to their therapy, such as an interview with a significant other; they can be invited to use a camcorder during a session, as well.

Isaac: Filmmaking as Therapy

For a boy named Isaac, film was central to his therapy at various points in his youth, and eventually in his life. As a timid little boy, conflicted about anger at his critical parents, he enacted dramas with the small clay creatures he created (11.6D). Later, he used them in animated films that he made using a super-8mm camera on a tripod.

When he returned to therapy as a depressed adolescent, Isaac modeled the large head of a creature, which he then dramatically provided with a victim (11.6E). Following this period of work, he was able to leave home to attend college, where he studied filmmaking. His graduation project was an autobiographical movie about a fearful little boy, which included a claymation segment of a large monster (11.6F).

The monster reminded me of the creature-head, but this time it had a body and limbs. It was also active rather than passive, and growled as it destroyed buildings (which were linked, in the film, to the boy's demeaning mother).

Creative Uses of Language

Drama Therapy

Probably because of my exposure to drama therapy in the study group described earlier, I began to notice spontaneous shifts of modality in art therapy (DVD 11.7), as when a clay sculpture would become a puppet, and the child would make it move or speak, or when it stimulated a drama (11.7A). I became more aware of the drama in art itself, as when finger-paint or clay images were created, destroyed, and replaced by others (11.7B).

When I first started seeing children in art therapy, I used a small tape recorder so I could accurately record what they said about their work. Much to my surprise, adding a small hand-held microphone (Figure 11.3) not only made the recordings clearer; it sometimes helped inhibited children to overcome their shyness (11.7C).

I also found that even when no tape recorder was available, pretending that a pencil or brush was a microphone was equally motivating for many youngsters. With those who were acutely uncomfortable or resistant about discussing their creations, I would sometimes dramatize. Often I pretended to be interviewing them for a television program, enlisting their natural

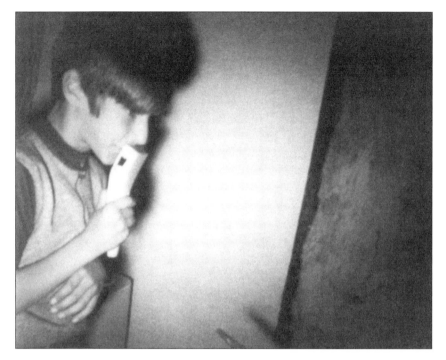

11.3 A Boy Using a Microphone to Describe His Painting

exhibitionism. This degree of aesthetic distance, along with the pleasure of being in the spotlight, helped them speak more freely and at greater length about what they had made (11.7D).

My drama-therapist colleague inspired me to get some ready-made puppets and miniature life toys—family, animal, and fantasy figures—for my playroom. She taught me that, if children were not able to play spontaneously with the puppets or toys, helping them along by participating in the play—always under their direction—was a way both to support and to teach.

I was probably most pleasantly surprised to discover that the use of drama in therapy need not be confined to children, but was actually appealing to some adolescents and adults. Although psychodrama is a technique that I believe must be studied and mastered before you can safely employ it, I was able to help patients use some of the dramatic techniques of Gestalt therapists—like talking to a significant person imagined to be in an empty chair, or taking the role of each element in a dream, or a drawing.

Some adults and adolescents were willing to use the puppets to make up stories (11.7E), especially in family and group therapy (11.7F, G; cf. Gerity, 1999). Many were also able to use the black-and-white cardboard characters and simple backgrounds from the *Story-Telling Card Game* designed by psychiatrist Richard Gardner (1988), even though it was created for children.

Gardner (1971) also invented another clever game, the *Mutual Story-Telling Technique*. While also originally meant for children, it, too, was useful with many adolescents and adults. Like Winnicott's *Squiggle Game*, it is an interactive method, in which the patient first tells a story and the therapist responds with a modification, based on his or her judgment about a more adaptive ending.

Creative Writing Therapy

Making up stories requires no special equipment, and can be done in the office or between sessions by patients of any age. Any storytelling or writing done in the context of psychotherapy is a use of words that allows more space and aesthetic distance than ordinary verbal discourse (cf. Allan & Bertoia, 1992). Perhaps you have already had patients bring in something they've written to show you. If you are receptive and encouraging, you will discover how rich such creations can be, and how much they can add to therapy.

Sometimes the youngsters I saw wanted not only to tell stories about their art, but to have them written down as well. If they couldn't write as fast as they could generate ideas, I would volunteer to be their secretary, and would type the dictated story on a typewriter (later, a laptop computer).

Although this practice began with young children, I soon found myself offering my secretarial services to adolescents and adults as well, and was surprised by how often they took me up on it. After a story or poem was completed, I would make one or more copies, which could then be illustrated and elaborated. I found that being a scribe worked for patients of all ages, who were able to be more fluent with their poems or stories.

Sam's Halloween Story

Twelve-year-old Sam, who often got in trouble, had worked hard in therapy to find socially acceptable outlets for his aggression, especially his intense rivalry with his younger sister, who was always being praised at home and school for her good behavior. Sam's healthy use of humor was evident in the following dictated story, in which he managed to joke about his sister's grandiosity, his hostility, and his fearsome fantasies.

One Halloween my sister, Sally, was telling the same story that she tells every year. In it my two cousins, my sister and myself are captured by an evil monster while trick-or-treating. When this story was first told, about 4 or 5 years ago, my sister accidentally saved us all. Sally has now changed the story so she calmly saves the day. In my favorite version of this story Sally is eaten alive by wolves.

While Sally was telling this story, a mirror that was hanging on the wall began to buckle and warp outward. The mirror finally broke. Through what was left of the mirror roared an alien monster determined to kill us all. As my sister continued her story, the unstoppable blue juggernaut began to tear the room apart. Soon, the destructive evildoer left our furniture and walls alone and turned on us. At that moment the dangerous behemoth staggered and fell.

I cautiously approached the fallen four-foot fiend. I realized that it had been bored to death by Sally's story. For an unaccustomed body, the sudden shock of so bad a story is deadly. At that point, I woke up. "Sam, Sam, wake up," my sister said. "You missed part of my story!" I groaned.

Eleanor's Sad Tale

Eleanor, who had been abandoned by her natural mother, feared that her stepmother—who she was sure preferred her own two biological children—had rejected her as well. Eleanor's story, which reflected her painful situation, was entitled "Why Me?"

Cindy was your average 11-year-old, except for one thing. Her mother. Most mothers like their children, as well as love them. But Cindy's didn't. Cindy's mom never seemed to be happy with what Cindy did. She told Cindy one thing, but meant another. Cindy tried to please her mother, but got very frustrated with her because it usually didn't work.

For instance, one day when Cindy woke up she told her mom that she was going to the basement to get a pair of pants that were dry. Her mother said, "Why didn't you do that last night?" "Because I forgot," Cindy said. "Well you can't go downstairs now," her mother said. "You'll have to wear something else."

Cindy sighed, and opened her mouth to protest, but then quickly shut it when she saw the look on her mother's face. Silently she walked into the other room, found the only other pair of pants that were clean, and put them on. "I hate these pants!" she grumbled to herself. Then she thought again, "Is it really these pants I hate? Or is it my mom? No, I don't HATE my mom," she thought quickly. "I just get mad sometimes." "Cindy," her mother called from the next room. "Go downstairs and put the puppy in the basement." Now Cindy felt really mad!

At this point Eleanor abruptly ended the story, realizing that it was not as fictional as she had thought when she started dictating it to me. In fact, it was so close to home that it stimulated a more open discussion than ever before of how furious she was about being treated differently, yet how help-less she also felt about being able to please her mom. It was my notion that it was not primarily the stepmom of the present who seemed impossible to please, but the real mom of the past who had walked out on her, and with whom Eleanor had finally ended visitations, because the weekends there were so lonely.

Several years later, the rage that had been so hard to feel toward those upon whom she was still dependent was turned inward for a period, during which she had impulses and thoughts about suicide. It has been said that every suicide is a failed murder, and no doubt that was part of her motiva-tion.

But it is also true that this lonely, unhappy youngster had indeed felt re-jected by the two women who were supposed to love her in a maternal way, so that she felt ugly, unlovable, and hopeless. Happily, she was eventually able to establish a loving, respectful relationship with her family, and most especially with her stepmother.

Andy's Alienated Poetry

Andy, a boy who never quite fit in with his adoptive family, had a very difficult time in adolescence, trying to find and to define his identity. He frequently turned to writing as a way of dealing with his anguish. At one point, his distress caused so much mental dissonance that even his chosen outlet—writing poetry—became really difficult.

> *Writing Block*
> I want to write,
> I'd like to write,
> But somehow my brain is all tied up.
> The things I think are all jumbled.
> They just don't fit together.
> Little bits of thoughts
> with no meaning at all.
> My mind is melting,
> My memory filled.
> I can no longer remember anything.
> I am full of ideas
> With no way to release them
> I'm going to explode!

Sally's Writings about Change

Sally, a woman in her early 40s, came for what she announced would be her last of 16 tries at psychotherapy. After a few weeks of testing the waters, she shyly shared some poems with me, stimulated by her excitement about discovering an unexpected onrush of optimism in therapy. Because she feared destroying me with her anger, she idealized me and the therapy in an attempt to find, through what was offered, her own potential for growth. Although she was very articulate, she could not speak directly to me as eloquently as she could through her poems, as in these excerpts.

> This sorry world has found one point of hope
> The single ray of light in this long, deep chasm of pain . . .
>
> It glides through a tormented river
> Rushing to a hardened core, releasing the heart of truth and love . . .
>
> Light is freed from its prison of hell . . .
>
> You have touched the soul of a troubled one.
> This light will remain . . .
>
> Oh Oh Oh
> It's scary business here.
> You are the strong one,
> The one in control.
>
> I'm shaking, shivering, teeth chattering.
> Upside down, not what I expected.
>
> You're the cool one.
> Too cool, way cool, way too cool.
>
> And what if you decide that I'm no good?
>
> "I'm not judgmental!"
> Oh.
> Oh?
>
> What if What if What if . . .
> My ameoboid self can finally start to grow . . .

After she had been in therapy for about a year, Sally decided, despite much anxiety, that she wanted to leave a sado-masochistic relationship in which she had been trapped. As hard as the decision had been, acting on it was even more difficult. A few months later, she wrote a story for a friend's little girl, then realized that it was really a message from her adult self to her own inner child. She said that writing it enabled her to see things more clearly, and to move closer to autonomy.

Sally's Story

Once, there was a little rabbit that got lost in the woods and couldn't find her Mommy and Daddy. It got dark and cold, and the rabbit was so frightened, and she cried for a long, long time.

Then she met a big porcupine, who smiled at the rabbit and said, "You can trust me." So the rabbit trusted the big porcupine, and tried to be nice to him, and hoped that he would be the new Daddy. The rabbit tried to hug the porcupine, but he didn't like that, and he got mean, too. The rabbit kept trying to hug the porcupine, but she got hurt many times. The rabbit didn't even realize how much the porcupine was hurting her, because she really wanted to hug him. But she was getting sad, and she didn't know why. So she cried for a hundred days.

And it was so cold and dark, and Winter came, and stayed for five years.

Then one day, the rabbit saw the most beautiful bird she had ever seen, and she thought she must have been dreaming. This bird was so colorful, and she looked very exotic. The rabbit loved watching her fly. But even though the bird could fly very well, sometimes she just walked, or sat down. So, the rabbit and the bird started to talk to each other, and they each had lots to say. They talked about all kinds of things, and the rabbit could tell that this bird had seen so much, and was very, very smart. And the rabbit knew that the bird was very kind, too. The rabbit loved her, and was wishing that the bird could be her Mommy. Sometimes, the bird would start to fly so far away that the rabbit couldn't even see her, but this never got too scary, because she knew that the bird would always come back.

And the bird always came back, and this made the rabbit very, very happy.

The bird had so many good stories to tell. And she taught the rabbit so many things about The World, and she even told her about other rabbits, and other birds, too. Sometimes, the bird would tell the rabbit a story about The World that surprised her, and the rabbit wouldn't believe the bird. But the bird never got angry, even when the rabbit disagreed. But sometimes when this happened, the bird would just smile and say, "You'll see. Someday, you'll go into The World, and it will be fun, and not too scary. You will be ready."

And the rabbit knew that the bird was probably right, and this was exciting. The rabbit began to look forward to the day when she could take her first trip into The World. Each day, the rabbit felt happier and happier.

Then one day, the porcupine found out about the bird, and he was very angry, and said, "That bird is bad and stupid. You cannot talk to the bird any more." And then he said, "Besides, you can never be a bird. You are only a rabbit.". . . Every time she saw the bird, she was happy. But when she saw the porcupine, she was sad. And she felt very sorry, so she tried to be nicer and nicer to the porcupine. But every time she tried to hug him, he hurt her. OUCH! And every time she tried to be happy, he said to her, "You can never be happy like the bird. You will never fly. You should quit trying. You are only a rabbit." And this made the rabbit very sad.

One day, in the Spring, the rabbit was thinking about these things. Even though the bird wasn't there, the rabbit was feeling happy, thinking about the bird, and all her good stories and ideas. But she was still wishing that she could fly, like the bird. Then, she looked at the pretty blue sky, and felt the warm sun, and smiled. She felt so comfortable that she fell asleep.

And while she was sleeping, she had an interesting dream. In the dream, the bird was flying, and saying to the rabbit, "Come on, you can fly, too. You have to try." And the rabbit saw the porcupine laughing, and he said, "You can NEVER fly. You will never get off the ground. You are only a rabbit. You can never be like the bird. You will have to stay with me FOREVER."

But the rabbit looked up in the sky, and the bird was still there, and said to the rabbit, "Come on, you really can fly. It just takes a little practice. Even I had to learn to fly, once, a long time ago." And the rabbit knew that the bird had always told the truth, and so she could trust the bird. Then the porcupine said to the rabbit, "If you try to fly, you will fall down. You can never be a bird. Only birds can fly. And only birds can be birds." But the bird said to the rabbit, "You don't have to be a bird to fly. I know this. I've seen lots of flying rabbits, in The World."

The rabbit got scared, because she had to make a decision. And she got very jumpy. Then she remembered that, a long time ago, she had loved to jump. And maybe if she jumped up to the sky, she really could fly. So, the rabbit started to run, and she ran as fast as she could. She ran so fast that the porcupine couldn't keep up with her. She ran and ran. She was so quick that everything around her looked fuzzy. Then, she jumped as high as she could, and flew through the air until she finally landed softly in the grass. This was fun! And so she practiced again and again, and each time it got easier.

And the bird was smiling, and was happy, too. And this made the rabbit feel even happier. The bird said, "See? I told you that you could do it. Isn't it neat?" The rabbit felt so excited that she had learned something new. She giggled, and then she ran, and jumped, and flew again. But the porcupine was grumpy, and he said, "You are as silly as the bird. Why don't you go away and never come back?" This made the rabbit feel a little bit sad and frightened, but then she remembered that the bird had always come back, and it was O.K. to go away.

The bird must have known what the rabbit was thinking, because just then she suggested, "Maybe you'd like to go visit The World today. I think you're ready for a short trip." The rabbit felt shaky, but she said, "O.K., I'll try. Which way is The World, from here?" And the bird pointed with her wing, saying, "Over there, to the left. Have fun. I'll see you later."

So, the rabbit jumped and flew all the way to The World, and it was so pretty there. She saw lots of new animals, like deer and mice and bears and giraffes and snakes and dogs and alligators and goats, and even a few alpacas. And she saw some nice skunks and foxes and porcupines, and a couple of sharks. And all of these animals were having a big birthday party, with music and dancing, and flowers. When she got to the field where the party was being held, she saw the nicest thing of all. There were nineteen flying rabbits, and fifty-seven little ones that were waiting to learn to fly. And she knew that she could help them, and this made her so happy that she woke up from the dream.

At first, she felt sad, because the dream was over, and she was wishing that she really could go to The World, right then, and see it for herself. But then, she heard music in the sky, and looked to see the bird, chirping and smiling. What a nice day to go to The World! Then the bird said to the rabbit, "Come on, you can fly, too. You have to try."

And guess what happened?

Fortunately, the patient (rabbit) was eventually able to *fly* with her own wings, to leave the man who had browbeaten her (porcupine), to go into "The World," and to find new and healthier relationships. Much to her surprise, she was also able to leave her therapist (bird) after 2 years, without the anguish she had once feared. One of the ways she coped with termination was by writing a humorous book, which affectionately mocked psychotherapy. She gave me a copy of the manuscript as a parting gift.

A Patient's Reflections on Writing and Art

Marjorie, who was going through a very difficult time in her life, wrote between her sessions, mainly to manage the stress. She was also doing art at home and bringing it in to share with me. When she finished therapy, she decided that she didn't want me to reproduce her artwork, which had become a valued avocation, but that it would be all right to share her written reflections. The following excerpts convey some of the differences in how she was able to use the two modalities, both of them therapeutically.

"The Art" [after 8 months of therapy]
the different functions of the writing and the art . . .

—The writing serving to clarify, express, contain, communicate; a vessel for the articulation of the pain.
—The art feeling very different, seeming to be primarily expressive, from a different part of the internal landscape, enhancing the strong and healthy components, communicating only in the sense that those areas have become more accessible to Judy as well as to me, no small accomplishment.
—Explaining why I have held onto the art, because it is healthy and satisfying and diverting, all of which have been important. At a time when I needed to feel healthy, needed to be diverted.
—And as quickly and easily as all of the above has flowed when I began writing about the art, the analysis is removed from the experience. Really a simple

decision to continue with something that felt right and constructive, allowing it to unfold in its own way and its own time.

Seven months later, she wrote the following:

Speaking of filling up the time, the art has to be watched. It has been so satisfying, is so "safe," that it can be counterproductive. There is a genuine desire to share what has been happening with Judy, my sense of excitement and pleasure. Certainly an unexpected consequence, that the art would emerge and develop in this way, take on a life of its own. Assuming it must be satisfying for Judy too, to have opened such a door under these circumstances, to see the art unfold and flourish. A very small artistic territory, but one that seems to be teeming with activity and satisfaction for me.

And then, 10 months later, she wrote "More on the Art":

Re-reading what I wrote earlier about the art, glad that I captured the experience then. Because it has been evolving, feels different now.

—Feeling then that it was art rather than art therapy, certainly true on the surface. But recognizing now that it has also been art therapy, on many levels. Most important has been the sense of the "art as prototype," that it has symbolized much that is important about me, in therapy as in life.
—Just as it was with my adolescent struggle for identity. I had to forge out my own path, during a turbulent adolescence. The struggle was worthwhile, ultimately meeting both of our needs, Judy having served as midwife to the creative offspring, having had the opportunity to watch it develop, at least in its infancy.
—A much stronger proprietary sense now, of "my things," instantly recognizable as they emerge . . . the continuing recognition of the small artistic territory that I inhabit, but also a sense of its sufficient expandability, that it will be as large as it needs to be, as I explore my personal artistic landscape."

And, during the termination phase:

As I write about the art, for probably the last time in therapy, feeling the connection with termination. A sense of impending loss, an empty space, where the therapeutic alliance has been. And the art a bridge . . . And now with Judy, taking the art with me as I prepare to depart, leaving the writing in case it can be of use. Feeling enormously thankful for the therapy, for the art, both having enriched my life in unexpected ways. . . .

It has been a fascinating and satisfying artistic journey for me, at a time when my journey in life was filled with pain and turmoil. As Judy has been the midwife for the artistic process for me, I seem to have served as the midwife for the art. Because it really has seemed to have a life of its own from the beginning, needing room to emerge and define itself, to unfold and evolve, resisting my efforts to intervene and transform. The process has seemed much like my life (thinking of my adolescence), trusting my intuitions, willing to explore uncharted territory, an inherent sense of direction and goodness (or poorness) of fit as things emerged. The process similar in life and in therapy and in art. . . .

An extremely bright woman, Marjorie was able to get past her initial distrust of psychoanalytic therapy and to enjoy the transference-learning available in the process. The art, initiated in part to please, became an oasis, something she was able to keep as her own along with the therapeutic gains she had accomplished through her hard work. I am grateful for what she taught me, and for her willingness to teach others through giving me permission to share her written reflections.

Music and Movement Therapy

As noted earlier, I found simple instruments and a keyboard to be stimulating for many children and adolescents, and even a few adults; and patients of all ages made use of the various machines for playing music—phonograph, tape player, and CD player. Sometimes a person wanted to record something he or she had composed on the keyboard or another instrument, or singing a tune themselves. Occasionally people brought in instruments they played, using them like records and tapes to tell me something about themselves they wanted me to know. As a nonmusician, I could only listen.

The same was true for movement. As a klutz, I couldn't teach or show much of anything; but I could certainly affirm anything that someone wanted to communicate in dance or movement. Both music and movement tended to occur more often in groups, where people could stimulate, show, and sometimes teach one another.

There are professions which specialize in all many of the areas noted in this chapter, from sandplay therapy to phototherapy, poetry therapy, movement therapy, music therapy, drama therapy, psychodrama; and there are some who are trained to be able to facilitate activities in multiple modalities, such as those in the Lesley University training program in expressive therapies founded in 1974 by Shaun McNiff. In that program, incidentally, students can either specialize in one of the major art forms and be eligible for registration in art, drama, movement, or music therapy; or they can choose to be generalists, and be trained as expressive therapists, for which many have spelled out a rationale, including Paolo Knill.

There is no question that to become proficient in any of these therapies takes specialized training, which is of course true for art therapy as well.

What I am proposing is that, even if you have no particular skill or background in an art form, you can be receptive to what your patients might be able to say. In some instances, this means simply responding in an affirmative fashion, as to a poem or drawing someone brings in. In others, it means having some expressive materials available, like paper and markers or puppets, which will enhance the possibility that your clients will be able to take advantage of an even wider range of possibilities for expression, in order to get the most out of your work together.

Conclusion

I believe that, at their source in human beings, there are no hard and fast lines between expressive modalities. Instead, they are more like points on a continuum: from the body to the sound to the image to the word—dance, music, art, and drama. This is similar to what Natalie Rogers (1993, 2001) calls the "creative connection" among all expressive modalities.

As someone who had studied both dance and art, Rogers, using her father Carl's person- (originally client-) centered approach, discovered

11.4 A Young Woman Is Proud of Her Work

serendipitously that working in one modality (such as dance/movement) seemed to facilitate expression in another (such as art), which could then be further extended by adding writing or talking.

I tend to agree with Winnicott (1971a), who wrote that all therapy takes place in the "play space" between patient and therapist. As he also said, part of the therapist's task is to enable a person of any age to be able to play, in the broadest sense of the word.

While this is possible through strictly verbal therapy, it becomes even more likely when the patient can play with hands, eyes, body, and heart, as well as with the head. Being receptive to expression in all of the arts make this much easier (DVD 11.8).

Frida Kahlo, for example, needed to use both art and poetry in her diary, in order to cope with an impending leg amputation (11.8A). Similarly, the adolescents in our art-drama therapy group moved fluidly from one art form to another as needed, in their healing process (11.8B).

If you are respectful of all efforts at self-expression, if you show a sincere and sensitive interest in anything and everything created by those you are seeing, you will be rewarded with material that, like dreams, reveals the deepest layers of their souls. When someone writes a poem or paints a picture, it is an expression of the self; and the way in which it is received is felt as a response to the person who created it (Figure 11.4).

This is so simple and so obvious, yet so full of potential benefit (as well as risk). I believe that Carl Rogers (1951, 1961) was right about the need for "unconditional positive regard" as a necessary condition for growth. Conveying that kind of affirmation to people through your response to their creative products can only enhance their feeling of being safely "held" by you for the therapeutic journey.

CHAPTER

12

Using Mental Imagery

The soul never thinks without an image.
>—ARISTOTLE, *On the Soul* (4th century B.C.;
>quoted in Arnheim, 1969, p. 12)

*My mind, in its ordinary operations, is a fairly complete picture gallery —
not of finished paintings, but of impressionist notes.*
>—TITCHENOR, *Lectures on the experimental psychology of the
>thought processes* (1909; quoted in Arnheim, 1969, p. 107)

Why Mental Imagery?

Depending on your training and orientation, you may already be using mental imagery in your work. Like art, mental imagery is compatible with any theoretical or technical approach. Similarly, it can be used at any stage of assessment or treatment, and is helpful with a wide variety of patients of all ages and conditions.

While this book is primarily about using art in diagnosis and therapy, it also recommends the use of mental imagery. Even though it was a focus of early psychologists using introspection, and even though there was a significant revival of interest in the late 20th century, mental imagery remains underutilized in psychotherapy. Yet, as you will see, there are many reasons to consider incorporating it more often and more actively (cf. Nucho, 1995; Singer, 1974; Singer & Pope, 1978).

189

One is that imagery is one of our main ways of encoding both inner and outer experience as we strive to make sense of the world. This is especially true before we have language, or when an experience is primarily visual. Trauma, which overwhelms the ability to cope, can trigger both dissociation and regression, leading to a dominance of sensory modes of recording the event—which itself is often tactile, auditory, and visual as much as it may also be verbal. Thinking in images is also constructive, and is frequently reported by both scientists and artists as part of the creative process (Singer & Pope, 1978).

Another reason for using imagery in therapy is that we so often describe our emotional life in visual terms, from feeling "blue," to being "green" with envy, or having a "sunny" disposition. We use similes with a strong visual/affective component, like calling a play "dark" and gloomy, or a movie "bright" and cheerful. These metaphors often carry more weight than their linguistic equivalents, suggesting that like a picture, an image, too, is "worth a thousand words."

It is striking that so many of the words we use to describe the awareness we strive for in psychotherapy are visual—such as *illuminate*, to make something visible, or to "see," meaning not only to perceive, but to grasp, as well. *Imagine*, something one has to do in order to change, includes the word "image." Thinking of something in a new light is called *reframing*, referring to the visual context in which a pictorial image is presented and, therefore, better perceived.

Both mental and artistic imagery derive considerable power from their capacity to condense affectively rich meaning into finite forms. Perhaps that is why Ernst Kris (1956) called a certain kind of vivid understanding in therapy "id insight"—insight experienced with a sense of emotional intensity, a *Wow!* instead of an *Oh!* After all, the word "insight" includes a reference to vision, to "seeing-in."

In addition, a number of studies have confirmed that some people think more often in images (*visualizers*), while others think more often in words (*verbalizers*) (Richardson, 1977). Psychotherapy, like academic education, has traditionally been biased in favor of verbal behavior, to the detriment of those whose preferred mode of cognition is visual. It makes sense that, when treating someone who thinks more often and more easily in pictures, it would help to inquire, to invite, and to suggest imagery, and to do so as often as seems clinically appropriate.

Perhaps an even more important reason to incorporate mental imagery into therapy is that it is actually present all the time in everyone, including you and your patients. In experimental studies of ongoing thought processes, when subjects were instructed to record (when prompted) whatever was on their minds, it turned out that a surprisingly large proportion of our mental life is in the form of images. In fact, more than half—almost two thirds—of spontaneously occurring waking thoughts, both in and out of the laboratory, are "moderately or very visual" (Klinger, 1978, p. 243).

Since there are always images in our minds, using mental imagery can simply mean finding ways to pay attention to what is already there. In other words, directing patients to report any internal images they notice, with eyes closed or open, is yet another way of accessing what is on their minds. There are many other possibilities, which require no special training, but which yield rich rewards for practitioner and patient alike.

History: Imagery in Therapy

Despite the interest of ancient philosophers like Aristotle and psychology pioneers like Titchenor in mental imagery, the glaring light—or was it the dark cloud?—of behaviorism, which dominated psychology for half a century, all but obliterated work with these internal pictures. When people finally began to pay attention to imagery again, psychologist Robert Holt wrote an article accurately entitled "Imagery: The Return of the Ostracized" (1964).

Yet, in the very beginning of the field of psychotherapy, when Freud and Breuer first discovered what they called the "talking cure," imagery was central. During the period between 1893 and 1895, Freud actively requested images, using what he called the "pressure" or "concentration" technique to evoke forgotten memories:

> I placed my hand on the patient's forehead or took her head between my hands and said: "You will think of it under the pressure of my hands. At the moment at which I relax my pressure you will see something in front of you or something will come into your head. Catch hold of it. It will be what we are looking for—well, what have you seen or what has occurred to you?" (Freud & Breuer, 1893–1895, p. 110)

Even when he had abandoned this method in favor of free association, he couched his instructions in visual terms, asking the patient to "act as though you were a traveler sitting next to the window of a railway carriage and describing to someone inside the carriage the changing views which you see outside" (1913, p. 135).

Similarly, Jung developed "active imagination" largely as a way of paying close attention to internal images pressing for expression (Chodorow, 1997; Edwards, 2001; Wallace, 2001). In a 1931 letter to someone who had consulted him about irrational experiences, Jung advised the writer to "Let it [the unconscious] speak. Then switch off your noisy consciousness and listen quietly inward and look at the images that appear before your inner eye. . . ." He went on to suggest that "Images should be drawn or painted assiduously, no matter whether you can do it or not" (Adler & Jaffe, 1973, pp. 82–83).

Since Freud and Jung—even during the dark ages of the behaviorists' ostracism—visual imagery has been used by clinicians to stimulate memory, fantasy, and an awareness of feelings and ideas. Now that cognitive-behavioral techniques are dominant, the use of mental imagery for the treatment of many different problems, from phobias to failures, has become even more common (cf. Lazarus, 1981, 1984; Nucho, 1995).

Personal History: Imagery in Therapy
Images on the Couch

My own interest in this area stems from personal experience. In 1973 I enrolled in the Pittsburgh Psychoanalytic Institute for training, first in the analysis of adults and adolescents, then in child analysis. During my training analysis I was fascinated not only by dream imagery, but also by the vivid images that emerged so often in the course of free association.

I was keenly aware that my thoughts were frequently in pictorial form, and that they were sometimes very hard to translate into words for my analyst. These experiences had an impact on me that was more intense than a conceptual realization; and although I finished that analysis many years ago, I still recall with feeling some of those on-the-couch visions.

One day I attended a dance therapy workshop in what is known as "authentic movement." We were invited to close our eyes, and without any music or instructions from the leader, to do whatever our bodies felt like doing in moving and making sounds. This free association in movement was powerful, leading to vivid images of significant others, along with strong affects and memories of early childhood. It was an extremely primal and potent experience, full of auditory, tactile, and visual associations.

I was relieved that I had an analytic session during the lunch break, so I could process the wordless events of the morning. I found it helpful to revisit those movements and the powerful visual and somatic images they had evoked. While relaxed and lying on the analytic couch, I could look at what had been an overwhelming emotional experience, now free to re-view it and to do my best to metabolize and to grow from it.

A Study of Spontaneous Imagery

The training required that I analyze three adults and three children, including one adolescent. For the required graduation project, I studied their spontaneous visual imagery and its role in our work over time (Rubin, 1983). Reviewing the literature on mental imagery in psychoanalysis and psychotherapy, I found myself questioning those who saw it as primarily resistant or regressive.

For the study, I reviewed the first, middle, and last occurrences of spontaneous mental imagery in two of my adult patients (a man and a woman), within its analytic context. Reading about what had happened in both analyses actually convinced the skeptical faculty members reviewing the material that the appearance and analysis of mental imagery had served to reveal more than to conceal.

In other words, although the patients' spontaneous images might well have had a defensive function and, like all mental products, were the result of compromise and disguise, it seemed as though their emergence and subsequent exploration had facilitated the progress of each individual's treatment. I also examined instances of spontaneous mental imagery in the analyses of the youngsters I was seeing, with similar results.

Ways of Using Imagery in Therapy

Spontaneous Imagery

Because of my experience in analysis and authentic movement, I began by focusing on images that arose spontaneously. I am sure that my attentive reaction to such images was reinforcing, and I have no doubt that it stimulated more frequent reporting of mental images by all of my patients. The method is simple: Just listen for images with a keen ear and a sharp inner eye, and when they come up, inquire about them in order to extend their possible meaning and usefulness in the therapy.

Daydreaming, another kind of mental imagery that occurs spontaneously in most people, is as useful in therapy as nighttime dreams—Freud's (1900) "royal road to the unconscious" (DVD 12.1). One of his most famous patients was the Wolf-Man (12.1A), who brought him a drawing of the dream for which the case is named (12.1B). Drawing a dream can help greatly in understanding it, both during its execution (12.1C) and afterward as well (12.1D). One of many kinds of normal waking imagery you can inquire about, it is especially useful during the assessment phase.

As with dreams, monitoring daydreams periodically in the course of psychotherapy can provide a useful index of how things are changing in the patient's inner world. Other normal kinds of mental imagery you can inquire about include any sort of fantasies a patient is willing to disclose, whether positive or negative, like those during masturbation.

Unusual imagery experiences can be scary for people, and patients may not be able to tell you about them without an explicit invitation. This can be true for the vivid images we all have but rarely pay attention to while falling asleep and waking up (known as *hypnagogic* and *hypnopompic* images, respectively). Images that emerge during such altered states of consciousness can be especially useful in treatment, and are rarely disclosed without being requested.

A Series of Images

The notion of *free association* in imagery became especially appealing to me during my analytic training. While doing my graduation project, I discovered that there had been several psychologists who had investigated requesting such free image association, which was then reported verbally.

Joseph Reyher, for example, invited "clients to describe only pictures of images that come into their mind's eye" (1977, p. 27). He also presented experimental evidence that such free association in imagery produces "heightened GSR [galvanic skin response] activity, more primary process, more direct representation of drives, and less effective defense" than does free association in words (Reyher & Smeltzer, 1968, p. 218).

Inquiring about Imagery

By the time I graduated, I had begun to request information about mental imagery not only with analytic patients, but from others of all ages, usually finding the answers fascinating as well as fruitful. What I discovered was that spontaneous and requested mental imagery could be as helpful and revealing as making art, in the context of psychotherapy as well as analysis.

It was so useful, in fact, that it would be wrong to exclude mental imagery from this book, as it is indeed the sibling—or perhaps more accurately, the parent—of making images with art materials. In the years since that study, I have found it extremely useful to direct a patient's attention to the underlying, omnipresent image world. This logical next step from my interest in spontaneously reported images also seemed to promote more such reports. Although the technique is one I have used more often with adults and adolescents, there are times when it is also helpful with children, whose capacity for eidetic (vivid) imagery is even greater.

I have especially found myself inquiring about possible mental imagery during periods of silence. This is remarkably productive, and is a practice I can heartily recommend. Of course, the language used needs to be clinically appropriate to the particular individual, but the following questions and variations thereof often yield extremely useful responses:

"Is there a picture (or image) that goes with that idea?"
"What image comes to mind when you think about that?"

If the response is negative, like "Not really," or "I don't know," you can follow up with the suggestion to "Just tell me whatever pops into your mind." Such questions are useful, not only when the flow of words seems blocked, but when verbal reports are unclear. Requesting a visual description of something someone has told you about also seems to yield different data than are available from a verbal description alone.

The two questions just noted are general, and are analogous to open-ended questions about people's artwork, like "Can you tell me about it?" Just as it is often useful to pursue more specific questions to help patients project more ideas onto their art ("How old might that person be?" or "What might she be feeling?"), the same avenues are appropriate when dealing with mental imagery.

You can also evoke mental imagery by asking questions like the following about whatever topic is being discussed:

"What color would fit your mother best?" ("What sort of a red?")
"If your husband were a shape, what sort of shape would he be?"

Since imagery is not just visual, but includes all of the senses, especially smell, hearing, touch, and kinaesthesis, your questions can include those as well:

"As you contemplate that feeling, what texture would it be?"
"Is there a sound (odor, movement, feel) that goes with that idea?"

The more general questions noted earlier, as well as those that narrow down and specify, can be asked about events, places, people, feelings, ideas, memories—in fact, anything you are hoping to understand better.

Related questions that are less abstract invite projection in categories that, while they could be strictly verbal, generally evoke visual or other sensory associations:

"If that person were an animal (instrument, song, rhythm), what would he (or she) be?"

The possible metaphoric areas are limited only by your imagination, and will come to mind as you think and feel with your patients. Most important, if your request to assign an image to something on the patient's mind seems difficult, asking him or her not to think too hard about it but to report "whatever pops into your head" can reduce anxiety and enhance spontaneity.

A playful approach to inviting imagery can be as effective as suggesting that someone "fool around" with art materials. It relaxes the person, it minimizes worry, and it is also most likely to evoke meaningful responses. In some ways, mental imagery is even easier to invite than art, because there is none of the performance anxiety that can be so inhibiting. As with art, it makes sense to first test the water with open-ended questions. If that seems too threatening, you can offer some help by suggesting or requesting something more specific and less anxiety-provoking, like the examples noted previously.

Requesting Specific Images

Another possibility is to request specific images in response to the patient's verbalization, which is similar to asking people to draw what they have been discussing. Psychiatrist Mardi Horowitz described a teenage girl whose responses in a history-taking interview were meager, but who was able to tell more and with much greater affect when she was asked to form an image of herself with her mother, her father, or her friends (1983, pp. 228–229).

Suggesting that someone imagine him- or herself in a particular situation, whether it is wished or feared, is sometimes called *trial action* by psychodynamic therapists. Behavioral and cognitive therapists use a similar technique, sometimes called *rehearsal*, to help modify behaviors and feelings.

Guided Imagery

What is generally known as *guided imagery*, first developed by a German psychologist named Hanscarl Leuner (1969) in 1948, now covers a broad range of techniques. All begin by helping the client to achieve a physically relaxed state, usually with eyes closed—conditions that facilitate an awareness of mental imagery.

The techniques themselves stem from those that are quite open ended (encouraging the person to find and describe a "safe place") to those that are quite directive, and that lead the person to a specific fantasy location suggested by the therapist usually something like a beach, a meadow, or some other relaxing spot.

Although there are many variations, it is significant that the full name of Leuner's original approach was "guided *affective* imagery," and, as I observed with on-the-couch spontaneous images, such events do seem to carry great emotional loading. Like many who invite mental imagery in therapy, Leuner also asked patients to sketch or paint what they had seen.

Imagery in Cognitive-Behavioral Therapy

If you do cognitive-behavioral therapy, you are probably familiar with the use of imagery in a variety of techniques designed to aid individuals in overcoming phobias, modifying maladaptive behaviors, solving problems, or some other agreed-upon goal. In *systematic desensitization*, for example, the patient imagines a series of scenes, each one a little more anxiety provoking than the last. By encountering each in turn in a deeply relaxed state, the patient becomes more comfortable with the formerly phobic images.

Cognitive-behavioral *art* therapists invite patients not only to think about but also to draw images of the fearful scene. Similarly, in attempts to eliminate unwanted behaviors like addictions, imagining and drawing the particular behavior paired with negative experiences (either imagined or actual) can lead to that behavior's becoming aversive, so that the individual can give it up more easily (cf. Rosal, 2001; Rozum & Malchiodi, 2003).

Imagery in Alternative Medicine

Many of the uses of imagery in alternative or complementary medicine are similar, in that the patient is invited to imagine, for example, his or her immune system attacking cancer cells, as in the work of the Simontons (Simonton, Mathews-Simonton, & Creighton, 1978), Siegel (1986), and Achterberg (1985). These practitioners, like others, often include the drawing of such images, on the theory that this additional visualizing activity will further promote the impact of the mind on the body, a relationship that is now well confirmed.

Many approaches to the use of imagery in healing are focused: The patient visualizes or draws the disease, as well as his or her body's efforts to fight it (cf. Epstein, 1989; Malchiodi, 1999a). My gifted young colleague, Susan Aach-Feldman (DVD 12.2), used mental and artistic imagery as one of many tools in her battle with ovarian cancer (12.2A).

One year after her first operation, and a course of chemotherapy which brought a welcome period of comfort and energy, Sue was due to have a routine follow-up called "second-look" surgery. Just before she went into the hospital, she requested a meeting at my office. During an intense two-hour session, she drew and discussed a series of three chalk drawings, which, like her courageous spirit, were realistic, yet full of hope.

The first was a glowingly healthy portrait of her body, "What's Happening Inside: Visualizing the Best" (12.2B). The second was a representation of her T-cells, entitled "My Fighters: the Swordsmen" (12.2C), and the third was a boat plowing its way through rough waters: "The Narrow Path: An Odds-Beater on a Sturdy Ship" (12.2D). Although the disease eventually won out, she lived considerably longer than the doctors had predicted; and there is no way to know whether her energetic efforts served to assist her immune system.

In a study presented at an imagery conference at Yale 20 years ago, a researcher first asked subjects to visualize their T-cells multiplying. He then asked them to draw what they had imagined. The slides he showed of their blood—extracted before and after the imaging and the art activity—were so clearly and visibly different that even a skeptic could not deny that creating mental and pictorial images had somehow helped to increase the number of fighter cells.

Subsequent research has confirmed the powerful impact of visualized and drawn images on physiological functioning. Although the field of psychoneuroimmunology is young, findings so far are very encouraging. They support the use of mental imagery in physical medicine, in such areas as pain reduction, as well as the value of adding drawing, with its active component (cf. Malchiodi, 2003a).

Mental Imagery and Art

As noted earlier, clinicians who use a great deal of mental imagery in therapy often invite people to draw as well, like psychiatrists Mardi Horowitz (1983) and Gerald Epstein (1981), psychologist Jeanne Achterberg (1985), or social worker William Steele (2003). If, in fact, the concretizing of the mental image by capturing it in line and color does help us to process it more deeply, then it makes sense that adding drawing may enhance the patient's ability to learn from the imaginary experience, and to be able to generalize that learning to the real world.

One of the areas in which both mental imagery and art have proved to be astonishingly effective is that of trauma. Understanding the need for individuals of any age not only to remember the trauma, but to be reexposed to it in a new way, clinicians have found that the visual image and its representation in a drawing are extremely helpful in the reworking and reframing of the traumatic event (Steele, 2003).

Art therapist James Consoli (1991) called his approach "psychimagery," and illustrated it in his work with a woman who had experienced sexual abuse as a child. In a filmed reconstruction of their work he demonstrated the use of relaxation, hypnosis, mental imagery, and art in a therapeutic effort that helped her to heal and to get on with her life (DVD 12.3).

198

Indeed, relaxation and the invitation to imagine are employed by many art therapists, as in the work with a boy with ADHD conducted by a student of Marcia Rosal, who used guided imagery to help him to focus before creating.

Art therapists also sometimes evoke visual imagery to stimulate artistic creativity. Selma Ciornai, a Brazilian art therapist, invited members of her class to relax, to imagine a special person, and then to draw and later describe their creations (DVD 12.4).

The Don Jones Assessment

Working at the Menninger Foundation, art therapist Don Jones developed an assessment that combined guided imagery with drawing. The patients, in a relaxed state, are invited to imagine a journey, stopping at four key points. At each point, they are asked how they would proceed, and are told that they will be drawing a picture of their answer. Each imaged situation is carefully designed to represent a different kind of universally stressful problem. They are then asked to draw a picture of what they imagined. Both exercises are followed by a series of structured questions.

Like many such techniques, both Jones and his colleagues who studied the protocol found it to be as useful in treatment as in assessment (Jones, Vinton, & Wernick, 1999; Vinton & Wernick, 2000; Don Jones & Maria Vinton, personal communications, August 14 & August 17, 2004). Like Jones, most clinicians using mental imagery along with art request drawing or painting an image after it has been seen.

Free Association in Art Imagery

Stimulated by my analytic training, I experimented with free association in art imagery, inviting free image association using a different art process each week: drawing, painting, modelling, and making a collage (Rubin, 1981a). The participants were enrolled in a course on spontaneous imagery taught through the Psychoanalytic Center. Although I had worried that the task might be too difficult, it turned out that it was possible for people to suspend thinking in words, and to follow each image with another, letting them emerge as spontaneously as possible (Figure 12.1).

When someone is invited to draw images in a sequence, each one being stimulated by looking at the last, we can suppose that a mental image might have been part of the transition to the next drawing. Some participants reported just such a sequence, while others were either unaware of or did not experience it that way.

In addition to being fascinating, the process turned out to have unexpected fringe benefits. Post-course interviews with some of the partici-

12.1 Workshop Participant Describes Free Image Series

pants revealed that for several of them, the experience had had unexpected therapeutic effects. Two people found that the images discovered in this way helped them to move ahead in their therapy, and two others overcame longstanding creative work blocks (Rubin, 1981a).

Like psychoanalysis, free association in art or mental imagery requires a pretty healthy person. In workshops where people can go on with the image series until they feel finished, it usually takes more time than most therapy sessions (DVD 12.5). A manageable variation, which I have used with patients who can handle it, is to ask what sort of image would follow the first one drawn, and to encourage two or more sequential pictures, which can then be viewed and discussed.

Hypnosis and Imagery

Freud's requested imagery, when he was using the "concentration technique," occurred during a period of transition in his work from hypnosis to free association. Like most art therapists, I am not trained in clinical hypnosis (DVD 12.6) or meditation. Reading, however, about the fascinating work of Australian psychiatrist Ainslie Meares (12.6A; 1957, 1960), who invited patients to paint (12.6B) and model (12.6C) while hypnotized, long ago impressed me with the potential value of creating during an altered state of consciousness. In 1992 psychologist John Watkins devoted a book chapter to what he called "hypnography" (drawing) and "sensory hypnoplasty" (modeling).

In recent years, art therapist Karen Schock has developed a procedure she calls "hypno-art therapy," inspired by Meares' investigations (12.6D). If you are trained in clinical hypnosis, you already use visual imagery, but you may not have thought to have patients draw what they have seen. According to Schock, the combination is remarkably powerful, and is useful with a variety of problems, including chronic pain (personal communication, August 13, 2004).

Meditation and Imagery

Visualization techniques have been used in the East much longer than in the West, usually in association with some form of meditation or yoga. Although one can think of meditation as emptying or clearing the mind, it (like relaxation) also enables easier access to inner experience. Meditative relaxation is used by many practitioners, including expressive arts therapist Natalie Rogers (DVD 12.7). Michael Franklin, a practitioner of a contemplative, image-centered approach to art therapy, has been exploring ways to integrate the practice of yoga with the making of art (Franklin, 2001).

Using Your Own Imagery

One reason to include mental imagery in your therapy is that you yourself are probably utilizing it all the time as a way of thinking about your patients, though you may not be labeling such moments as imagery. When conducting purely verbal psychotherapy, for example, you are constantly using your own imagination to construct mental pictures of what people are describing or reporting.

Whether someone is giving a history, telling about a recent event, or describing a person or place, you are probably visualizing whatever is being verbalized. This is especially true when hearing reports of dreams, which are largely in the form of images. So, even if you do not literally doodle while you listen (a useful pastime, by the way, for monitoring your own reactions), you are constantly forming mental pictures as you interact verbally with those you treat.

Just as I have suggested that you pay attention to the images people report, and that you invite them as part of your work, so it is helpful to pay attention to your own spontaneous mental imagery. You may even want to draw it, either at the time (if you can do so discreetly in your notebook) or later, as a way of better understanding what your patients have stirred up in you, which will hopefully help you to understand more about them.

Conclusion

The reason for including this chapter in a book mainly about art is that mental imagery, with or without art, seems to enhance therapy. It is used in all sorts of approaches, ranging from psychodynamic to humanistic to cognitive, behavioral, spiritual, and transpersonal. This is probably true because, as noted earlier, imagery is one of our major human ways of encoding both inner and outer experience.

In fact, it is one of the main ways we make sense of the world. Gestalt psychologist Rudolf Arnheim (1969) spent the better part of his career exploring what he called "visual thinking," both in the mind's eye and in art. A wood sculptor as well, he noted that working with wood involved "thinking with the hands instead of the eyes" (Gypsycat Productions, 1994).

Whatever the explanation for their effectiveness, there is no question that the usefulness of art and mental imagery has been demonstrated in a wide range of therapeutic applications, from psychotherapy to alternative medicine. It seems almost foolish not to use both in our efforts to help other human beings to feel better and to improve their lives. Neither can do any harm, in my opinion, and either or both might help a great deal. Fortunately, you don't need specialized training to ask a person who has been quiet for a while whether he or she is aware of an image. Nor do you need special training to invite people to close their eyes, relax, and see what images come to mind.

The effectiveness of art and mental imagery will probably be explained scientifically some day, perhaps as being a result of the impact of imagery on the autonomic nervous system, as theorized by some who use art and imagery in medicine. Or we may come to understand that it is the interaction between the two cerebral hemispheres—which happens automatically when we think about or create images—that promotes integration at the cortical level, accounting for the power of pictorial problem-solving.

Whatever the explanation, mental imagery seems to be ubiquitous, one excellent reason for tapping it in therapy. And whether its effectiveness when invited in therapy is due to its "magic power" (Kris, 1952, p. 200) for our primitive minds, and/or its physiological effect on our biological brains, there is considerable evidence that—like the arts—visual imagery can help human beings to solve problems as well as to overcome anxieties, to think creatively as well as to heal the mind and the body.

202

Although psychoanalytic theory is currently perceived as incompatible with biological and cognitive approaches, Freud was comfortable from the beginning with an understanding that the necessary scientific tools for examining the mind did not yet exist. With his usual optimism, he expected that someday they would, and I believe that he would have been the first to employ modern technologies in the service of understanding the mind (Sulloway, 1979).

In fact, in 1895, during the early years of his research into mental functioning using the psychoanalytic method, Freud wrote a work that was discovered and published posthumously (in 1950) and is now known as the *Project for a Scientific Psychology* (Freud, 1955b). As you might imagine from the title, he hypothesized that all of the phenomena he was describing as metaphorical parts or forces in the mind would eventually be explained and understood biologically (cf. Siegel, 1999).

Similarly, the effectiveness of placebos, faith healing, and image magic is no doubt due to the fact that whatever chemicals or neurons are activated in belief, they have a positive effect on mental processing and the immune system. I am not a neuroscientist, but I eagerly await their findings—which, since imaging and measuring techniques have become increasingly powerful, are likely to validate what those of us who use art in therapy have long observed (cf. Kaplan, 2000; Malchiodi, 2003a).

CHAPTER

13

Assigning the Arts

Introduction

From time immemorial, the arts have been therapeutic in the broadest sense of the word. Simply making contact with an art form can provide escape, soothing, or clarity. Listening to music can give solace, reading a novel can promote understanding, and watching a movie can offer a respite from stress. Going to a concert, a poetry reading, a play, a gallery, or a museum gives us access to that special magic that has kept the arts alive for centuries.

It has already been noted that patients sometimes arrive at a therapy session with art they have created at home or in school, either currently or in the past. They are also likely to bring in things they have written at different times in their lives, such as journals, poems, or stories. This happens not only because they see its relevance to their therapy, but also because you've expressed an interest in them and what they create.

Assigning the Arts as Homework

The arts are especially well suited to homework assignments, as both responsive and creative activities. Poetry therapy involves not only writing poems, but also reading or hearing the poetry of others; similarly, a great deal of music therapy involves listening to or playing others' compositions—and the field of bibliotherapy is literally recommending specific readings, as you feel they might be useful.

Some patients will rebel against such assignments, but you can always look, read, or listen together if you feel that an important message is best delivered through an art form. Others will be delighted to be able to continue the work on their own, to get more out of it and perhaps to shorten the length of their treatment. Although you will be deprived of observing and hearing patients' responses while they create or react, you will be fostering autonomy, which is a goal of all psychotherapy regardless of theoretical orientation. While you have less control over the process than when someone is in your office, for those who take to this mode it can be remarkably fruitful.

Even though homework assignments can be either responsive or creative, suggesting that patients watch a video or read a book is appropriate to the art form, and to its complexities as well. After all, most people are not likely to want to make a video or write a book without help; but they already watch videos and read books on their own. Thus, neither is much of a stretch, and you're even helping them in the always-difficult task of selecting which book to read next or which videotape to rent for the coming weekend.

As for what to recommend, I suggest that you draw upon the books, films, television shows, music, and theater with which you yourself are familiar. There is such a vast pool of creative material from which to choose that it makes the most sense to use your own favorites, since your knowledge of what you've suggested will also help the assignment to be useful. I shall note some of those I have found helpful in the past, to give you an idea of the kind of thinking that goes into such selections—not to impose them. Of course, it goes without saying that whatever you assign to be listened to, read, or viewed needs to be something the patient can comprehend. And, by the time you make such suggestions, you will hopefully know enough about the individual to be able to select something that reflects his or her interests and frame of reference.

Books

Over the years, I've found myself lending or recommending a variety of books, usually at a point where a patient was dealing with similar issues. In addition to amplifying our work, reading about others who were dealing with the same things was usually quite reassuring to the clients. I suggested fiction as well as nonfiction, as long as it was written so that it could be understood by lay audiences.

The Magic Years, by Selma Fraiberg (1996), was especially useful to preschoolers' parents who were worried about the degree of their children's involvement in fantasy play. For parents struggling to deal with an adolescent's confusing oscillation between progression and regression, *On Ado-*

lescence, by Peter Blos (1962), often provided assistance as well as reassurance.

A study in which the subliminally projected phrase "Mommy and I are one" helped patients with a wide variety of disorders, was described in the book, *The Search for Oneness* (Silverman & Lachmann, 1982). Reading that book was helpful to sophisticated patients who were struggling with early attachment deficits.

In the popular psychology realm, a book called *Imaginary Crimes* (Engel & Ferguson, 1990), which summarized a large-scale research study on the curative elements in dynamic psychotherapy, was most helpful to the many patients struggling with irrational guilt. Similarly, Judith Viorst's *Necessary Losses* (1986) was useful to those working through feelings about separation and loss, especially when those feelings involved unresolved issues from earlier developmental stages. *My Mother, My Self* (Friday, 1977) was helpful to women trying define their identities as separate from those of their mothers.

Other psychology books addressed to ordinary people that I found myself often recommending included those by Harriet Lerner, especially *The Dance of Anger* (1990). For patients with depression, *Feeling Good* (1999) by David Burns, was often helpful, along with some of the related workbooks that have been developed.

When I first became a therapist, Haim Ginott's books—*Between Parent and Child* (1965) and *Between Parent and Teenager* (1969)—reinforced my work with parents, by showing how they might better relate to their youngsters. A few decades later, the same topic was dealt with in *How to Talk So Kids Will Listen and Listen So Kids Will Talk* (Faber & Mazlish, 1999).

Your Child Is a Person, by a child psychiatrist (Chess, 1977), was helpful to parents having a hard time dealing with children whose temperaments were different from their own. *The Difficult Child*, by a pediatrician (Turecki, 1985), was comforting as well as informative for parents whose children had been more challenging from the beginning than other youngsters. And *Teach your Child to Behave* (Schaefer & Digeronimo, 1991), a book about discipline, included helpful descriptions of behavioral interventions that parents could successfully apply.

Many couples found *You Just Don't Understand*, by a sociologist (Tannen, 2001), to be quite helpful in differentiating normal gender differences from their own specific interpersonal problems. *Men Are from Mars, Women Are from Venus*, by a psychologist (Gray, 1990), was also useful for couples trying to understand some of their interactional difficulties in the context of typical male and female roles.

In addition to psychology books addressed to the general reader, I also found myself drawing on literature, both classic and contemporary, in the effort to help patients to grasp and accept difficult understandings. Since the vast majority of creative writing deals with human psychological issues, the range of possibilities is great. For adolescents struggling to master the tremendous biological and emotional upheavals of that period, reading Walt Whitman's *Leaves of Grass*, Thomas Wolfe's *Look Homeward, Angel*, or J. D. Salinger's *Catcher in the Rye* can be both informative and reassuring (i.e., that they're not going crazy, even though it sometimes feels that way).

Fairy tales and myths are often used for amplification by Jungian analysts, since they express eternal themes. Even if you aren't a believer in *archetypes*, you can still suggest that patients (re)read stories that contain universal issues as they emerge in their therapy. These include fairy tales like "Snow White" when people are dealing with rivalry between mothers and daughters; they also include myths, like that of Sisyphus, whose struggle to get the boulder to the top of the hill mirrors what many a discouraged patient experiences in the course of psychotherapy.

Although it might be seen as promoting avoidance, there were times when I would prescribe something humorous for someone in the throes of a depression, something silly like Pogo or Ogden Nash. Another favorite, probably because I was once a teacher (as were a number of my patients), was a satire called *The Sabre-Tooth Curriculum*, written by the dean of Columbia University Teachers' College (Benjamin, 1939).

Films

As with literature, there is such a vast pool from which to draw that it makes sense to select from your own favorites, since here, too, your familiarity with them will enhance the assignment's usefulness in therapy. I shall note some of those I found helpful in the past, but, as with the books, these are just examples to help you in rummaging through your shelves or your memory for what might help.

In family therapy, members often have trouble realizing that one person's experience of a shared event can be radically different from another's. The Japanese film *Rashomon*, in which the same story is told from the point of view of each of the four people involved, can be very useful.

For children dealing with fears and fantasies, it is hard to improve on *The Wizard of Oz*, with its sharply defined good and bad witches, as well as its story of a little girl finding her way home with the help of friends.

For parents and youngsters who are coping with the ostracism of a child who is different, *The Boy with the Green Hair* and *Ma Vie en Rose* can be helpful. For people of all ages who are visibly different, it is hard to improve on the sensitivity and humor of *Shrek* and *Shrek 2*. For those whose disabilities are invisible, *Rain Man* can be helpful as well.

For people who have or who know someone who has HIV or AIDS, *Philadelphia* is both moving and instructive, regarding not only prejudice, but also courage. For those struggling with illness and death, *Ordinary People* can be a meaningful assignment. When someone is coping with loss, *Steel Magnolias* is extremely helpful.

For patients who are dealing with depression about the aging process, Ingmar Bergman's *Wild Strawberries* is useful, as is the wishful fantasy of *Cocoon*, with its modern-day fountain of youth. A humorous and touching treatment of both aging and eccentricity is found in the delightful film *Harold and Maude*.

Television

Since the majority of Americans have not only VCRs but also television sets, this is another modality you can think of prescribing. If you are seeing parents of young children, both of the long-running PBS programs for preschoolers—*Sesame Street* and *Mister Rogers' Neighborhood*—are also helpful for adults. Although *My So-Called Life* was a short-lived series, it has been rerun on cable and is now available on DVD; and is extremely informative for parents of adolescents.

In addition to providing information, television—like other art forms—can provide much-needed distraction from physical and psychological pain. Fritz Perls, the founder of Gestalt therapy, based his theories in part on the findings of Gestalt psychology, which included studies of figure-ground perception. Perls (1969) noted that when one thing comes to the forefront of our consciousness, it becomes figurative, and other things (like pain) tend to recede into the background. Thus humor can provide escape—and it may even affect the immune system in some therapeutic fashion.

Norman Cousins' physicians, who had no cure to offer, were pessimistic about his prognosis when he was hospitalized with a puzzling ailment. In *Anatomy of an Illness* (1981), Cousins described his self-designed and successful fight against the disease, which included watching comic films with the Marx brothers in his hospital room. Jackie Kennedy is said to have enjoyed watching episodes of *I Love Lucy* when she had terminal cancer. And a teenager I know who has been battling leukemia for several years really loves watching the *Three Stooges*, which is about as slapstick and silly as you can get.

I once prescribed a comedy routine by Mel Brooks and Carl Reiner, *The 2000 Year Old Man*, for a severely depressed woman, in order to tide her over a long and difficult weekend. While listening to the recording, which she did a number of times over the three days, did not cause her suicidal ideation to vanish, it did provide a welcome antidote, at least while she was playing it.

As with books and films, it makes most sense for you to select from television programs with which you are familiar. The offerings have grown so vast that you are sure to be aware of some that might meet patient needs, including the many special reports on topics that may be pertinent to their therapy.

Theater

Although the availability of live theater in any community varies considerably, and it has become quite costly to attend, you may still want to consider this art form as well. Because of the expense, it makes more sense to simply mention a play or other live performance, rather than prescribing it. Reading a play, unfortunately, doesn't have the same impact, although seeing one on film or television can be helpful.

Some that I have mentioned to patients over the years include *Death of a Salesman*, *Peter Pan*, *The Iceman Cometh*, *The Importance of Being Earnest*, *The Skin of Our Teeth*, and *Pygmalion*.

The classic Greek dramas, such as *Oedipus Rex* and *Electra*, were used by Freud to name the conflictual situations he identified in human development, Shakespeare was also a psychological genius, although not everyone can grasp the subtleties in his Elizabethan language. Some of his plays, such as *Hamlet*, *Romeo and Juliet*, and *Julius Caesar*, are more accessible than others.

Musical comedy and opera are other forms of theater that can also be suggested, especially when they have pertinent themes, as with *Carmen*, *Othello*, or *My Fair Lady*. Gilbert and Sullivan operettas are especially useful in regard to power and pomp, and are also extremely funny (cf. *Topsy Turvy*, a film about the collaborators).

Envy and ruthless competition are the themes of *Chicago*, which makes them palatable because it is so tuneful. And for escapist humor, along with a fine satire about ambition and cynical manipulation, it is hard to beat *The Producers*. *The Lion King* is highly creative, and its messages—about intrafamilial rivalries and the interconnectedness of life—come across even more forcefully in the stage version than in the original film.

Since performances of many plays, musicals, and operas have been recorded on film, videotape may be the easiest format for patients to access. In any case, drama, with or without music, is an art form that embodies so many themes and levels of meaning that you will want to keep it in mind.

Music

From Biblical times, when David calmed King Saul by playing on his harp, music has been thought of as being able to "soothe the savage beast"—and there is no question that hearing a Bach cantata or a Beethoven symphony is among the most moving of human experiences. Some compositions excite rather than calm, like the marches of John Philip Sousa or the ragtime of Jelly Roll Morton.

I have also discovered that some song lyrics are extremely useful in psychotherapy. Although I was the Art Lady on *Mister Rogers' Neighborhood* (PBS) for its first 3 years, and am grateful to Fred Rogers for many things, I didn't realize how very wise he was until I went into full-time private practice (DVD 13.1). Much to my surprise, I found myself quoting him frequently, not only to children, but also to adults. Some lyrics popped into my head more often than others, like "Scary mad wishes don't make things come true," "I like you as you are," "Some are fancy on the outside," or "What do you do with the mad inside when you feel so mad you could bite?"

As with live theater, concerts are usually costly, so you may be better off suggesting recordings of music you think might be helpful. This is one art form in which your tastes can easily be different from those of your patients. Nevertheless, calling their attention to any music that you feel might echo or improve their mood, or help them to see something more clearly, cannot hurt and may indeed help.

Art and Photography

Even though this book is mainly about the visual arts, that is probably the area you are least likely to assign as homework—mainly because it is so easy to bring art and photography directly into therapy through books and reproductions. Nevertheless, there may be an exhibit you feel would be of special interest to a patient, because of either the theme, the style, or the technical process involved. Art exhibits are generally not as costly to attend as plays or concerts, so I have occasionally recommended a show at a museum or gallery to someone, usually because when I went to see it, I was reminded of that individual (DVD 13.2).

On very rare occasions, and with children for whom the transference meanings and gratifications were less loaded than with most adults, I have taken a youngster (Figure 13.1) or a group (Figure 13.2) to an art exhibit during a therapy session. This is mainly because viewing a sculpture or painting full size is radically different from the experience of seeing a reproduction.

As suggested in Chapter 6 on assessment in the section "Responding to Visual Stimuli," you first note the spontaneous response to whatever is on display, and then invite more specific reactions. In a museum or gallery, you can also ask patients to stand in front of something they really like or dislike, which feels quite different from telling you.

In addition, you may want to suggest that they take the position of a sculpture or painting of a person, a helpful exercise for getting at the feeling the artist wished to convey. Similarly, you can invite them to stand or sit in any way they desire in response to an artwork, an association in body movement rather than in words (Figure 13.1). As depicted in Figure 13.2, when a sculptor invited a group of blind children to come and to touch her artwork, they were thrilled (13.2A[1, 2]). Like the adults and adolescents who take "Touch Tours" at the Philadelphia Museum of Art (13.2A[3]), it was therapeutic to be allowed to touch without restraint or rebuke.

Working with adults from Danvers State Hospital in the 1970s, Shaun

13.1 A Boy Poses with a Statue

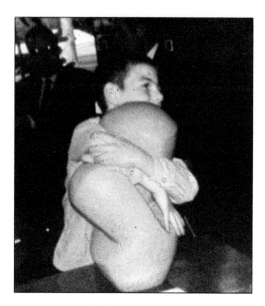

13.2 A Blind Boy Loves a Sculpture

McNiff took them to the Addison Gallery (13.2B), where they viewed the art and made their own art as well. According to McNiff (1981), who also videotaped the experiences, it was liberating as well as educational for the patients, most of whom had been in the hospital for many years.

Patient Recommendations

It is most likely that your patients will have their own musical tastes firmly in place, and that you are as likely to have them suggest concerts or recordings to you as the other way around. While some therapists do not feel that it is a good idea to do what a patient wants them to away from the office, due to boundary and control issues, I believe that such decisions are best made on a case-by-case basis.

There have certainly been instances when a patient's request that I read, see, or listen to something proved to be extremely helpful, enhancing my understanding of the individual and furthering our work. While I didn't always find the recommended music, film, book, or television show personally appealing, it was generally useful as part of my homework on their behalf, sometimes more so than reading some of the relevant professional literature.

I hope that you will consider doing the same, and will welcome—or at least consider—such recommendations. In fact, when training child therapists I have often suggested that they watch the television shows their young patients are viewing, at least a few times, so that they can understand references to the characters and themes in them. The same is true for books, music, and films they refer to frequently, since it is virtually impossible to know what they mean to the youngster without actually reading, hearing, or seeing them yourself.

Creating at Home

Creations Brought from Home

Sometimes, in the course of therapy, patients will bring in art they have created at different times in their lives (DVD 13.3). A troubled young woman once brought in a large collage done in high school. It represented the self she was turning over to me, as well as the memory of a happier period in her life. She did a good deal of art in therapy, usually to express her most unspeakable feelings and impulses.

Unlike the collage, which was a calm and beautiful still life, her therapy art was usually chaotic and full of pain. In the course of our work, the collage took on different meanings, depending on the state of the transference at the time. When she thought she was my favorite patient (child), she was sure that I adored the picture. When feeling jealous of others, she would demean their artwork, but also worried that I preferred it and them.

During a time of devaluation and rejection of me as a "bad" therapist (mother), she threatened to take the collage back, finally in a moment of rage angrily tearing it off the wall. Like the self trying to be reborn in treatment, it had been a temporary loan, to be reclaimed at a time when she needed to rip herself away from me in order to separate and become more independent. When she later returned for further therapy, she said that she planned to hang the collage on the wall of her first apartment, reclaiming her life, as part of moving on.

Usually art done at home in the course of treatment has been stimulated by the therapy, like John's dinosaur drawings (13.3A) or Mrs. B's self-collage (13.3B, C). Even if a patient never creates in your presence, the fact that you have materials available and encourage their use will make bringing in old or current artwork much more likely. However, there may be some patients who will agree to draw or paint as part of their therapy, but who are so uncomfortable about being watched that they ask whether they can do the work at home. While you will lose the observational data, it is wise to agree, and to make the most of what they offer. Thus, if people flatly refuse to use the art materials, asking whether they're willing to do so at home is worth a try.

Marjorie, whose reflections on art and writing you read in the last chapter, was reluctant to waste her valuable therapy time doing art. But she was curious about art therapy, and wanted to try it out. So she experimented at home, following my advice to "just fool around." After trying several media and finding one she preferred, she began to spend more and more of her spare time using it, surprised by how rewarding it was. At one point she decided to take a class, but left because it seemed to be interfering with her own self-initiated creative process.

Though she brought her work in every week, I respected her request not to look at it analytically. In truth, her art developed so nicely and so organically, as she found not only her voice (the medium) but also her language (the style), that I didn't want to interfere in that process, for it had its own integrity and obvious therapeutic benefit. For Marjorie, making art became an unexpected bonus, something she was able to continue to develop when therapy ended. In her reflections on the benefits she received from art and writing (cf. Chapter 11, pp. 184–186), it is clear how meaningful it was for her to create.

Creating as Homework

In addition to accepting art made at home, you may find it sometimes makes sense to assign it as well. I have found such assignments most desirable during interruptions in therapy, especially if I was the one leaving the patient. Under those circumstances, suggesting that someone do artwork for you to look at when you return helps them to stay connected (DVD 13.4) and to feel less abandoned. In her treatment of an adolescent, Helen Landgarten did the just that (13.4A).

Similarly, encouraging journal writing can also be helpful for people in therapy, especially during interruptions. In addition to written reflections, you can suggest a *doodle diary*, an idea proposed by Janie Rhyne (1995) and adopted by some of her pupils, including Natalie Rogers (1993), who called it an "art journal."

There are many possible variations on this idea. One involves having patients draw in a sketchbook each day, then having them write whatever comes to mind when they look at what they have created. It seems as if requesting a *doodle* reduces the self-consciousness that might be felt if it were called a "drawing diary," and invites the sort of spontaneity that is most helpful in treatment. When Sandra Graves gave a bereaved boy a sketchbook to use between sessions, she asked him not only to draw, but also to "scribble" (13.4B).

Because some art forms—like short stories or poems—can take more time to create, especially for adults, you may want to suggest these as something to be done during interruptions (and if it appeals to the patient, between sessions as well). It is best to wait and see how they want to handle the writing they bring in. They may want to read it to you or have you read it in their presence, which are the best options. However, sometimes you may need to be willing to read what they've written as *your* homework assignment, especially if the patient urgently needs to talk about something else that day.

In general, assigning a creative project, whether in art or another modality, makes the most sense to me during interruptions, or for those who strongly prefer creating at home. The exceptions are when the art or imagery assignment is part of cognitive-behavioral therapy, or is an activity that must be done away from the office. This would include such assignments as taking photographs of subjects like their home, a trip, things they love, hate, fear, and so on. You can also suggest that patients interview significant others and, if they agree, bring in the audio- or videotapes for use in their therapy.

Prescribing the Arts as Therapy

On rare occasions, usually at termination, I have recommended that a patient consider doing some further therapeutic work in another expressive arts modality, such as movement therapy or psychodrama. This is especially helpful for individuals who would benefit from something like dance, but who need more support than is available in a class. It is also helpful for those who are now ready to work on an area (such as body image) that would have been too threatening earlier.

In addition to incorporating art into your work as a therapist or suggesting work with a creative arts therapist, I hope that you will also consider reinforcing, even promoting, the involvement of your patients in various art activities outside of therapy. If you are as convinced as I am of the inherently therapeutic values in all of the arts, you might even consider prescribing them, either during or after treatment, as a way of enhancing and maintaining mental health.

Depending on your feelings about your proper therapeutic role, you might suggest that someone you see would do well to take a class or a workshop in whatever art form is appealing. The arts have, after all, been with us since prehistoric times, largely because they serve fundamental human needs. I have no question that having the arts in your patients' lives is one of the best vitamin supplements you can recommend—excellent medicine for the human spirit.

Based on interests people have expressed, and what has been helpful in their therapy, you may want to suggest that they consider taking classes in art, dance, photography, or filmmaking; that they think about learning a musical instrument or joining a choral group or community theater; or that they study creative writing, or a craft, such as quilting, weaving, or wood-working.

Although looking at art, listening to music, or seeing a film can be extremely therapeutic and may indeed help to further someone's therapy, there is something quite different to be gained by direct involvement in a creative activity. Hearing a choir is not the same as singing in a chorus; and while both are good for the soul, I believe that participating, albeit minimally, is much more therapeutic than being in the audience. My husband, who listens to music all day long and greatly enjoys attending concerts, comes home even more exhilarated after his weekly sessions in the community chorus.

Similarly, in spite of the fact that I have always loved going to museums, experiencing such visits as wonderful visual treats, they are not in the same class as doing my own painting. Creating involves more of *me*—body, mind, spirit, energy, call it what you will—and I believe it promotes internal integration for that very reason.

Thus, while I still enjoy attending dance recitals, I'm delighted that I decided to take up tap dancing in my 60s. Although my doctor was nervous, I find that tap offers not only good aerobic exercise, but also a wonderfully exhilarating experience of moving the body in a rhythmic and expressive way. Indeed, I find any kind of dancing to be deeply renewing, despite the fact that I have always been and probably always will be a klutz.

Many find that creative work in a craft, such as quilting, weaving, embroidery, or woodworking, is greatly therapeutic. Others prefer to play an instrument, or to write in their journals. Some are amateur painters, like British Prime Minister Winston Churchill, whose art was an essential release valve for the unbearable tensions of World War II. Since it now appears that he suffered from bipolar disorder, painting was probably also helpful to his emotional equilibrium.

Why the Arts Are Therapeutic

Depending on your theoretical orientation, there are many ways of conceptualizing the therapeutic values inherent in creative experiences. If you are a psychoanalytic therapist, for example, you probably value the power of sublimation as an adaptive coping mechanism. You will therefore be pleased if a patient turns to sculpture rather than to street fights as a way to channel otherwise-destructive aggressive impulses.

If you are a humanistic therapist, you appreciate the power of artistic creativity to lead to self-actualization, and to provide healthy "peak ex-

216

periences" (Maslow, 1959; May, 1975). You are therefore likely to applaud both receptive and expressive arts activities on the part of your patients. In many ways, the art is as unique and original as the person; in fact, it *is* the person.

If your orientation is existential or transpersonal, you are likely to promote arts activities as you would meditation, because of their potential for transcending the self. And if you believe in the spiritual connection of creativity with the universe, you will be pleased when a patient becomes engaged in learning in any of the arts.

If your orientation is behavioral, cognitive, developmental, or solution focused, you can appreciate the organizing potential of the behaviors required to create or perform in any of the arts. For example, learning how to use watercolors, charcoal, or clay demands focused attention, the learning of specific skills, goal setting, problem solving, frustration tolerance, self-evaluation, and much more that is essential for healthy functioning. Learning any art form requires considerable patience and discipline, and can be extremely helpful to those who have been unable to plan, to organize, or to delay gratification.

In addition, as Arnheim (1969) has emphasized, thinking with the hands, eyes, or body is another form of cognition that can supplement, augment, and enhance thinking with the mind in words. Perhaps even more important, there is no right or wrong in the arts, so that the self-definition and self-expression possible in the creative process can often enhance a person's self-esteem, almost as much as learning the necessary skills (see Figure 11.4).

In other words, no matter what your preferred theory and technique of psychotherapy, you probably have some ways of understanding the intrinsically therapeutic value of authentic arts activities. If you agree, then you will consider prescribing them. As often happens, it was a patient who gave me this idea, when she said that one way she planned to deal with the loss involved in the impending termination of her therapy was to take an art class. And many a patient takes art therapy home as a way to cope with stress (DVD 13.5).

Grandma Layton: An Art Class Cures Depression

Sometimes art classes turn out to be amazingly therapeutic (DVD 13.6). Elizabeth "Grandma" Layton was a Kansas housewife who overcame a lifelong depression at the age of 68, while taking a class in contour drawing (13.6A). Even though she had enrolled to distract herself from grief over her son's death, doing contour drawings of herself while looking in the mirror led to an amazing result: the end of a depression that had been resistant to all of the usual therapies (13.6B), including hospitalization, shock treatment, medication, and various kinds of psychotherapy (Lambert, 1995; 13.6C).

Although we don't yet know the scientific explanation for her remarkable recovery, we do know that it was probably both neurological and psychological (Ault, 1996). At this point we are still hypothesizing the reason that the arts are therapeutic, though we have no doubt that they are, and have been for centuries

Conclusion

Creative arts experiences also enhance one's quality of life, hardly negligible in this troubled and troubling world (DVD 13.7). Most people, given encouragement and support, can enrich their lives through the arts, whether the focus is on learning skills, expressing themselves, or both (13.7A). Although participants in the *parent play* groups (13.7B) we ran at our clinic, for example, did learn valuable things about parenting, they often said that the greatest fringe benefit was the energy and renewal they felt following a creative experience.

Art therapist and glass artist James Minson recently demonstrated that the Guatemalan children to whom he taught glass craft skills grew measurably in many areas of their lives (13.7C).

It is no accident that the human-potential movement of the 1960s utilized so many art activities in its growth workshops, also true of its revival in the 1990s. One of the values of the arts is that they promote a deep sense of being in touch with the self, of exploring one's potential for becoming a fully alive and creative person. Perhaps the poet Schiller (1875) was right, after all, when he wrote "Man is human only when he plays."

14

Using Art Therapists

A Brief Introduction to Art Therapy

History

Although the roots of art in healing are ancient, the profession itself is quite young. Many circumstances created a fertile environment for the birth of art therapy in the 20th century—especially the depth psychology of Freud and Jung, with its emphasis on the power of the unconscious and the language of the symbol. This led, in art, to movements like expressionism and surrealism, and in psychiatry to an interest in the spontaneous artwork of the mentally ill, some of whom were pacified by painting and drawing long before there were effective antipsychotic medications (Rubin, 2004; cf. DVD 1.12).

In the heyday of projective techniques, art was incorporated by a number of psychodynamic clinicians as a form of expression in the treatment of adults (Azima, Cramer-Azima, & Wittkower, 1957; Baruch & Miller, 1951; Fleming, 1940; Hulse, 1949; Lewis, 1925; Mosse, 1947; Stern, 1952) as well as children (Appel, 1931; Baruch & Miller, 1952; Elkisch, 1948; Harms, 1948).

Some of the most successful instances occurred at the initiation of a patient who brought his or her artwork into the treatment. You may want to read the fascinating case studies by Australian psychiatrist Ainslie Meares (*The Door of Serenity,* 1958), British analyst Marion Milner (*The Hands of the Living God,* 1969), Norwegian psychiatrist Ingrid Naevestad (*The Colors of Rage and Love,* 1979), Swiss analyst Marguerite Sechehaye (*Symbolic Realization,* 1951), and Dutch therapist Anneliese Ude-Pestel (*Betty: History and Art of a Child in Therapy,* 1977).

The first art therapists, however, were artists who had been hired by psychiatrists to set up studios in mental institutions, like Mary Huntoon (1939) at the Menninger Clinic in the United States and Edward Adamson (1984) at Netherne Hospital in Great Britain in 1946.

And the two individuals most responsible for defining and founding the field of art therapy were educators. One was Margaret Naumburg, who founded a progressive school where the arts were central (Naumburg, 1928) and later worked in a psychiatric hospital (1947, 1950, 1953).

The other was Edith Kramer, who worked in a residential school for disturbed boys (Kramer, 1958) and later in a school for the blind and on an inpatient child psychiatric unit (1971, 1979). Both were Freudian, but each used different aspects of psychoanalytic theory as the foundation for her ideas about the therapeutic use of art.

For Naumburg (1955), art was a form of *symbolic speech* emanating from the unconscious like dreams, to be evoked in a spontaneous way, and to be understood through free association, always respecting the artist's own interpretations. Art was therefore conceived of as a "royal road" to unconscious symbolic content, a means of both diagnosis and therapy (the latter involving verbalization and insight as well as art expression). Her approach, which she called "dynamically oriented art therapy" (1966), led to what is known as *art psychotherapy*.

For Edith Kramer, on the other hand, art was viewed as a "royal road" to sublimation, a means of integrating conflicting feelings and impulses in an aesthetically satisfying form and thus helping the ego to control, manage, and synthesize via the creative process itself (Kramer, 1958, 2001). She called her approach *art as therapy* (1971, 2000), a term by which it is still known (Rubin, 2004).

Both approaches remain visible in a field that has grown rapidly since the founding of the American Art Therapy Association (AATA) in 1969 and the development of training programs as well as ways to recognize excellence in both education (approval) and practice (registration and board certification).

Growth

Since British art therapist Adrian Hill (1945) first coined the term in 1942, the field has grown in many ways. Art therapy is still offered to those in the inpatient psychiatric hospitals where it began; but over the years it has moved into many other settings, such as day hospitals and outpatient clinics, treatment centers for those with mental and physical disabilities, partial programs for the aging, nursing homes, and long-term care facilities.

In addition to its place in educational institutions for students with disabilities, art therapy is now found in schools at all grade levels, from preschool to college. Art therapy is frequently offered in drug and alcohol treatment programs, both inpatient and outpatient. Moreover, art therapy is found in hospitals and clinics for patients with medical problems from burns to AIDS, in both acute care and rehabilitation. Art therapists also work in hospices, and in programs serving the bereaved. Art therapy is offered in detention centers as well as in prisons, including maximum-security settings.

In many ways, art therapy has moved from the clinic to the community. Art therapy is sometimes offered in storefront settings, like ArtStreet, an open studio for the homeless in Albuquerque, NM. In Baltimore, an art therapist helped a group of homeless women to paint a mural, and in Pittsburgh an art and a drama therapist led a group at a community arts center for women fighting substance abuse.

In Turin, Italy, some developmentally delayed adults collaborated with artists on creative projects, supervised by an art therapist. In Vancouver, British Columbia, art therapist Kate Collie developed a computer program so that homebound adults could participate in group art therapy. There are now art therapy associations in many countries on every continent in all parts of the globe, and the field continues to expand around the world, as reflected in the growth of the International Networking Group of Art Therapists (ING/AT; cf. Table 14.1 and Rubin, 1999, 2004).

Definition

Defining art therapy has always been difficult because it is a hybrid, the child of both psychology and art. Despite changes over the years, especially the growing sophistication of the literature and the practitioners, it is hard to improve on the definition proposed in 1961 by Elinor Ulman, founder and editor of the first journal in the field, the *Bulletin of Art Therapy*. Basically, Ulman insisted that *anything that is to be called art therapy must genuinely partake of both art and therapy*—which is as true now as then.

Since art therapy overlaps many other areas, it is useful to compare and contrast it with closely related disciplines. Despite the fact that art therapy is much better known today than ever before, it remains a mystery to many. Even when people have heard of it, they are often unclear about just what it is (DVD 14.1). Many people think, for example, that art therapy means doing art with those who are disabled or in distress. But the definition of art therapy does not depend on *who* is being seen, any more than it is a function of *where* the work occurs, but rather *why* it is being offered (Rubin, 1999).

When art materials are given to sick or troubled individuals, the activities may well be educational or recreational. Providing art for the purpose of constructively filling leisure time is not art therapy. Even in a psychiatric setting, if the primary purpose of the activity is learning or fun, it is certainly *therapeutic*, but it is not art therapy. The essence of art therapy is— as Elinor Ulman so wisely said—that it must be true to both parts of its name: art and therapy. Thus the primary *goal* of the art activity must be *therapy*, which for most clinicians includes assessment as well as treatment.

Of course, there is an element of education involved in art therapy, just as there are therapeutic aspects of art education. But if an art therapist teaches techniques, it is not for the sake of the skill itself, but rather in order to help the person to achieve (for example) a more articulate expression of a feeling, or a higher level of sublimation. Just as a verbal therapy session can seem to the untrained observer to be simply a conversation with a sympathetic listener, a session of group art therapy might look like a class (DVD 14.2).

The differences, as in talk therapy, are invisible—inside the minds of the therapist and the participant. Another way to think about this sort of distinction is that in art therapy and art education, the *modality* (art) is the same, but the *goal* (therapy vs. education) is different. Similarly, play therapists usually have some art materials in their playrooms. In child art therapy and play therapy, however, the *goal* (therapy) is the same, but the *modalities* (art vs. play) are different, despite considerable overlap.

Other professionals, such as occupational, recreational, activity, and speech therapists, also use art materials in their work. However, these disciplines tend, for the most part, to provide art for some circumscribed purpose, often prescribed by a referring physician. Although the social and emotional well-being of the patient is of interest to other activity-based therapies, art therapists' focus is on the psychological aspects of their work.

Even though it is easy to tell the difference between art therapy and its close relatives—like music, movement, dance, drama, or poetry therapy— when each is offered separately, there is as yet no consensus about approaches that use multiple modalities. They are usually called by names like *expressive [arts] therapy* or *creative [arts] therapy*. Although there are some individuals who can evoke and facilitate expression in more than one art form, such people are rare. More often, a therapist has training in one creative modality, along with an openness to and comfort with others.

The 30-year-old training program at Lesley University trains expressive therapists, both generalists and those with a specialization in one primary modality. Whether their graduates have expertise in one or more art forms, they are open to, and comfortable with, working in all.

The National Coalition of Creative Arts Therapy Associations (NCCATA), formed in 1979, includes organizations in all of the arts therapies: music, dance, drama, poetry, and psychodrama. In contrast, the International Expressive Arts Therapy Association (IEATA), formed in 1995, has a multimodal (or intermodal) focus (Malchiodi, 2003b).

Art Therapists

Before the development of a professional association, training programs, standards of practice, and a code of ethics, "anyone with a paintbrush and a patient" could call him- or herself an art therapist (Howard, 1964). Although it is still possible for someone to do so, the difference between an artist or a teacher who fancies him- or herself a therapist, and someone who has undergone the rigorous training now required is considerable.

Training and Credentials

Undergraduate programs and courses in art therapy typically prepare students for graduate study, which is the entry level in the field. Most training programs recommend or require undergraduate study in both art and psychology. These master's degree programs are usually full time for 2 years, covering the required subjects in both lecture and studio classes.

In addition to coursework and observation, students must complete at least 700 direct-contact hours of supervised clinical practicum. The Educational Program Approval Board (EPAB) of the AATA publishes guidelines for both undergraduate (preparatory) and graduate training. It also grants approval to training programs meeting its criteria, which must be renewed at least every 7 years.

In order to become a *Registered Art Therapist (ATR)*, an individual must have a master's degree in art therapy or a related field and must demonstrate that he or she has had the required number of direct-contact hours of supervised clinical work after the degree (1,000 for approved programs, 2,000 for programs that are not approved or are in a related field).

If their program was not approved when they graduated, or if their degrees are in related fields, applicants are required to show that they have taken the required 24 core credit hours in graduate art therapy courses (plus 15 credit hours in studio art and 12 in psychology, which can be undergraduate). They also need to submit three letters of reference from individuals familiar with their clinical work.

In order to become *Board Certified (ATR-BC)*, a registered art therapist needs to pass a national examination. Professional credentials are awarded by a separate organization, the Art Therapy Credentials Board (ATCB). To maintain board certification, an art therapist must submit evidence of at least 100 hours of continuing education credits every 5 years. Art therapists are also expected to adhere to AATA's *Ethical Standards* and *Standards of Practice*.

Quite a few art therapists, particularly those in higher education and in private practice, have earned advanced degrees in related fields, such as social work, counseling, and psychology; some are licensed in those disciplines. Certain training programs prepare students for licensure, as with programs in California whose graduates are eligible to become licensed as marriage and family counselors. Efforts to achieve eligibility for licensure in art therapy are under way in many states, and have been successful in quite a few, most often as a specialty under the umbrella of a master's-level counseling license. Relevant professional associations are listed in Table 14.1.

What an Art Therapist Can Offer

Although the main goal of this book is to help you use art and related visual and creative modalities in your own work as a therapist, there are times when you might want to turn to an art therapist. Most often, it would be to help you achieve your goal of incorporating art into your work with the greatest effectiveness.

Sometimes, as in a referral for adjunctive art therapy, you might decide to turn to an art therapist for a service you are unable to provide. What art therapists have to offer, which is unique to the discipline, is a highly developed expertise in the use of art as a central modality in therapy. This is true whether the art therapy is adjunctive to verbal psychotherapy, or is the primary treatment

Working Together

Adjunctive Art Therapy

Before the development of the field of art therapy, some psychotherapists sent their patients to art classes, with the idea of using their expressions in the ongoing therapeutic work. René Spitz (1954), for example, hired an artist to teach his patients, who brought their paintings to group therapy. Spitz, a psychiatrist and psychoanalyst, would then look at the art with the patients in order to see whether, as with dreams, understanding it could move the therapy forward. Since he believed unconscious material was likely to be expressed in images prior to becoming conscious, having an artist facilitate the patients' creative expressions made very good sense.

Table 14.1 Professional Associations

American Art Therapy Association (AATA)
1202 Allanson Rd.
Mundelein, IL 60060
(847) 949-6064
http://www.arttherapy.org/

American Association for the Study of Mental Imagery (AASMI)
http://www.uml.edu/dept/psychology/aasmi/

American Society of Psychopathology of Expression (ASPE)
Irene Jakab, MD, PhD
74 Lawson St.
Brookline, MA 02146
(617) 738-9821

Art Therapy Credentials Board (ATCB)
http://www.atcb.org/

Association for Play Therapy, Inc.
2050 N. Winery, #101
Fresno, CA 93703
(559) 252-2278
http://www.a4pt.org/

International Expressive Arts Therapy Association (IEATA)
P.O. Box 641264
San Francisco, CA 94164
(415) 522-8959

International Imagery Association (IIA)
Phone: (914) 476-0781/Fax: (914) 4765796
http://www.imagery-iia.com/
e-mail: info@imagery-iia

International Networking Group of Art Therapists (ING/AT)
http://www.emporia.edu/ingat/

International Society for Sandplay Therapy (ISST)
http://www.sandplay.org/

National Coalition of Creative Arts Therapy Associations (NCCATA)
c/o AMTA
8455 Colesville Rd.
Silver Spring, MD 20910
http://www.nccata.org/

Sandplay Therapists of America
http://www.sandplayusa.org

Early art therapists in the 1930s and 1940s like Edward Adamson (1984) in Great Britain and Mary Huntoon (1939) in Topeka, Kansas, were artists who performed a similar function of providing creative opportunities for hospitalized patients. By the 1950s, those artists invited into hospitals were usually supervised by the psychologists and psychiatrists under whom they worked, as Elinor Ulman was trained by Bernard Levy at D.C. General Hospital, or Hanna Kwiatkowska by Lyman Wynne at NIMH. These psychiatrist/psychologist promoters of art therapy were most helpful in its growth and development; like Irene Jakab, M.D., Ph.D., founder and president of the American Society of Psychopathology of Expression (DVD 14.3).

In the beginning, almost all art therapists worked *adjunctively*. That is, the primary therapist was either a psychiatrist, a psychologist, or a social worker. The patient would be referred for individual or group art therapy, as an adjunct to the ongoing psychotherapy. Often, the art therapist would report to the primary therapist on a regular basis, so that what was expressed in the art could be utilized in the therapy. In less well-integrated situations, the art therapist functioned more independently, and whatever benefit was enjoyed by the patient was separate from the psychotherapy.

Inpatient and Residential Settings

Art therapists who work in hospitals and other inpatient settings nowadays are still frequently in an adjunctive role. However, in some situations they may be designated as the primary therapist, especially for nonverbal patients. When I worked on an inpatient unit in a psychiatric hospital in 1963, I saw all of the schizophrenic children individually once a week.

Each child was being followed by a resident in child psychiatry, who did individual and sometimes family therapy with the youngster. Group activities were offered by the occupational therapist, parent counseling was done by the social workers, and diagnostic testing was done by the psychologists. Everyone attended the daily morning meetings, in which each child's condition was presented. In addition, anyone working with the child or family attended case conferences that were held regularly, as part of treatment planning.

Because we were also free to collaborate individually with one another, the situation provided a setting in which to learn about the contributions of each discipline to the functioning of the unit and the treatment of the children. Those schizophrenic children whose therapists wanted to meet regularly got a good deal more out of art therapy than those whose therapists were not interested. Not only did the psychiatrist have the information from the art sessions, but I too knew more about each youngster when his or her therapist and I collaborated. I am quite sure it helped me to respond more helpfully in the art therapy sessions. Although time and money pressures in inpatient care currently make collaboration more difficult, it is still worthwhile if you can arrange it.

Over the years, I worked as a consultant to several residential schools for multiply handicapped children whose primary disabilities were orthopedic, sensory (blindness and deafness), or cognitive (mental retardation). If it was not possible for the art therapist, who was usually adjunctive, to have a formal relationship with the others treating the children, I urged that an informal connection be made. Meetings with psychologists; social workers; speech, occupational, and physical therapists; and teachers often led to regular collaborations.

If you are working in an inpatient or residential setting where there is an art therapist, and you have not yet had an opportunity to get to know one another, try to arrange a meeting. At that time, you can explore the possible ways in which the two of you might work together. One such way would be to refer one or more patients for adjunctive art therapy.

Outpatient Clinics

As the art therapist at the Pittsburgh Child Guidance Center from 1969 to 1981, I had the opportunity to work alongside a number of child psychiatrists, psychologists, and social workers. Many of them referred their patients for art evaluations, either individually or as families.

If this is available to you, it may be a useful option. In addition, a number of those professionals referred patients for adjunctive individual or group art therapy. If it was individual, it was sometimes on the same day, sometimes on a different day, and sometimes alternated with the child's psychotherapy. In all cases, the primary therapist and I met regularly to compare notes.

In one instance, described briefly in Chapter 2, both of us saw a mother and her child on a weekly basis. As noted, we met immediately after their sessions, an ideal arrangement. Dr. Mann found the art to be a preview of what would soon come up in his work. For this reason, he felt the art therapy was complementing the verbal and play therapy by allowing each patient to explore ideas and feelings symbolically before they became conscious. He called it a "preview of coming attractions."

There are many possible variations on the adjunctive theme. You can ask an art therapist to see people individually, as a couple, in family therapy, or in a group, no matter how you are currently treating them. Although having two therapists introduces other issues, and requires maturity and security on the part of both clinicians, there is often considerable benefit to patients who participate in art therapy at the same time that they are in psychotherapy.

While it is generally best to collaborate on a regular basis, there are exceptions where it makes more sense for patients themselves to integrate the two experiences by being in charge of the therapists' contacts. In one such instance, the art therapy began as adjunctive, became parallel, and was eventually the primary therapy.

Elaine: From Adjunctive to Primary

Elaine was a woman in her 40s who had battled depression since her college years, and who was in twice-weekly psychotherapy with a male psychologist (DVD 14.4). At one point, she became aware of previously suppressed memories of sexual abuse that, despite trusting her therapist, she could not bring herself to say aloud. He suggested that she try representing the memories in finger paint, so that she could wipe out the images if they were too upsetting.

Elaine was able to produce a series of finger paintings at home, expressing in simple but powerful terms the memories of what had happened to her (14.4A). Bringing the pictures to her next session, she was finally able to tell her therapist about the events. Since she had found the painting process to be so helpful, he suggested that she might want to try adjunctive art therapy. He also felt that, since she had unresolved issues with both parents, working with a woman as well as a man might accelerate her treatment.

She therefore came for art therapy on a weekly basis, with considerable trepidation and anxiety about what else might emerge. It was clear that she needed the safety of our shared time and space in order to confront some of the more primitive and terrifying image/body/memories and feelings that began to surface. Elaine used all media, but soon gravitated to clay, which proved to be appropriate for a series of eloquent sculptures, most of them rather primitive heads (14.4B).

Within a month of starting art therapy, Elaine had reduced her verbal therapy sessions to once a week. Even though she liked and trusted both therapists, she requested that we not talk to each other, but that she be the one to communicate with each of us. After a year of working on parallel tracks, Elaine decided that she was ready to share her artwork and space with her other therapist.

This session was immensely powerful, as she showed him around my office, filled with her sculptures and paintings (14.4C). Since her divorced parents had never been able to deal with her together, or with each other, either, the joint meeting resonated on many levels. We agreed to have such sessions whenever Elaine felt that she needed to. It is difficult to describe the intensity of those meetings, during which very little was said in words, while a great deal was shared through images. When her male therapist moved to another city, art therapy became the primary treatment, twice a week.

Several years later, Elaine decided to join a survivors' group at a local agency. As she began to trust and to learn from the group therapist, she wanted that woman as well to know and to see her continuing search for healing through art. She, too, visited my office while Elaine, by then better able to talk about her creative experiences and the images she had made, gave her a guided tour.

A few months later, Elaine discovered that the trancelike states in which she usually modeled the clay (14.4D) were a repetition of the dissociation with which she had defended against early abuse. Like others, she had developed *alters* (multiple personalities related to the age and nature of the abuse), who began slowly to emerge, sometimes while she was creating art.

As she was having a very hard time knowing all of these split-off parts, I asked a psychiatrist friend whether the techniques he was then developing might help her. Lou Tinnin of the Trauma Recovery Institute thought they would, but because they were so intense and the regression so potentially disorganizing, it would be best if she could be hospitalized for the procedure.

Eager to have a conscious awareness of all of the alters, Elaine agreed. Dr. Tinnin and I therefore consulted with the psychiatric nurse Elaine had been seeing in connection with her medication at a community mental health center. Fortunately, that therapist was also affiliated with an inpatient setting, which is where Elaine went for the videotherapy feedback sessions described in Chapter 11 (p. 175).

It was important for me to be in contact with this woman, who was with Elaine in the hospital as she watched the videotapes and was introduced to all of her "parts." Several months later, this therapist was also invited to my office to be shown Elaine's art, by then more varied and livelier than before (14.4E).

Since the patient no longer needed to erect such rigid boundaries between the parental figures helping her, she gave permission for us to have telephone collaborations as indicated, which we did. Fortunately, when I retired from full-time practice, this therapist was able to continue with Elaine. Perhaps most significant for this book, we all knew that if necessary, she could carry on with the art therapy. Elaine herself was experienced, knew the media, and mainly needed someone to bear witness while she created her art.

I have told Elaine's story in considerable detail, because it became necessary over time for me to work collaboratively with a series of therapists involved in her care. My role would not have become so central, had not her first therapist referred her for adjunctive art therapy. And there is no question that art therapy, which was parallel for a long time and became primary for a number of years, also allowed her to get to know and to express aspects of her history and disowned parts of herself, which she might not have found out about as soon, or in the same way.

Doing Cotherapy

The child guidance center where I worked for more than a decade was affiliated with a large university. Trainees included psychiatrists, psychologists, and social workers, who provided the individual, group, and family therapy to clinic patients. Fortunately, they were as curious about the use of art in diagnosis and therapy as I was about their disciplines. As a result, I had the privilege of working as a co-therapist with many of them, an arrangement that provided a wonderful opportunity for mutual learning as well as for patient treatment and research.

Even if you have none in your setting, it is still possible to work with an art therapist, whether that person is in training or is elsewhere, including private practice. Let me share with you some of my own experiences, not as literal models, but to give you an idea of some ways of working with an art therapist and of providing patients with the benefit of your expertise as well as theirs. One of the best ways to learn from each other is to do cotherapy. As with adjunctive art therapy, this works best if both clinicians are secure, and able to collaborate honestly and openly.

Mother-Child Art Sessions

After almost a year of separate individual work with 8-year-old David and his mother, both her therapist and I were discouraged, feeling that we had progressed precious little in loosening their powerful symbiotic attachment. We decided on a joint half hour, to be followed by separate half hours with each. They were asked to work together in art (DVD 14.5).

With little discussion, they proceeded to paint a calm, peaceful picture of a lake (14.5A), uttering hardly a word. At the end, each said they had known what the other one was thinking. As mother put it, "I always know what he's thinkin', sometimes before he does." David smiled and nodded his head in agreement, and his mother went on to complain about his messiness and his peculiar habit of collecting junk.

After his mom left to meet separately with her therapist, David created a series of "beautiful mess" paintings (14.5B) and talked about how hard it was to feel mad at a mother with whom he also felt so close (14.5C). His mother, on the other hand, was able to see more clearly, perhaps for the first time, how the intimacy between David and herself might not be such a good thing. Her therapist gently introduced the idea that David might even be expressing angry feelings by doing things like collecting junk and "messing up."

Art in Mother-Child Therapy Groups

On a different occasion, after meeting several times to see what sort of collaboration we could come up with, a social worker and I had the idea that occasional joint art sessions for groups of mothers and children might be useful in treating both. We therefore invited referrals of young children (ages 5 to 6), where it was felt that there were major problems in the mother-child relationship. After interviewing prospective candidates, we ended up leading parallel groups (Rubin, 1974).

Since the groups met at the same time every week, it was easy to schedule periodic joint sessions. On the basis of our weekly collaborations, the social worker and I decided when to have such sessions, and how to conduct them. They ranged from being open ended, which was diagnostically informative, to asking the mother-child pairs to work together in a variety of ways.

During the discussion time, the pairs eventually interviewed each other as well. The week after each of the joint sessions, the mothers would process their reactions as a group, while the children would talk about theirs in the art therapy group, which I co-led with a male child psychologist (DVD 14.6). His motivation—to learn more about art therapy—had led him to request the arrangement. I was pleased, because the group included both boys and girls. He and I also met weekly to collaborate.

Family Art Therapy

The chief of psychology at the clinic was the person with whom I designed the family art evaluation described in Chapter 11, as well as co-leader of the Family Art Study Group (Rubin & Magnussen, 1974). We also decided to work as co-therapists with a family, which we did on a weekly basis for 32 sessions over the course of a year (DVD 14.7).

We recommended this modality on the basis of their response to a family art evaluation, and because of the fact that the boy's stuttering, which was virtually absent in the children's group and at school, was still evident at home and a source of distress for the parents (Rubin, Magnussen, & Bar, 1975).

Most of the time, the members were free to use whatever they wanted, and to make whatever they wished. With two therapists in a large space and many working surfaces, we were able to conduct some individual and couple therapy, as well as talking with the family as a whole in the sharing time at the end of each session. In addition to free choice, we also assigned topics based on our weekly postsession collaborations.

The first topic we assigned was "the *main problem in the family* that you would like to work on," asking that they not look at each other's drawings until the sharing time. Father drew the mother abandoning him with the two screaming kids at the supper table (DVD 10.4A[1]), and complained that "She never joins us." Mother drew him reading while the kids argue and she wearily does the dishes, begging him to intervene in the children's fight (10.4A[2]). Since both were shocked by the similarity in their feelings of abandonment and mutual resentment, they were able to begin to be less defensive and more understanding.

In response to a request several months later to "draw things the way you *wish they were*," mother made a picture in which a maid is cooking a meal in the kitchen while she and her husband have a drink on the sofa (10.4B[1]). They are romantically planning a trip to Africa, as she thanks him for the beautiful flowers he has sent her. The children are notably absent.

Father, however, had a very different wishful image. In his picture, his wife is happily cooking the meal, both children at her side. On the other side of his drawing she is sending him off to work with a kiss, while the angelic youngsters—complete with halos—wave goodbye from their windows (10.4B[2]).

Their conflicting images of perfection and their mutual dissatisfaction, poignantly evident in these drawings, became an increasingly open topic for discussion. By the latter part of the work, the focus had shifted from the boy and his now-absent symptom to stresses in the marriage. When family art therapy ended, the parents agreed to our recommendation of individual and/or couples therapy, both of which they pursued with positive results.

Group Art Therapy

Another way to work with an art therapist is to co-lead a group. I have done so with colleagues from many disciplines, and it has usually been both enjoyable and mutually beneficial. As with dyads and families, you need to conduct your work according to whatever approach is comfortable for both of you.

If you do co-therapy with an art therapist, whether it is with a couple, family, or group, it is critical to meet regularly, preferably after every session. Even if your collaboration meetings are shorter than you would desire, what matters is to be as honest and open as you can about what you were uncomfortable with, as well as to review what happened and to plan for the future. This is especially important in group therapy, in which the group dynamics and the multiple transferences put great pressure on the leaders.

Consulting with an Art Therapist

If you have access to an art therapist who can consult with you and perhaps other clinicians on a regular basis, it may be well worth the investment of time and money. I have met with many groups of experienced social workers, play therapists, psychologists, psychiatrists, and others for various periods of time at their request

It works best if you can learn together, go back and try things out with patients, and then return to explore what happened with the help of the art therapist consultant. Doing this in a group is a good idea, even if you put together a small one privately, because you can learn much more from each other than by yourself alone.

In either case, it is a good way to get started or to get help at any stage, and will certainly amplify what you can learn from this book. One of the nice things about using art in therapy is that, in addition to being able to tell the consulting or supervising art therapist what happened between you and the patients, you can also present the artwork—a most helpful feature.

Collaborating on Research

Although the emphasis in this book is on practice, I would be remiss if I didn't mention something you might very well want to do with an art therapist: to design and conduct research. Some of the best investigations that have been done have been generated by multidisciplinary teams, which take advantage of the resources and knowledge of different professions.

I have done a number of studies over the years, almost always in collaboration with one or more professionals from other fields. When the chairman of the Child Development Department who first invited me to work with schizophrenic children asked whether their art work was diagnostic, the psychologist at the Child Study Center and I designed a way to collect data from a matched group of nonschizophrenic youngsters.

When I later worked at the Child Guidance Center, the director of research, who was a psychiatrist and psychologist, helped me to take the next step: to design the judgment part of the study, which was then implemented (Rubin & Schachter, 1972). While there I also worked with others to study intra-individual variability in children's human figure drawings (Rubin, Schachter, & Ragins, 1983), as well as what you could tell about schizophrenic and nonschizophrenic mothers and their children from their drawings (Rubin, Ragins, Schachter, & Wimberly, 1979). We also collected data for a study (unpublished) that attempted to look at what you could validly infer from family drawings.

In addition, two speech therapists and I once designed a study with parallel tasks: comparing the development of art and speech in preschoolers (Rubin & Rubin, 1988). A clinical psychologist helped me to design a study of a "tactile aesthetic" in blind children, using blind, partially sighted, and sighted judges of wood-scrap sculptures produced by all three groups (Rubin, 1976).

Another clinical psychologist and I did a study designed to look at the relationship between group drawings and group dynamics (Rubin & Rosenblum, 1977). The drama therapist and I compared art and drama productions from same-day interviews with latency and adolescent youngsters along a number of dimensions (Rubin & Irwin, 1975). A study of change in blind children after they experienced a pilot art program was designed with the woman who was in charge of their schooling and whose training was in special education (Rubin & Klineman, 1974).

In other words, no matter what field you are trained in, there are probably areas that you and an interested art therapist could productively investigate, which would add to the knowledge base in both fields. There are indeed many issues that cry out for well-designed and carefully implemented research.

One vital area is that of the potentially curative mechanisms in the artistic process. Investigations in this field are now more possible than ever, thanks to advances in imaging technology (Kaplan, 2000; Malchiodi, 2003a). Another area, which badly needs investigation in art therapy as in psychotherapy, is that of outcome studies. Here, too, recent technology may allow us to measure the effectiveness of treatment with and without art in a more objective and verifiable manner.

Conclusion

It should be clear by now that you can work with an art therapist in any of a number of ways, from consultation to collaboration to co-therapy to research. In addition, you can always take a course or a workshop in art therapy if you decide you want to pursue more training in the field. In fact, as you may have noted, you can even become Registered and Board Certified as an art therapist, if you take the required credit hours of courses (as well as doing thousands of hours of supervised clinical work).

One person who decided to do that was Eliana Gil, who took her art therapy training at George Washington University at a point in her career when she already had both a PhD and a thriving practice, and was the author of two highly respected books on play therapy with children and families (Gil 1991, 1994). Gil is an authority on work with children who have been abused. Perhaps it was that specialization which stimulated her desire to expand her offerings of art materials and to deepen her understanding of creative products (DVD 14.8).

In any case, while you are welcome to travel that route should you so desire, the purpose of this book is not to recruit or create more art therapists. It is, instead, to convince you to add art, mental imagery, and other creative modalities to the work you do with others. Not only do I believe that you can help them more if you do; I am also sure that you will find doing so both fascinating and enjoyable. Good luck!

Postscript

Should you decide to follow the recommendations of this book, you will be following in the footsteps of many illustrious professionals from various disciplines who, in the years before art therapy developed as a separate profession, did use visual modalities in their work.

In fact, in 1958, when I first searched the literature for articles on the psychology of art, I found papers by psychiatrists, psychologists, social workers, occupational therapists, counselors—indeed, mental health professionals from all disciplines. It was their work that inspired me, well before I discovered the early art therapy literature.

Should you decide to explore the use of art and imagery in assessment and therapy, therefore, you will be following in the footsteps of such illustrious workers as Kenneth Appel (1931), J. G. Auerbach (1950), Fern Azima (Azima et al., 1957), Dorothy Baruch and Hyman Miller (1951, 1952), Gustav Bychowski (1947), Paula Elkisch (1948), Milton Erickson and Lawrence Kubie (1940), Joan Fleming (1940), Ernest Harms (1948), Molly Harrower (1958), Frederick Hulse (1949), Irene Jakab (1998), Nolan D. C. Lewis (1925), Eric Mosse (1940), and Max M. Stern (1952).

So don't feel that since you are not an artist or an art therapist, the use of art media is too technical or too difficult. I fact, if you were to read the articles just noted, I suspect that you would be as inspired as I was to find them almost 50 years ago.

For, in spite of all the wonderful technological and biological advances of our era, it is still true that the image is the language of the human soul, and that is eternal. Irene Champernowne was a Jungian analyst who started a new treatment center in Great Britain called Withymead, where all of the arts were central (Stevens, 1986). She wrote some very wise words for a newsletter published about 35 years ago by the British Association of Art Therapists. They seem to me to be appropriate to end this book.

> As far back as the second century a Greek physician, Galen by name, became aware of the power of the visual image on the life of the individual. He said: "I am of the opinion that those who by a process of reasoning convince themselves that some evil is present or impending are not moved to fear or grief by that process but by conjuring up visions of these things. For how can the irrational be affected unless it be moved by some analogous imagining, some picture brought to the senses." (1970, p. 2)

Champernowne (1970, p. 2) wisely concluded with a statement that supports the message of this volume: "It is quite useless for us to speak from our head to the head of the sick person, and expect it to be taken up at any deep, emotional level. Only the image will suffice."

More about Art Materials

Things to Draw or Paint On

Papers

Whether you are inviting people to draw, to paint, or to make a collage, sturdy paper is essential. Newsprint is not a good idea, because it is thin and tears too easily. As a rule, it is best to have *medium-weight white drawing paper* (60 to 80 lb.), which is adequate for most drawing and painting media.

It is also a good idea to have *more than one color* of paper, so packages of *white drawing paper* and assorted colors of *construction paper* are a good start. The best size to begin with is 9″ × 12″. If you have the space to be able to offer larger sizes of paper, it's nice to have alternatives, so I'd recommend both white drawing paper and assorted construction paper in size 12″ × 18″, as well.

If you want people to be able to work large, or to have groups or families work together on a single surface, a package of 18″ × 24″ paper (white for sure, assorted colors if you wish) is very helpful. This larger size is also desirable if you see children or adolescents, but it requires that you have a working surface big enough to accommodate it.

You don't really *need* any other kinds of paper, though if you want to provide more, *tissue paper* is great for high-success torn-paper collages. If you want to offer finger paints, then a package of 11″ × 16″ *glossy finger-paint paper* is desirable. While there is special paper with more tooth and absorbency for charcoal, chalk, and watercolor, 60-lb. paper works well enough, while 80-lb. paper is even sturdier.

You might wonder whether it makes more sense to buy paper in packages or in pads. In general, packages are best, because they allow each piece of paper to be used separately with any drawing or painting medium.

Also, even though you can tear single sheets out of pads, it's sometimes difficult to do so without creating an uneven edge. Finally, buying any kind of paper in packages, even small ones, is less costly. It is most economical to buy white drawing paper by the ream (500 sheets), while construction and finger-paint paper are sold in smaller packages of 50 or 100 sheets.

You may also want to buy *pads of white drawing paper* for use with individual clients. These can be purchased in bulk from art supply houses, and are best if they are around 9″ × 12″ in size and contain medium-weight paper (at least 60 lb.).

Even though you may have a table available, people who have become most comfortable sitting on your couch or chair may prefer to stay there to make a drawing or a doodle. For them, it helps to have their own personal, private pad, which they can even carry home for between-session drawing or writing if they wish.

When I first suggested drawing to analytic patients, I offered simple media (colored pencils, thin markers, oil crayons) and a pad. It worked remarkably well, even while they were reclining. An alternative to a pad, if someone is working on a chair or couch, is to use cardboard as a backing for a piece of drawing paper.

Things to Draw With

Pencils

These are a wonderful way to begin, and indeed, may be sufficient for your needs. Many patients prefer to start with a pencil or pen, since they are such familiar writing instruments. A *soft drawing pencil*, like an Ebony, makes it possible to make both light and dark lines very easily; and a good eraser is a must.

Colored pencils are also nice to have, because they are still neat and controllable, but expand the tonal repertoire; it is a good idea to buy a set with more than eight colors, as the choice itself is stimulating. You need to buy a good brand, like Mongol, since many sets of colored pencils can be quite frustrating, and ultimately discouraging. For adults and adolescents you may want to add *charcoal* and *pastel pencils*.

Pens

If someone wants to draw with a pen, it is best to offer *roller-ball pens* of different thicknesses for ease of flow and choice in size. You can also buy

240

such pens in different colors, and those at the drugstore are good enough. In addition, there are felt-tip pens of different thicknesses and colors, for which those available in stationery sections are also adequate. Using a responsive pen or pencil is dramatically different from trying to use one that isn't.

Markers

Felt-tip markers are probably the easiest drawing tool for most people to use. They are versatile, too, since fine ones allow the artist to represent precise details, while broad ones can rapidly cover a large area. As long as you buy a good brand, *watercolor markers* flow freely and have intense colors. Although a set of eight colors is sufficient, sets of 12 or more are stimulating enough to warrant the extra outlay.

When properly cared for by putting the caps tightly back on each color immediately after each use, they can last a very long time. If the boxes start to wear out, the markers can be kept upright in jars or plastic cups, which makes it even easier for people to select colors. Since you won't want to get marks on surfaces from which they can't be removed, it's best to buy those markers labeled "washable" and to protect work surfaces by covering them with paper or plastic.

Be careful to buy watercolor—and not ink—markers, which are permanent and have a very strong odor. However, you may want to have a few *ink markers* on hand for those times when people want to work on glass, metal, or plastic. Moreover, older adolescents and adults enjoy using *paint markers* of various colors, including metallic ones.

Crayons

Wax crayons, like markers and colored pencils, should be made by a reputable company, like Binney & Smith. As with markers and colored pencils, sets of more than eight colors are more stimulating. Regular-size crayons are fine for most people of all ages, although little fingers and people with disabilities that impair their grasp may do better with larger crayons.

Oil crayons are more grown-up looking and therefore more appealing to adolescents and adults. They are really a kind of paint in stick form, and the colors are smoother to apply, are more intense, and can be blended as well. They are sometimes called oil pastels. One well-known brand is Sakura Craypas, which come in 12 or more colors. Like wax crayons, they also come in larger sizes, which may be better for fingers whose grasp is weak.

Chalk and Pastels

As with colored pencils and watercolors, you can rarely find good *drawing chalk* in the drugstore, and would do best to look for better-quality brands, like Alphacolor. A set of 12 or 24 colors can last a long time. *Dry pastels* can be blended easily with the fingers, and *wet pastels* are especially vivid on colored paper (either wet the paper first or dip the chalk in water).

There are also very large *poster chalks*, which are practical for covering big surfaces rapidly, as when a family creates a mural. If you like using chalk, you will want to buy a spray can of fixative, which holds the particles in place. The finished pastel drawings can be sprayed by the patient or by you when the patient has left, depending on which seems most clinically useful.

Things to Paint With

If you see children, paint is essential, while it is optional for work with adolescents and adults. There are five main kinds that will be most useful for art therapy: tempera, watercolor, gouache, finger paint, and acrylic. As with drawing materials, you need to buy reliable brands, like those in art supply catalogs (Prang, Alphacolor, etc.), because poor paints are extremely frustrating.

Tempera, a water-based paint, can be purchased in small sets of 6 to 12 colors, usually in 2-oz. jars. It can be used directly from the jars, as long as a cup of water is available to clean the brush before using a new color. These sets are easily portable, and work well when painting on a table.

Tempera (or *paint*) *markers* are little plastic squeeze bottles with a felt-covered tip that contain liquid tempera. They are held in the hand like a drawing tool and, after being squeezed, can be pressed onto the paper surface to make dots, lines, or masses. They are useful when the place or the person requires something less messy. They are easy to use for covering large surfaces, and can be pounded on the paper, which is helpful as an outlet for aggression.

If you see children, you may want to buy large (16-oz.) containers of tempera paint and pour the colors into plastic cups or muffin tins. I recommend a jar of each of the most commonly used colors (e.g., red, yellow, blue, green, purple, orange, black, brown, white, and flesh). Plastic palettes with small sections for different colors and large ones for mixing are also useful. Other alternatives are aluminum-foil trays and paper plates.

Water colors are always popular, because they come in small, easily portable containers. They are actually harder to use than tempera, which allows you to paint over something if you want to make a change. Despite the easy availability of cheap watercolor sets, only good brands, like Prang, are satisfying to use. A variety of colors (i.e., 16 to 24) is more stimulating, and oval pans are the most manageable.

Gouache is sold in tins or tubes like watercolors, but can be used to cover over something, and is often more satisfying for adults and adolescents. *Acrylics* are also appealing to mature patients. They resemble oil paints in their tubes, but are in fact water soluble. They require some sort of palette, however (pads of disposable paper palettes are available, or a paper plate will do), as well as a sturdy surface, like cardboard, canvas board, or canvas sheets in pads. (They can also be used on 80-lb. paper.)

Finger paints are the messiest of the lot, but are very useful with people of any age who have problems with their impulses—whether they are inhibited or out of control. One of the least messy ways to fingerpaint is to use it in shallow plastic trays, with or without paper.

If the person works directly onto a tray or table, you can make a monoprint of the image at any point by simply pressing a piece of finger-paint paper onto what has been drawn. Here, too, only reputable brands are reliable. While optional for work with adults, finger paints are highly recommended in child therapy.

Things to Model With

The kind of clay that is easiest to use in any setting is a man-made, oil-based modeling material called *plasticine*. It is often sold in quarter-pound sticks—like butter—and comes in a variety of colors. You need a decent brand, like Modeline, although lately most of what is available in drugstores is of adequate quality.

When my analytic patients wanted to model while lying on the couch, this proved to be the best medium, and it is always good when mess is a concern, either for the person or the place. A small piece can be held in the hand, squeezed (which reduces anxiety), and fiddled with, without requiring a work surface.

If the person wants to press down on a flat surface, a piece of cardboard is fine, or you can use printer paper or paper plates to protect a table. I recommend buying sets with different colors, as these are not only stimulating, but are also likely to lead to attractive products. Plasticine never hardens.

Clay (or *earth clay*) is the kind that forms naturally in the ground and is used in ceramics. It is messy, and it needs to be stored in plastic bags and kept moist (by periodically adding water). It is, however, much more responsive than plasticine, and can be modeled with the hands alone or with simple tools. Unlike plasticine, earth clay dries out and gets hard.

I recommend the smooth kind used in schools, ideally one bag of red (or brown) and one of gray (or white). You don't need to have a kiln (a special oven for firing clay at a high temperature to make ceramics), since clay can air dry, and can be painted and even varnished or shellacked if you wish.

If you want to spend more money, there are also *synthetic modeling media* that air dry like fired clay or that can be fired in an ordinary oven (special clays like Mexican Pottery Clay, Sculpey, or Fima) Another synthetic material that is even cleaner than plasticine is Model Magic. Most of these alternative clays come in a neutral tone as well as in a variety of colors, and most can be painted as well.

Many child therapists use *modeling dough*, either homemade or commercial (e.g., Play-Doh). While this is a very pliable medium, it does not hold its shape well or have a smooth surface when it hardens. The mixing process itself can indeed be therapeutic, however, and involves adding color to a flour, salt, and water combination. But it's no substitute for clay or plasticine when it comes to modeling.

Although a paper plate or a piece of cardboard is an adequate base for clay work, it is helpful to model on a small plastic *turntable* (available in hardware stores) so that people can easily see what they're making from different angles.

Things to Construct With

Two-Dimensional

For patients who find art intimidating, making *collages* of pictures they have chosen is often much less threatening. You can collect such images yourself and put them in a box to be selected, and you can also have available magazines with numerous photographs, like *National Geographic* or *People*.

Pictures can be torn or cut, and then glued on white or colored paper or cardboard, along with scraps of any other kind of paper, cloth, or yarn you want to put in your collage box. Drawing or painting media can be added to complete the image.

Three-Dimensional

There are many commonly available materials that can be easily used by people of all ages for three-dimensional construction, such as colored pipe cleaners (which promote a kind of 3-D linear doodling), craft sticks, tongue depressors, wood scraps without splinters, or soldering wire (which is easy to shape).

For both two- and three-dimensional construction, you need a glue that works (like Elmer's), staplers, tapes (masking and clear), and any other easy ways of successfully attaching one thing to another. Some materials, like soldering wire, pipe cleaners, and colored toothpicks, are easy to anchor in a piece of styrofoam (packing materials are fine). As with clay, a plastic turntable can be helpful when patients are working in three dimensions, depending on the size and nature of the construction.

Tools to Work With

Brushes

If you offer tempera paints or watercolors, you will need to buy some brushes. This is another area where quality makes a huge difference. It is a good idea to buy both pointed and flat brushes, and to get several sizes. A set of assorted sizes of each (pointed and flat) is a good way to start out.

Short-handled brushes are easiest to use, even at an easel. If you order from an art supply catalog (like those listed at the end of this appendix) you will be safe with the least expensive ones. For the most part, brushes that are sold in the drugstore are not worth whatever they cost, since the hairs usually fall out and they don't hold the paint or their shape well.

It is important to wash brushes immediately after use. Twisting them gently into soap and water in the palm of your hand and then rinsing them in water until they are clean is a safe and effective method of removing the paint. Properly cared for, good brushes will last a long time.

Clay Tools

If you offer regular (earth) clay, even though your hands are wonderful tools, it's a good idea to get some clay tools as well. Wire or string is essential for cutting pieces of earth clay from a large block. You can actually get by with tongue depressors, craft sticks, or orange sticks. But it's not too costly to buy a basic set of clay tools, and as long as you wash them out right away like brushes, they'll last forever. You can buy wooden or plastic tools, and they should include one or two with wire ends for cutting out pieces of clay, as well as at least one that is serrated for making textures. Sponges are useful as well, for smoothing the surface.

Like pencils, pens, markers, and other drawing utensils, both brushes and clay tools can be stored in jars, cans, and plastic or cardboard cups of appropriate sizes, making them easy for patients to select and to use.

Sources of Art Supplies

Dick Blick Art Materials: (800) 447-8192, http://www.dickblick.com
Nasco Arts & Crafts: (800) 558-9595, http://www.nasco.com
Sax Arts & Crafts: (800) 558-6696, http://www.sax.com
Triarco Arts & Crafts: (800) 328-3360, http://www.triarco.com

More about Different
Approaches

In the book *Approaches to Art Therapy: Theory and Technique* (Rubin, 2001a), art therapists who have studied particular orientations describe how they have applied the thinking therein to their work. What follows here is a brief description of the book's contents.

Since art therapy was born during a time when Freudian thinking dominated psychiatry, it is not surprising that the earliest theories came from this orientation. Some theorists were interested in making the unconscious conscious, some focused on developing ego capacities, and some emphasized the development of a self that could function independently in the world.

The ability of art to express censored, unconscious material in a safe way is at the core of all of these approaches. They differ in part because of the contexts in which they were developed—that is, art therapy as adjunctive or primary. They also differ because of the patients with whom they were developed, especially the degree and developmental origin of those patients' problems.

The first section of *Approaches to Art Therapy* covers *Psychodynamic* approaches, and includes five chapters written by art therapists with a Freudian point of view, three of whom are also practicing psychoanalysts. The chapters contain case examples of work with both children and adults, whose problems include anxiety disorders, reactive depression, behavior disorders, substance abuse, borderline disorder, and narcissistic disorder.

In the first chapter, I describe the use of art therapy in work with a neurotic young woman suffering from both anxiety and a reactive depression, using her spontaneous drawings and paintings as springboards for associations and discussions, similar to what an analytic therapist might do with dreams. In Chapter 2, Edith Kramer describes doing art therapy with deeply disturbed psychotic and borderline patients, both children and adults, with the ultimate goal is the fostering of sublimation through the achievement of formed expression. In Chapter 3, Laurie Wilson discusses how making art can help in work with those whose symbolic function is impaired or undeveloped, describing its use with a retarded woman, an aphasic man, and a schizoid boy.

In Chapter 4, Arthur Robbins talks about how object relations theory informs his way of conducting art therapy, and why it is especially helpful with patients suffering from borderline and narcissistic disorders, as illustrated in a case example of a woman.

In the fifth chapter, Mildred Lachman-Chapin describes her unique application of Self psychology to art therapy with a young woman suffering from a failure in preoedipal development, reflected in a history of substance abuse. A commentary by Sandra Kryder amplifies this chapter.

Psychoanalyst Eleanor Irwin then offers a brief description of object relations theory, the area in psychoanalytic therapy undergoing the greatest amount of discussion and change in recent years, evolving into such approaches as interpersonal, relational, intersubjective, and social constructivist.

The following two chapters are by Jungians. In Chapter 7, art therapist and Jungian analyst Michael Edwards describes his application of analytical psychology with both individual patients and workshop participants. Chapter 8, by psychiatrist and analyst Edith Wallace, describes her way of using active imagination with workshop groups and in the treatment of a young woman.

Finally, a commentary by Jungian analyst and art therapist Joy Schaverien considers the relevance of each of the seven approaches described in the psychodynamic section to her own work with a hospitalized anorexic man, noting the continuing relevance of psychoanalytic thinking to art therapy.

The second section covers *Humanistic* approaches, and includes art therapy from phenomenological, Gestalt, person-centered, humanistic-holistic, and spiritual (transpersonal) points of view. Four of the authors are licensed psychologists as well as art therapists, and have studied their theories in depth.

The importance of art in humanistic approaches, which focus on people's capacity to take charge of their own lives, lies in its unique ability to help human beings realize the goals of both self-actualization and self-transcendence. Rather than being the object of transference or the source of interpretations, the art therapist in these approaches is viewed mainly as a companion, a guide, or a witness.

Chapter 8, by psychologist and art therapist Mala Betensky, emphasizes a very special kind of looking—in an intense and phenomenological way—at the art that is made in therapy, using an example from the out-patient treatment of an anorexic teenage girl.

Janie Rhyne, who studied psychology with Frank Barron and Gestalt with Fritz Perls, then discusses the relevance of Gestalt therapy to art therapy in growth groups for healthy adults, which she calls the "Gestalt art experience." She also describes her individual treatment of a very confused young woman, using "mind state" drawings based on George Kelly's personal construct theories (Chapter 9).

In Chapter 10, Josef Garai talks about humanistic-holistic approaches to art therapy, using examples of tasks he has given to training groups; he also discusses his work with spontaneous paintings in the therapy of an alcoholic young man struggling to be more autonomous.

In the 11th chapter, Natalie Rogers describes her application of her father Carl's client- or person-centered approach to expressive arts therapy with groups, as well as in her own life at a time of crisis.

Pat Allen then conceptualizes a highly disciplined and spiritually centered approach in an art studio, noting the similarities with and differences from transpersonal art therapy (Chapter 12). Finally, existential art therapist Bruce Moon reflects on the continuing relevance of humanistic modes to the practice of art therapy.

In the third section, broadly labeled *Psycho-Educational*, there are descriptions of behavioral, cognitive-behavioral, and developmental approaches to art therapy. These are followed by a chapter on the assessment and teaching of cognitive skills through art. First, Ellen Roth (Chapter 13) tells about how she used "reality shaping" in behavioral art therapy with emotionally disturbed, retarded children. Then, in Chapter 14, Marcia Rosal describes cognitive-behavioral art therapy with a depressed adult who was alexithymic, unable to identify her feelings. Both chapters are based on work in psychiatric settings.

The next two chapters describe approaches used in both clinical and educational settings: Susan Aach-Feldman and Carole Kunkle-Miller first (Chapter 15) explain their broad-based developmental approach to assessment and treatment in work with blind and retarded children who were also emotionally disturbed. Then Rawley Silver, in Chapter 16, describes her work in the assessment and development of cognitive skills through art, detailing her experience with a hearing-impaired youngster. Finally,

Frances Anderson, who herself has articulated an "Adaptive" approach to art therapy, comments on the section as a whole.

In the fourth section, which concerns *Systemic* approaches, Barbara Sobol and Katherine Williams describe the history and present state of family and group art therapy, with examples of their work from a psychodynamic perspective, incorporating understandings of group dynamics and family systems. In her commentary, Shirley Riley then talks about the relevance of systemic and postmodern approaches to family art therapy, especially those that are narrative and solution-focused.

The fifth section includes three descriptions of approaches broadly described as *Integrative*, although it is true that some of those in earlier sections integrate more than one perspective as well. These four chapters deal more explicitly with the issue of choice for the therapist. Two are about the problem of selecting from among different theories, and the challenge of shifting as needed in terms of the needs of the situation and the patients. Elinor Ulman (Chapter 18) describes the dilemma of choosing between art as therapy and art psychotherapy, while Harriet Wadeson discusses the evolution of her eclectic approach to art therapy (Chapter 19).

The third chapter (20) in this section, by Shaun McNiff, concerns the integration not of different orientations, but of different art forms in an expressive therapy approach to art therapy carried out in a studio setting. (The chapter by Natalie Rogers, although it is in the humanistic section, also deals with shifting from one creative modality to another.) While it could be argued that multimodal approaches differ more in technique than in theory, they are based on a belief in the unique expressive potential of different art forms. Finally, in Chapter 21, David Henley outlines his treatment of disturbed adolescents through a therapeutic curriculum infused with activities in all of the arts.

The book is framed by an introduction and a conclusion written by the editor, in which general issues about translating any theory into an art therapy technique are considered.

A recent volume edited by Cathy Malchiodi, the *Handbook of Art Therapy* (2003c), includes brief discussions of some of the approaches noted previously, as well as a number of those that are currently being explored extensively, such as solution-focused and narrative ways of doing psychotherapy.

More about Art Activities

An Ambivalent Appendix

Throughout my career, whether in the training of art therapists or of people from other disciplines, I have avoided the temptation to satisfy the frequent pleas for a list of activities that would tell the therapist which materials to use or what to do with a certain population. It is natural for clinicians, like everyone else, to want to know exactly what to do, just as it is natural to want to be told precisely what artwork means.

I, too, wish it were that simple, and that I could give you a list of art materials or activities to be used with specific populations for specific purposes. That doesn't mean that you always need to offer free choice, or that there are no ways in which you can think of media and tasks according to your goals. Not at all.

In fact, although I can't tell you what to do each week in individual art therapy with a 14-year-old anorexic girl for each of 10 sessions, I can offer you some guidelines about making decisions on what to offer and what to request. I've suggested throughout that many of these decisions will be guided by your preferred orientation and way of conducting psychotherapy. Others will be dictated by the circumstances of the situation, and by what you yourself are comfortable with.

My first book, *Child Art Therapy* (first edition published in 1978), was subtitled *Understanding and Helping Children Grow through Art*. It was full of detailed descriptions of art therapy with individuals, families, and groups. The only specific advice I offered, however, was a "Cautionary Note" at the end of the book, reminding readers that, while the procedures in it sounded simple, art in therapy was powerful and practitioners needed to realize that using it could be something of a two-edged sword. Probably one reason I wrote that in 1978 was that there were not as many sophisticated training programs, and therefore very few experienced and knowledgeable art therapists. I am less concerned about the readers of this book, since I am assuming that you have been well trained in your own discipline, and recognize the power you have to do harm as well as to do good in psychotherapy.

My next book was *The Art of Art Therapy* (1984), in which I spelled out the basic understandings art therapists needed to have about the "Art Part," the "Therapy Part," and "Putting It Together" in the art of conducting art therapy.

I wrote that I could not tell anyone how to *do* art therapy, but rather how to *think* about doing it. I am still of that opinion. That means that I don't feel I can tell you exactly *how* to include art in your own work, but I can help you to *think* about doing it. I hope that the chapters in which I have tried to suggest possible ways of proceeding, at each step of the way—from getting started, to introducing art activities, to what you can do during and after the process—have helped to give you some ideas of how you might proceed, but in ways that are syntonic for you.

Since you are likely to be interested in using art and visual stimuli in assessment, I have included two chapters offering an overview of the area, as well as various ways in which art therapists and other clinicians have used drawing and other modalities for that purpose. As with what you can do to initiate, observe, and reflect on the creative process with patients, these chapters are also meant to stimulate and to give you ideas that you can modify as you wish—not to tell you precisely what to do. Similarly, the chapters on using art in your work with adults, children, families, and groups are meant to give you ideas of ways you might proceed. The same is true of the chapters suggesting that you consider including opportunities in other art forms, inviting mental imagery, and working with art therapists.

The Need for Flexibility

For the most part, I have always found doing psychotherapy, even from my preferred analytic orientation, to be a highly unpredictable endeavor. I have recently likened it to sailing, since the clinician needs to catch the wind when it comes up, often with little notice. There may be long periods when we must wait for the wind and tides to shift, so that the course of the therapy voyage can be a safe one.

It takes alertness to sense when the patient is ready to move in a new direction. Any therapist tunes in to multiple frequencies for evidence of readiness to go deeper: artwork, dreams, mood, attitude, and behavior in and out of the sessions. As is true when sailing, there are inevitably rough as well as smooth periods, during which the therapist must hold firm to the rudder in order to keep the boat of treatment as steady as possible.

Whether a therapist is seeing an individual, a couple, a family, or a group; whether the goal is assessment or treatment; whatever the age, and wherever the setting; the creative challenge of this work consists in deciding what to do and how to do it. The artistry of the work lies in helping people to become engaged in the therapeutic process in ways that enhance their personal growth. A good therapist is selective and sensitive, trying to accomplish the goals of any particular intervention within whatever constraints are present. This may involve using one or another technical approach, but always doing so with the deepest respect for the human beings involved.

Effective and thoughtful psychotherapy is at least as much an art as it is a science. As in other art forms, only practice can help the practitioner to develop both skill and spontaneity. Well-developed technique is not so much a collection of ideas as it is deeply ingrained and easily available. Elinor Ulman (1971) made this point when she wrote that "a little learning may be worse than none. Our understanding must be well digested if it is to inform lightning decisions" (p. 28). A good therapist—like the psychoanalyst Donald Winnicott or the psychiatrist Milton Erickson—has both theory and technique "in her bones."

On the Other Hand . . .

If you saw *Fiddler on the Roof*, you may remember how Tevye would frequently make a statement and then say, "But on the other hand," which allowed him to look at the other side of the issue. Despite the fact that I am uncomfortable telling you exactly what to do, and would probably be unable to write a book that was composed of nothing but lists of activities with art media, I must admit that there are certainly a number of examples of art activities in this book and the others I have written.

It is in fact possible to find lists of art activities for different therapeutic purposes, and I would encourage you to look at them—not for a prescribed plan, but for stimulation as you think about what you might do to further your work with an individual, couple, family, or group. As it happens, several art therapists have given considerable thought to making lists of possible activities, in many cases along with the probable or possible purpose of each activity. Although I am convinced that, as you become comfortable with art media, you will be able to think of tasks and themes that will meet your goals and that you will be comfortable with, I also imagine that you may find the stimulation of others' thinking and ideas to be helpful.

Therefore, despite my ambivalence about providing such lists myself, I am pleased that others have done so, and understand that you may want to know about them. The following books and articles containing such activities are far from exhaustive. However, having looked at those noted here, I am comfortable providing them for you, and hope that they will indeed be useful.

Drawing Workbooks and Guides

Like fairy tales and art in therapy, the cartoon story drawings proposed by Crowley and Mills in *Cartoon Magic* offer both disguise and distance, enabling loaded themes to be dealt with more comfortably. The popularity of such self-help materials, for both adults and children, has not been lost on art therapists.

Some have developed creative workbooks that suggest various drawing and writing activities. The pioneer in this area was Lucia Capacchione, whose *Creative Journal* (second edition published in 2001) was the first of her many drawing workbooks. Other art therapists have also contributed to this genre. Barry Cohen and his colleagues (Cohen, Barnes, & Rankin, 1995) have published a creative workbook for those suffering from PTSD; Sandra Graves (1994) has created one for the bereaved; and Nichols and Garrett (1995) wrote one for those who are depressed.

Marge Heegaard's series of workbooks for children—and her guide for facilitators (1992)—deal with specific problems, like death or divorce. More than 20 years ago, I tried out a variety of drawing books with children, including one on reality testing (*Make-Believe Drawing Book*), one on self-concept (*My Book about Me*), and a *Hospital Drawing Book* for children in a medical hospital. My young subjects' responses were uniformly positive, confirming the need for such tools. A few years ago, the American Psychological Association published one for children whose parents were separated or divorced, *My Mom and Dad Don't Live Together Anymore* (Rubin, 2002).

Closely related to drawing workbooks are books that encourage readers to explore their own creativity. Art therapists have contributed to this literature, most notably Pat Allen (1995), Shaun McNiff (1998), and Cathy Malchiodi (1998a). Janie Rhyne, an art therapist who began her work in the human potential movement, devoted a large part of her book (1995) to helping readers gain access to their own creativity.

As for art activities to be used by therapists, there are a number of books by authors such as Marian Liebmann, for work with adult groups (1986); Carol Ross, for work with children (1997); and most recently, Susan Makin (1999). In addition, many have included some consideration of activities along with the purpose for which they might be used, as Harriet Wadeson did in two of her books (1980, pp. 334–336, and 2000, pp. 404–438).

If you want something for stimulation, these are fine. What is most important, however, is to keep in mind that whatever you decide to do in art, as in verbal therapy, needs to make sense for the patients, their treatment, and the goals thereof. As long as you remain attuned and flexible, you need not worry. And once again, bon voyage!

References

Aach-Feldman, S., & Kunkle-Miller, C. (2001). Developmental art therapy. In J. A. Rubin (Ed.), *Approaches to art therapy* (2nd ed., pp. 226–240). New York: Brunner-Routledge.

Achterberg, J. (1985). *Imagery in healing.* Boston: New Sciences Library.

Adamson, E. A. (1984). *Art as healing* London: Coventure.

Ader, R. (Ed.). (2001). *Psychoneuroimmunology* (3rd ed.). New York: Academic Press.

Adler, G., & Jaffe, A. (Eds.). (1973). C. G. *Jung letters* (Vol. 1). Princeton, NJ: Princeton University Press.

Ahsen, A. (1973). *Basic concepts in eidetic psychotherapy* (2nd ed.). New York: Brandon House.

Akeret, R. U. (1973). *Photoanalysis.* New York: Peter H. Wyden.

Allan, J. (1988). *Inscapes of the child's world.* Dallas, TX: Spring Publications.

Allan, J., & Bertoia, J. (1992). *Written paths to healing.* Dallas, TX: Spring Publications.

Allen, P. B. (1995). *Art is a way of knowing.* Boston: Shambhala.

Allen, P. B. (2001). Art making as spiritual path: The open studio. In J. A. Rubin (Ed.), *Approaches to art therapy* (2nd ed., pp. 178–188). New York: Brunner-Routledge.

Allen, P. B. (2005). *Art is a spiritual path.* Boston: Shambhala.

American Psychiatric Association. (1994). *Diagnostic and statistical manual of mental disorders* (4th ed.). Washington, DC: Author.

Anderson, F. E. (1992). *Art for all the children* (2nd ed.). Springfield, IL: Charles C. Thomas.

Appel, K. E. (1931). Drawings by children as aids in personality studies. *American Journal of Orthopsychiatry, 1,* 129–144.

Arnheim, R. (1969). *Visual thinking.* Berkeley: University of California Press.

Auerbach, J. G. (1950). Psychological observations on "doodling" in neurotics. *Journal of Nervous and Mental Disease*, 304–332.

Ault, R. E. (1996). *Drawing on the contours of the mind*. Unpublished manuscript. Topeka, KS: The Menninger Foundation.

Azima, H., Cramer-Azima, F. J., & Wittkower, E. D. (1957). Analytic group art therapy. *Journal of Projective Techniques, 7*, 243–260.

Bar, A., & Jakab, I. (1969). Identification of the stuttering episode as experienced by stutterers. In I. Jakab (Ed.), *Psychiatry and art* (Vol. 2, pp. 2–15). New York: S. Karger.

Barnes, M., & Berke, J. (1971). *Mary Barnes: Two accounts of a journey through madness*. New York: Ballantine Books.

Barnes, M., & Scott, A. (1989). *Something sacred*. London: Free Association Books.

Baruch, D. W., & Miller, H. (1951). The use of spontaneous drawings in group therapy. *American Journal of Psychotherapy, 5*, 45–58.

Baruch, D. W., & Miller, H. (1952). Developmental needs and conflicts revealed in children's art. *American Journal of Orthopsychiatry, 22*, 186–203.

Benjamin, H. (1939). *The sabre-tooth curriculum*. New York: McGraw-Hill.

Benson, H. (1975). *The relaxation response*. New York: Morrow.

Betensky, M. G. (1973). *Self-discovery through self-expression* Springfield, IL: Charles C. Thomas.

Betensky, M. G. (1995). *What do you see?* London: Jessica Kingsley.

Betensky, M. G. (2001). A phenomenological approach to art therapy. In J. A. Rubin (Ed.), *Approaches to art therapy* (2nd ed., pp. 121–133). New York: Brunner-Routledge.

Bing, E. (1970). The conjoint family drawing. *Family Process, 9*, 173–194.

Blos, P. (1962). *On adolescence*. New York: Free Press.

Bradway, K., & McCoard, B. (1997). *Sandplay: Silent workshop of the psyche*. New York: Routledge.

Bradway, K., Signell, K., Spare, G., Stewart, C. T., Stewart, L. H., & Thompson, C. (1990). *Sandplay studies: Origins, theory, and practice*. Boston: Sigo Press.

Brooke, S. (2004). *Tools of the trade: A therapist's guide to art therapy assessments*. Springfield, IL: Charles C. Thomas.

Brown, W. (1967). *Introduction to psycho-iconography*. New York: Schering.

Buck, J. N. (1948). The H-T-P technique: A qualitative and quantitative scoring manual. *Journal of Clinical Psychology, 4*, 317–396.

Buck, J. N. (1992). *The House-Tree-Person projective drawing technique: Manual and interpretative guide* (Rev. by W. L. Warren). Los Angeles: Western Psychological Services.

Burns, D. O. (1999). *Feeling good: The new mood therapy* (Rev. ed.). New York: Avon Books.

Burns, R. C. (1987). *Kinetic house-tree-person drawings*. New York: Brunner/Mazel.

Burns, R. C. (1990). *A guide to family-centered circle drawings*. New York: Brunner/ Mazel.

Burns, R. C., & Kaufman, S. H. (1970). *Kinetic family drawings.* New York: Brunner/ Mazel.

Bush, J. (1997). *The handbook of school art therapy.* Springfield, IL: Charles C. Thomas.

Butler, R. N., Lewis, M. I., & Sunderland, T. (1998). *Aging and mental health.* Boston: Allyn & Bacon.

Bychowski, G. (1947). The rebirth of a woman. *Psychoanalytic Review, 34,* 32–57.

Cane, F. (1983). *The artist in each of us.* Chicago: Magnolia Street Publishers. (Original work published 1951)

Capacchione, L. (2001). *The creative journal: The art of finding yourself* (2nd ed.). Franklin Lakes, NJ: New Page Books.

Cardinal, R. (1972). *Outsider art.* New York: Praeger.

Carey, L. (1999). *Sandplay therapy with children and families.* Northvale, NJ: Jason Aronson.

Case, C., & Dalley, T. (Eds.). (1990). *Working with children in art therapy.* London: Tavistock.

Champernowne, I. (1970). Commentary. *Inseape,* vol. 5, pp. 1–2.

Chess, S. (1977). *Your child is a person.* New York: Penguin. (Original work published 1965)

Chodorow, J. (1997). *Jung on active imagination.* London: Routledge.

Cohen, B. M., Barnes, M.-M., & Rankin, A. B. (1995). *Managing traumatic stress through art.* Lutherville, MD: Sidran Press.

Cohen, B. M., & Cox, C. T. (1995). *Telling without talking: Art as a window into the world of multiple personality.* New York: Norton.

Cohen, B. M., Hammer, J. S., & Singer, S. (1988). The Diagnostic Drawing Series: A systematic approach to art therapy evaluation and research. *The Arts in Psychotherapy, 15*(1), 11–21.

Cohen-Liebman, M. S. (2003). Drawings in forensic investigation of childhood sexual abuse. In C. A. Malchiodi (Ed.), *Handbook of art therapy* (pp. 167–180). New York: Guilford Press.

Colarusso, C. A. (1992). *Child and adult development: A psychoanalytic introduction for clinicians.* New York: Plenum Press.

Coles, R. (1992). *Their eyes meeting the world: The drawings and paintings of children.* New York: Houghton Mifflin.

Consoli, J. J. (1991). *Psychimagery: Healing the child within.* Norfolk, VA: Psychimage Productions.

Cousins, N. (1981). *Anatomy of an illness.* New York: Bantam.

Cox, C. T. (2003). The MARI assessment. In C. A. Malchiodi (Ed.), *Handbook of art therapy* (pp. 428–434). New York: Guilford Press.

Crowley, R., & Mills, J. (1989). *Cartoon magic.* New York: Brunner/Mazel.

Damasio, A. (1994). *Descartes' error.* New York: Putnam.

Denny, J. M. (1972). Techniques for individual and group art therapy. *American Journal of Art Therapy, 11,* 117–134.

Edwards, M. (2001). Jungian analytic art therapy. In J. A. Rubin (Ed.), *Approaches to art therapy* (2nd ed., pp. 81–94). New York: Brunner-Routledge.

Elkisch, P. (1948). The "Scribbling Game": A projective method. *Nervous Child, 7*, 247–256.

Engel, L., & Ferguson, T. (1990). *Imaginary crimes: Why we punish ourselves and how to stop.* Boston: Houghton Mifflin.

Epstein, G. (1981). *Waking dream therapy: Dream process as imagination.* New York: Human Sciences Press.

Epstein, G. (1989.) *Healing visualizations: Creating health through imagery.* New York: Bantam.

Erikson, E. H. (1950). *Childhood and society.* New York: Norton.

Erickson, M. H., & Kubie, L. S. (1940). The use of automatic drawing in the interpretation and relief of a state of acute obsessional depression. *Psychoanalytic Quarterly, 9*, 443–466.

Faber, A., & Mazlish, E. (1999). *How to talk so kids will listen and listen so kids will talk.* Perennial Currents. (Original work published 1985)

Farrelly-Hansen, M. (Ed.). (2001). *Spirituality and art therapy.* London: Jessica Kingsley.

Fay, C. G. (1994). *At the threshold: A journey to the sacred through the integration of Jungian psychology and the expressive arts.* Dallas, TX: C. G. Jung Center.

Feinstein, R. E. (1981). The psychotherapeutic use of drawings in neuropsychiatric disease: A case study. In I. Jakab (Ed.), *The personality of the therapist: Proceedings of the 1981 international congress of psychopathology of expression* (pp. 161–168). Pittsburgh, PA: American Society of Psychopathology of Expression.

Fleming, J. (1940). Observations on the use of finger painting in the treatment of adult patients with personality disorders. *Character and Personality, 8*, 301.

Fraiberg, S. M. (1996). *The magic years: Understanding and handling the problems of early childhood.* New York: Scribner's. (Original work published 1955)

Franklin, M. (2001). The yoga of art and the creative process: Listening to the divine. In M. Farrelly-Hansen (Ed.), *Spirituality and art therapy* (pp. 97–114). London: Jessica Kingsley.

Freud, A., Nagera, H., & Freud, W. E. (1965). Metapsychological assessment of the adult personality. *Psychoanalytic Study of the Child, 20*, 9–41.

Freud, S. (1913). *On beginning the treatment* (Standard ed., Vol. 12). London: Hogarth Press.

Freud, S. (1916–1917). *Introductory lectures on psycho-analysis* (Standard ed., Vol. 12). London: Hogarth Press.

Freud, S. (1955a). *The interpretation of dreams* (Standard ed., Vols. 4–5). London: Hogarth Press. (Original work published 1900)

Freud, S. (1955b). *Project for a scientific psychology* (Standard ed., Vol. 1). London: Hogarth Press. (Original work written 1895, published 1950)

Freud, S. (1964). *The ego and the id* (Standard ed., Vol. 19). London: Hogarth Press. (Original work published 1923)

Freud, S., & Breuer, J. (1955). *Studies in hysteria* (Standard ed., Vol. 2). London: Hogarth Press. (Original work published 1893–1895)

Friday, N. (1977). *My mother, my self: The daughter's search for identity.* New York: Delacorte Press.

Fryrear, J. L., & Corbit, I. E. (1992). *Photo art therapy.* Springfield, IL: Charles C. Thomas.

Fryrear, J. L., & Fleshman, R. (Eds.). (1981). *Videotherapy in mental health.* Springfield, IL: Charles C. Thomas.

Gabriels, R. K. (1988). Art therapy assessment of coping styles in severe asthmatics. *Art Therapy, 5,* 59–68.

Gantt, L., & Tabone, C. (1998). *The Formal Elements Art Therapy Scale: The rating manual.* Morgantown, WV: Gargoyle Press.

Gantt, L., & Tabone, C. (2003). The Formal Elements Art Therapy Scale and "Draw a Person Picking an Apple from a Tree." In C. A. Malchiodi (Ed.), *Handbook of art therapy* (pp. 420–427). New York: Guilford Press.

Garai, J. (2001). Humanistic art therapy. In J. A. Rubin (Ed.), *Approaches to art therapy* (2nd ed., pp. 149–162). New York: Brunner-Routledge.

Gardner, H. (1980). *Artful scribbles: The significance of children's drawings.* New York: Basic Books.

Gardner, H. (1982). *Art, mind and brain.* New York: Basic Books.

Gardner, R. (1970). *The boys' and girls' book about divorce.* New York: Bantam Books.

Gardner, R. (1971). *Therapeutic communication with children: The mutual storytelling technique.* New York: Science House.

Gardner, R. (1988). *The Storytelling Card Game.* Creative Therapeutics, Inc. Available at http://www.rgardner.com

Gardner, R. (1991). *The parents book about divorce* (2nd ed.). New York: Bantam Books.

Gerber, N. (1996). *The brief art therapy screening evaluation (BATSE).* Philadelphia: Author.

Gerity, L. (1999). *Creativity and the dissociative patient: Puppets, narrative and art in the treatment of survivors of childhood trauma.* London: Jessica Kingsley.

Gil, E. (1991) *The healing power of play: Working with abused children.* New York: Guilford Press.

Gil, E. (1994). *Play in family therapy.* New York: Guilford Press.

Gillespie, J. (1994). *The projective use of mother-and-child drawings.* New York: Brunner/Mazel.

Ginott, H. G. (1965). *Between parent and child.* New York: Macmillan.

Ginott, H. G. (1969). *Between parent and teenager.* New York: Scribner's.

Gladding, S. T. (2005). *Counseling as an art* (3rd ed.). Washington, DC: American Counseling Association.

Gladding, S. T., & Newsome, D. W. (2003). Art in counseling. In C. A. Malchiodi (Ed.), *Handbook of art therapy* (pp. 243–253). New York: Guilford Press.

Goldstein, S. B., Deeton, K. D., & Barasch, J. (1975, March 7). The Family Joint

Mural: Family evaluation technique. Paper presented at the California State Psychological Association Convention, Anaheim, CA.

Golomb, C. (1974). *Young children's sculpture and drawing.* Cambridge: Harvard University Press.

Golomb, C. (1992). *The child's creation of a pictorial world.* Berkeley: University of California Press.

Golomb, C. (2002). *Child art in context: A cultural and comparative perspective.* Washington, DC: American Psychological Association.

Goodenough, F. L. (1926). *Measurement of intelligence by drawings.* New York: Harcourt, Brace, & World.

Graves, S. K. (1994). *Expressions of healing.* Van Nuys, CA: Newcastle.

Gray, J. (1990). *Men are from Mars, women are from Venus.* New York: Harper Collins.

Gypsycat Productions. (1994). *Rudolf Arnheim: A life in art* [Motion picture]. Berkeley, CA: Gypsycat Productions.

Hall, M. D., Metcalf, E. W., & Cardinal, R. (Eds.). (1994). *The artist outsider.* Washington, DC: Smithsonian Institution Press.

Hammer, E. F. (Ed.). (1958). *The clinical application of projective drawings.* Springfield, IL: Charles C. Thomas.

Hammer, E. F. (Ed.). (1997). *Advances in projective drawing interpretation.* Springfield, IL: Charles C. Thomas.

Hanes, M. J. (1997). *Roads to the unconscious.* Oklahoma: Woods 'n' Barnes.

Hare, A. P., & Hare, R. P. (1956). The Draw-A-Group Test. *Journal of Genetic Psychology, 89,* 51–59.

Harms, E. (1948). Play diagnosis. *Nervous Child, 7,* 233–246.

Harris, D. B. (1963). *Children's drawings as measures of intellectual maturity.* New York: Harcourt Brace & World.

Harris, J., & Joseph, C. (1973). *Murals of the mind: Image of a psychiatric community.* New York: International Universities Press.

Harrower, M. R. (1958). The most unpleasant concept test. In E. F. Hammer (Ed.), *The clinical application of projective drawings* (pp. 365–390). Springfield, IL: Charles C. Thomas.

Hays, R. (1979). The dot-to-dot exercise. Unpublished manuscript, American Art Therapy Association Annual Conference.

Hays, R., & Lyons, S. J. (1981). The bridge drawing: A projective technique for assessment in art therapy. *The Arts in Psychotherapy, 8,* 207–217.

Heegaard, M. E. (1992) *Facilitator guide for drawing out feelings.* Minneapolis, MN: Woodland Press.

Henderson, P., & Lowe, K. (1972). Reducing focus on the patient via family videotape playback. Paper presented at the annual meeting of the American Association of Psychiatric Services for Children.

Henley, D. (1992). *Exceptional children, exceptional art.* Worcester, MA: Davis Publications.

Hill, A. (1945). *Art versus illness: A story of art therapy.* London: George Allen & Unwin.

Holt, R. R. (1964). Imagery: The return of the ostracized. *American Psychologist, 19,* 254–264.

Homeyer, L. E., & Sweeney, D. (1998). *Sandtray: A practical manual.* Canyon Lake, TX: Linda Press.

Horovitz-Darby, E. (1988). Art therapy assessment of a minimally language skilled deaf child. *In Mental health assessment of deaf clients: Special conditions. Proceedings from the 1988 University of California's Center on Deafness Conference* (pp. 115–127). Little Rock, AK: ADARA.

Horowitz, M. J. (1983). *Image formation and psychotherapy.* New York: Jason Aronson.

Howard, M. (1964). An art therapist looks at her professional history. *Bulletin of Art Therapy, 4,* 153–156.

Hulse, W. C. (1949). Symbolic painting in psychotherapy. *American Journal of Psychotherapy, 3,* 559–584.

Huntoon, M. (1939). The creative arts as therapy. *Bulletin of the Menninger Clinic,* 198–203.

Irwin, E. C. (2001). Addendum. In J. A. Rubin (Ed.), *Approaches to art therapy* (2nd ed., pp. 79–80). New York: Brunner-Routledge.

Irwin, E. C., & Rubin, J. A. (1976). Art and drama interviews: Decoding symbolic messages. *Art Psychotherapy, 3,* 169–175.

Irwin, E. C., Rubin, J. A., & Shapiro, M. I. (1975). Art and drama: Partners in therapy. *American Journal of Psychotherapy, 29,* 107–116.

Jakab, I. (1998). *Pictorial expression in psychiatry: Psychiatric and artistic analysis.* Budapest: Akademiai Kiado. (Original work published 1956)

Jewish Museum of Prague. (1993). *I have not seen a butterfly around here.* Prague: The Jewish Museum.

Jones, D., Vinton, M., & Wernick, W. (1999, November 21). Three perspectives: Framing the Don Jones Assessment (DJA). Panel presentation, American Art Therapy Association Conference, Orlando, FL.

Jones, J. G. (1997). Art therapy with a community of survivors. *Art therapy, 14,* 89–94.

Kalff, D. M. (1980). *Sandplay.* Boston: Sigo Press.

Kaplan, F. (2000). *Art, science, and art therapy: Repainting the picture.* London: Jessica Kingsley.

Kaplan, F. (2003). Art-based assessments. In C. Malchiodi (Ed.), *Handbook of art therapy* (pp. 25–35). New York: Guilford Press.

Kellogg, J. (2002). *Mandala: Path of beauty* (3rd ed.). Belleaire, FL: Association for Teachers of Mandala Assessment.

Klepsch, M., & Logie, L. (1982). *Children draw and tell: An introduction to the projective use of children's human figure drawings.* New York: Brunner/Mazel.

Klinger, E. (1978). Modes of normal conscious flow. In K. S. Pope & J. L. Singer (Eds.), *The stream of consciousness.* New York: Plenum Press.

Klorer, P. G. (2000). *Expressive therapy with troubled children*. Northvale, NJ: Jason Aronson.

Koppitz, E. M. (1968). *Psychological evaluation of children's human figure drawings*. New York: Grune & Stratton.

Kramer, E. (1958). *Art therapy in a children's community*. Springfield, IL: Charles C. Thomas.

Kramer, E. (1971). *Art as therapy with children*. New York: Schocken Books.

Kramer, E. (1979). *Childhood and art therapy*. New York: Schocken Books.

Kramer, E. (2000). *Art as therapy: Collected papers* (L. A. Gerity, Ed.). London: Jessica Kingsley.

Kramer, E. (2001). Sublimation and art therapy. In J. A. Rubin (Ed.), *Approaches to art therapy* (2nd ed., pp. 28–39). New York: Brunner-Routledge.

Kramer, E., & Schehr, J. (2000). An art therapy evaluation session for children. In *Art as therapy: Collected papers* (L. A. Gerity, Ed., pp. 73–93). London: Jessica Kingsley.

Krauss, D. A., & Fryrear, J. L. (1983). *Phototherapy in mental health*. Springfield, IL: Charles C. Thomas.

Kris, E. (1952). *Psychoanalytic explorations in art*. New York: International Universities Press.

Kris, E. (1956). On some vicissitudes of insight in psychoanalysis. *International Journal of Psychoanalysis, 37*, 445–455.

Kwiatkowska, H. Y. (1978). *Family therapy and evaluation through art*. Springfield, IL: Charles C. Thomas.

Kymissis, P., & Khanna, P. (1992). The prospective kinetic family drawing. *American Journal of Art Therapy, 31*, 17–21.

Jung, C. G. (1964). *Man and his symbols*. New York: Doubleday.

Labovitz Boik, B., & Goodwin, E. A. (2000). *Sandplay therapy: A step-by-step manual for psychotherapists of diverse orientations*. New York: Norton.

Lachman-Chapin, M. (2001). Self psychology and art therapy. In J. A. Rubin (Ed.), *Approaches to art therapy* (2nd ed., pp. 66–78). New York: Brunner-Routledge.

Lambert, D. (1995). *The life and art of Elizabeth "Grandma" Layton*. Waco, TX: WRS Publishing.

Landgarten, H. B. (1981). *Clinical art therapy*. New York: Brunner/Mazel.

Landgarten, H. B. (1987). *Family art psychotherapy*. New York: Brunner/Mazel.

Landgarten, H. B. (1993). *Magazine photo collage*. New York: Brunner/Mazel.

Lazarus, A. (1981). *The practice of multimodal therapy*. New York: McGraw-Hill.

Lazarus, A. (1984). *In the mind's eye: The power of imagery for personal enrichment*. New York: Guilford Press.

Lerner, H. G. (1990). *The dance of anger*. New York: Harper Collins.

Leuner, H. (1969). Guided affective imagery. *American Journal of Psychotherapy, 31*, 4–22.

Levick, M. (2001). *The Levick cognitive and emotional art therapy assessment (LECATA)* (Rev. ed.). Boca Raton, FL: Author.

Levine, S. K., & Levine, E. G. (Eds.). (1999). *Foundations of expressive arts therapy.* London: Jessica Kingsley.

Levy, B. I., & Ulman, E. (1974). The effect of training on judging psychopathology from paintings. *American Journal of Art Therapy, 14,* 24–25.

Lewis, N. D. C. (1925). The practical value of graphic art in personality studies. *Psychoanalytic Review, 12,* 316–322.

Ley, R. G. (1979). Cerebral assymetries, emotional experience, and imagery: Implications for psychotherapy. In A. A. Sheikh & J. T. Shaffer (Eds.), *The potential of fantasy and imagination.* New York: Brandon House.

Liebmann, M. (1986). *Art therapy for groups.* Cambridge, MA: Brookline Books.

Liebowitz, M. (1999). *Interpreting projective drawings: A self psychological approach.* Philadelphia: Brunner/Mazel.

Linesch, D. (1988). *Adolescent art therapy.* New York: Brunner/Mazel.

Lowenfeld, M. (1979). *The world technique.* London: George Allen & Unwin.

Lowenfeld, V. (1957). *Creative and mental growth* (3rd ed.). New York: Macmillan.

Lowenfeld, V., & Brittain, W. L. (1982). *Creative and mental growth* (7th ed.). Englewood Cliffs, NJ: Prentice Hall.

Luborsky, L. (1984). *Principles of psychoanalytc psychotherapy: A manual for supportive-expressive treatment.* New York: Basic Books.

Lusebrink, V. (1990). *Imagery and visual expression in therapy.* New York: Plenum Press.

MacGregor, J. M. (1989). *The discovery of the art of the insane.* Princeton, NJ: Princeton University Press.

MacGregor, J. M. (1992). *Dwight Mackintosh: The boy who time forgot.* Oakland, CA: Creative Growth Art Center.

MacGregor, J. M. (1999). *Metamorphosis: The fiber art of Judith Scott.* Oakland, CA: Creative Growth Art Center.

Machover, K. (1949). *Personality projection in the drawing of the human figure.* Springfield, IL: Charles C. Thomas.

Makarova, E., & Seidman-Miller, R. (1999). *Friedl Deicker-Brandeis, Vienna 1891– Aschwitz 19—.* Los Angeles: Tallfellow Press.

Makin, S. R. (1999). *Therapeutic art directives and resources: Activities and initiatives for individuals and groups.* London: Jessica Kingsley.

Malchiodi, C. A. (1997). *Breaking the silence: Art therapy with children from violent homes* (2nd ed.). New York: Brunner-Routledge.

Malchiodi, C. A. (1998a). *The art therapy sourcebook.* Lincolnwood, IL: Lowell House.

Malchiodi, C. A. (1998b). *Understanding children's drawings.* New York: Guilford Press.

Malchiodi, C. A. (Ed.). (1999a). *Medical art therapy with adults.* London: Jessica Kingsley.

Malchiodi, C. A. (Ed.). (1999b). *Medical art therapy with children.* London: Jessica Kingsley.

Malchiodi, C. A. (2003a). Art therapy and the brain. In C. A. Malchiodi (Ed.), *Handbook of art therapy* (pp. 16–24). New York: Guilford Press.

Malchiodi, C. A. (2003b) Expressive arts therapy and multimodal approaches. In C. A. Malchiodi (Ed.), *Handbook of art therapy* (pp. 106–118). New York: Guilford Press.

Malchiodi, C. A., Kim, D., & Choi, W. S. (2003). Developmental art therapy. In C. A. Malchiodi (Ed.), *Handbook of art therapy* (pp. 93–105). New York: Guilford Press

Manning, T. M. (1987). Aggression depicted in abused children's drawings. *The Arts in Psychotherapy, 14*, 15–24.

Martin, E. (1997). The symbolic graphic life-line: Integrating the past and present through graphic imagery. *Art Therapy, 14*, 261–267.

Maslow, A. (1959). Creativity in Self-actualizing people. In H. H. Anderson (Ed.), *Creativity and its Cultivation* (pp 83–95). New York: Harper Row.

May, R. (1975). *The courage to create*. New York: Norton.

McGoldrick, M., & Gerson, R. (1985). *Genograms in family assessment*. New York: Norton.

McNally, S. P. (2001). *Sandplay: A sourcebook for play therapists*. Campbell, CA: Universe.

McNiff, S. (1981). *The arts and psychotherapy*. Springfield, IL: Charles C. Thomas.

McNiff, S. (1998). *Trust the process: An artistic guide to letting go*. Boston: Shambhala.

McNiff, S. (2001). The use of imagination and all of the arts. In J. A. Rubin (Ed.), *Approaches to art therapy* (2nd ed., pp. 318–325). New York: Brunner-Routledge.

Meares, A. (1957). *Hypnography*. Springfield, IL: Charles C. Thomas.

Meares, A. (1958). *The door of serenity*. London: Faber & Faber.

Meares, A. (1960). *Shapes of sanity*. Springfield, IL: Charles C. Thomas.

Mills, A. (2003). The Diagnostic Drawing Series. In C. A. Malchiodi (Ed.), *Handbook of art therapy* (pp. 401–409). New York: Guilford Press.

Mills, J. C., & Crowley, R. (1986). *Therapeutic metaphors for children and the child within*. New York: Brunner/Mazel.

Milner, M. (1969). *The hands of the living god*. New York: International Universities Press.

Mitchell, R. R., & Friedman, H. S. (1994). *Sandplay: Past, present and future* New York: Routledge.

Moon, B. L. (1995). *Existential art therapy* (2nd ed.). Springfield, IL: Charles C. Thomas.

Morgenthaler, W. (1921). *Madness and art*. Lincoln, NB: University of Nebraska Press.

Morris, D. (1962). *The biology of art*. New York: Alfred A. Knopf.

Mosse, E. P. (1947). Painting analyses in the treatment of neuroses. *Psychoanalytic Review, 27*, 65–81.

Naevestad, M. (1979). *The colors of rage and love*. London: Whitefriars Press.

Naumburg, M. (1928). *The child and the world*. New York: Harcourt, Brace, & World.

Naumburg, M. (1950). *Schizophrenic art: Its meaning in psychotherapy*. New York: Grune & Stratton.

Naumburg, M. (1953). *Psychoneurotic art: Its function in psychotherapy*. New York: Grune & Stratton.

Naumburg, M. (1955). Art as symbolic speech. *Journal of Aesthetics and Art Criticism, 12*, 435–450.

Naumburg, M. (1966). *Dynamically oriented art therapy: Its principles and practices*. New York: Grune & Stratton.

Naumburg, M. (1973). Studies of the "free" art expression of behavior problem children and adolescents as a means of diagnosis and therapy. *Nervous and Mental Disease Monograph, 1947, 17* (2nd ed.: *An introduction to art therapy*). New York: Teachers College Press.

Nichols, J., & Garrett, A. (1995). *Drawing and coloring for your life*. Overland Park, KS: Gingerbread Castle Publications.

Nucho, A. (1987). *Psychocybernetic model of art therapy* Springfield, IL: Charles C. Thomas.

Nucho, A. (1995). *Spontaneous creative imagery: Problem-solving and life-enhancing skills*. Springfield, IL: Charles C. Thomas.

Oaklander, V. (1969). *Windows to our children*. Utah: Real People Press.

Oster, G. D., & Crone, P. G. (2004). *Using drawings in assessment and therapy* (2nd ed.). New York: Brunner-Routledge.

Oster, G. D., & Montgomery, S. (1996). *Clinical uses of drawings*. Northvale, NJ: Jason Aronson.

Perls, F. S. (1969). *Gestalt therapy verbatim*. Lafayette, CA: Real People Press.

Piaget, J. (1952). *The origins of intelligence in children*. New York: International Universities Press.

Piaget, J., & Inhelder, B. (1971). *Mental imagery in the child*. New York: Basic Books.

Prinzhorn, H. (1922). *Artistry of the mentally ill*. New York: Springer.

Proulx, L. (2002). *Strengthening emotional ties through parent-child-dyad art therapy*. London: Jessica Kingsley.

Prout, H. T., & Phillips, P. D. (1974). A clinical note: The Kinetic School Drawing. *Psychology in the Schools, 11*, 303–306.

Reichard, G. A. (1977). *Navajo medicine man sand paintings*. NY: Dover.

Reyher, J. (1977). Spontaneous visual imagery: Implications for psychoanalysis, psychopathology, and psychotherapy. *Journal of Mental Imagery, 1*, 253–274.

Reyher, J., & Smeltzer, W. (1968). Uncovering properties of visual imagery and verbal association: A comparative study. *Journal of Abnormal Psychology, 73*, 218–222.

Rhyne, J. (1995). *The gestalt art experience* (2nd ed.). Chicago, IL: Magnolia Street. (Original work published 1973)

Rhyne, J. (2001). Gestalt art therapy. In J. A. Rubin (Ed.), *Approaches to art therapy* (2nd ed., pp. 134–148). New York: Brunner-Routledge.

Richardson, A. (1977). Visualizer-verbalizer. *Journal of Mental Imagery, 1*, 109–126.

Riley, S. (1999). *Contemporary art therapy with adolescents*. London: Jessica Kingsley.

Riley, S. (2001). *Group process made visible*. New York: Brunner-Routledge.

Riley, S. (2003). Art therapy with couples. In C. A. Malchiodi (ed.), *Handbook of art therapy* (pp. 387–398). New York: Guilford Press.

Riley, S., & Malchiodi, C. A. (2003). Solution-focused and narrative approaches. In C. A. Malchiodi (Ed.), *Handbook of art therapy* (pp. 82–92). New York: Guilford Press.

Riley, S., & Malchiodi, C. A. (2004). *Integrative approaches to family art therapy* (2nd ed.). Chicago, IL: Magnolia Street.

Robbins, A. (Ed.). (1997). *Therapeutic presence*. London: Jessica Kingsley.

Robbins, A. (2001). Object relations and art therapy. In J. A. Rubin (Ed.), *Approaches to art therapy* (2nd ed., pp. 54–65). New York: Brunner-Routledge

Robbins, A. (2002). *Dancing on my father's blood* [Motion picture]. London: Jessica Kingsley.

Rogers, C. R. (1951). *Client-centered therapy: Its current practices, implications, and theory*. New York: Houghton Mifflin.

Rogers, C. R. (1961). *On becoming a person*. Boston: Houghton Mifflin.

Rogers, N. (1993). *The creative connection: Expressive arts as healing*. Palo Alto, CA: Science & Behavior Books.

Rogers, N. (2001). Person-centered expressive arts therapy: A path to wholeness. In J. A. Rubin (Ed.), *Approaches to art therapy* (2nd ed., pp. 163–177). New York: Brunner-Routledge.

Rosal, M. (2001). Cognitive-behavioral art therapy. In J. A. Rubin (Ed.), *Approaches to art therapy* (2nd ed., pp. 210–225). New York: Brunner-Routledge.

Ross, C. (1997). *Something to draw on: Activities and interventions using an art therapy approach*. London: Jessica Kingsley.

Roth, E. (2001). Behavioral art therapy. In J. A. Rubin (Ed.), *Approaches to art therapy* (2nd ed., pp. 195–209). New York: Brunner-Routledge.

Rozum, A. L., & Malchiodi, C. A. (2003). Cognitive-behavioral approaches. In C. A. Malchiodi (Ed.), *Handbook of art therapy* (pp. 72–81). New York: Guilford Press.

Rubin, J. A. (1973). A diagnostic art interview. *Art Psychotherapy, 1*, 31–34.

Rubin, J. A. (1974). Mother-child art sessions: I. Treatment in the clinic. *American Journal of Art Therapy, 13*, 165–181.

Rubin, J. A. (1976). The exploration of a "tactile aesthetic." *New Outlook for the Blind, 70*, 369–375.

Rubin, J. A. (1980). Art in counseling: A new avenue. *Counseling and Human Development, 13*(3).

Rubin, J. A. (1981a). Art and imagery: Free association with art media. In A. E.

DiMaria (Ed.), *Art therapy: A bridge between worlds*. Falls Church, VA: American Art Therapy Association.

Rubin, J. A. (1981b). Art therapy in a community mental health center for children: A story of program development. *The Arts in Psychotherapy, 8,* 109–114.

Rubin, J. A. (1983). Art and imagery in adult psychoanalysis. In J. E. Shore, G. Sobel-Whittington, P. Robin, & J. A. Connella (Eds.), *Imagery* (Vol. 3, pp. 409–432). New York: Plenum.

Rubin, J. A. (1984). *The art of art therapy.* New York: Brunner/Mazel.

Rubin, J. A. (1999). *Art therapy: An introduction.* New York: Brunner/Mazel.

Rubin, J. A. (Ed.). (2001a). *Approaches to art therapy: Theory and technique.* New York: Brunner-Routledge.

Rubin, J. A. (2001b). Discovery, insight, and art therapy. In *Approaches to art therapy: Theory and technique* (pp. 15–27). New York: Brunner-Routledge.

Rubin, J. A. (2002). *My mom and dad don't live together anymore.* Washington, DC: 'Magination Press.

Rubin, J. A. (2004). *Art therapy has many faces* [Motion picture]. Pittsburgh: Expressive Media.

Rubin, J. A. (2005). *Child art therapy: Understanding and helping children grow through art* (3rd ed.). New York: Wiley.

Rubin, J. A., & Irwin, E. C. (1975). Art and drama: Parts of a puzzle. In I. Jakab (Ed.), *Psychiatry and art* (Vol. 4, pp. 193–200). New York: S. Karger.

Rubin, J. A., Irwin, E. C., & Bernstein, P. (1975). Play, parenting and the arts: A therapeutic approach to primary prevention. *Proceedings of the American Dance Therapy Association,* 60–78.

Rubin, J. A., & Klineman, J. (1974). They opened our eyes: An exploratory art program for visually-impaired multiply-handicapped children. *Education of the Visually Handicapped, 6,* 106–113.

Rubin, J. A., & Levy, P. (1975). Art-Awareness: A method for working with groups. *Group Psychotherapy and Psychodrama, 28,* 108–117.

Rubin, J. A., & Magnussen, M. G. (1974). A family art evaluation. *Family Process, 13,* 185–200.

Rubin, J. A., Magnussen, M. G., & Bar, A. (1975). Stuttering: Symptom-system-symbol (Art therapy in the treatment of a case of disfluency). In I. Jakab (Ed.), *Psychiatry and Art* (Vol. 4, pp. 201–215). New York: S Karger.

Rubin, J. A., Ragins, N., Schachter, J., & Wimberly, F. (1979). Drawings by schizophrenic and non-schizophrenic mothers and their children. *Art Psychotherapy, 6,* 163–175.

Rubin, J. A., & Rosenblum, N. (1977). Group art and group dynamics: An experimental study. *Art Psychotherapy, 4,* 185–193.

Rubin, J. A., & Rubin, H. (1988). Words and pictures: The relationship between graphic and verbal expression in young children. *American Journal of Art Therapy, 26,* 71–82.

Rubin, J. A., & Schachter, J. (1972). Judgements of psychopathology from art productions of children. *Confinia Psychiatrica, 15,* 237–252.

Rubin, J. A., Schachter, J., & Ragins, N. (1983). Intra-individual variability in human figure drawings: A developmental study. *American Journal of Orthopsychiatry, 53,* 654–667.

Safran, D. (2002). *Art therapy and AD/HD: Diagnostic and therapeutic approaches.* London: Jessica Kingsley.

Sardella, S. (1994). Drawing helps Croatian children cope. *APA Monitor* (January), 10–11.

Schaefer, C. E., & Digeronimo, T. F. (1991). *Teach your child to behave.* New York: Plume Books.

Schilder, P. (1950). *The image and appearance of the human body.* New York: Wiley.

Schiller, F. (1875). *Essays, aesthetical and philosophical.* London: George Bell.

Schreiber, F. R. (1974). *Sybil.* New York: Warner Books.

Sechehaye, M. (1951). *Symbolic realization.* New York: International Universities Press.

Siegel, B. (1986). *Love, medicine, and miracles.* New York: Harper & Row.

Siegel, D. J. (1999). *The developing mind: Towards a neurobiology of interpersonal experiences.* New York: Guilford Press.

Silver, R. A. (1978). *Developing cognitive and creative skills in art.* Baltimore: University Park Press.

Silver, R. A. (2001) *Art as language: Access to thoughts and feelings through stimulus drawings.* New York: Brunner-Routledge.

Silver, R. A. (2002). *Three art assessments: Silver Drawing Test of Cognition and Emotion; Draw a Story: Screening for depression; and Stimulus drawings and techniques.* New York: Brunner-Routledge.

Silverman, L. H., & Lachmann, F. M. (1982). *The search for oneness.* New York: International Universities Press.

Simonton, C. O., Mathews-Simonton, C. S., & Creighton, J. (1978). *Getting well again.* Los Angeles: Tarcher.

Singer, J. L. (1974). *Imagery and daydream methods in psychotherapy and behavior modification.* New York: Academic Press.

Singer, J. L., & Pope, K. S. (Eds.). (1978). *The power of human imagination.* New York: Plenum Press.

Sizemore, C. C. (1977). *I'm Eve.* New York: Doubleday & Company.

Sobol, B., & Williams, K. (2001). Family and group art therapy. In J. A. Rubin (Ed.), *Approaches to art therapy* (2nd ed, pp. 261–280). New York: Brunner-Routledge.

Spaniol, S. (2003). Art therapy with adults with severe mental illness. In C. A. Malchiodi (Ed.), *Handbook of art therapy* (pp. 268–280). New York: Guilford Press.

Spitz, R. (1954). Review of *Psychoneurotic art* by M. Naumburg. *Psychoanalytic Quarterly, 23,* 279–282.

Steele, W. (2003). Using drawing in short-term trauma resolution. In C. A. Malchiodi (Ed.), *Handbook of art therapy* (pp. 139–151). New York: Guilford Press.

Stern, M. M. (1952). Free painting as an auxiliary technique in psychoanalysis. In

G. Bychowski & L. Despert (Eds.), *Specialized techniques in psychotherapy*. New York: Basic Books.

Stevens, A. (1986). *Withymead*. London: Coventure.

Sulloway, F. J. (1979). *Freud: Biologist of the mind*. New York: Basic Books.

Tanaka, M., Kakuyama, T., & Urhausen, M. T. (2003). Drawing and storytelling as psychotherapy with children. In C. A. Malchiodi (Ed.), *Handbook of art therapy* (pp. 125–138). New York: Guilford Press.

Tannen, D. (2001). *You just don't understand: Women and men in conversation*. Perennial Currents.

Tinnin, L. (1990). Biological processes in nonverbal communication and their role in the making and interpretation of art. *American Journal of Art Therapy, 29*, 9–13.

Tinnin, L. (1994). Transforming the placebo effect in art therapy. *American Journal of Art Therapy, 32*, 75–78.

Turecki, S. (1985). *The difficult child*. New York: Bantam Dell.

Tyson, P., & Tyson, R. L. (1990). *Psychoanalytic theories of development: An integration*. New Haven, CT: Yale University Press.

Ude-Pestel, A. (1977). *Betty: History and art of a child in therapy*. Palo Alto, CA: Science & Behavior Books.

Uhlin, D. M. (1972). *Art for exceptional children*. Dubuque, IA: William C. Brown.

Ulman, E. (1961). Art therapy: Problems of definition. *Bulletin of Art Therapy, 1*(2), 10–20.

Ulman, E. (1965). A new use of art in psychiatric diagnosis. *Bulletin of Art Therapy, 4*, 91–116.

Ulman, E. (1971). The power of art in therapy. In I. Jakab (Ed.), *Psychiatry and art* (Vol. 3, pp. 93–102). New York: S. Karger.

Ulman, E. (1966). Therapy is not enough: The contribution of art to general hospital psychiatry. *Bulletin of Art Therapy, 6*(1), 3–21.

Ulman, E. (2001). Variations on a Freudian theme. In J. A. Rubin (Ed.), *Approaches to art therapy* (2nd ed., pp. 289–305). New York: Brunner-Routledge.

Ulman, E., & Levy, B. I. (1968). An experimental approach to the judgment of psychopathology from paintings. *Bulletin of Art Therapy, 8*, 3–12.

Vich, M. A., & Rhyne, J. (1967). Psychological growth and the use of art materials: Small group experiments with adults. *Journal of Humanistic Psychology*, (Fall), 163–170.

Vinton, M., & Wernick, W. (2000, November 9). Transitioning with the Don Jones Assessment: Research to application. Paper presented at the American Art Therapy Association Conference, St. Louis, MO.

Viorst, J. (1986). *Necessary losses*. New York: Simon & Schuster.

Volavkova, H. (Ed.). (1962). *I never saw another butterfly . . . Children's drawings and poems from Terezin concentration camp, 1942–1944*. New York: McGraw-Hill.

Wadeson, H. W. (1972). Conjoint marital art therapy techniques. *Psychiatry: Journal for the Study of Interpersonal Processes, 35*, 89–98.

Wadeson, H. W. (1980). *Art psychotherapy*. New York: Wiley.

Wadeson, H. W. (2000). *Art therapy practice: Innovative approaches with diverse populations*. New York: Wiley.

Wadeson, H. W. (2001). An eclectic approach to art therapy. In J. A. Rubin (Ed.), *Approaches to art therapy* (2nd ed., pp. 306–317). New York: Brunner-Routledge.

Wald, J. (1989). Art therapy for patients with Alzheimer's disease and related disorders. In H. W. Wadeson, J. Durkin, & D. Perach (Eds.), *Advances in art therapy* (pp. 204–221). New York: Wiley.

Wald, J. (2003). Clinical art therapy with older adults. In C. A Malchiodi (Ed.), *Handbook of art therapy* (pp. 294–307). New York: Guilford Press.

Wallace, E. (2001). Healing through the visual arts. In J. A. Rubin (Ed.), *Approaches to art therapy* (2nd ed., pp. 95–108). New York: Brunner-Routledge.

Waller, D. (1993). *Group interactive art therapy*. New York: Routledge.

Warren, L. A. (1995). An interview: Helen B. Landgarten. *American Journal of Art Therapy, 34,* 34–42.

Watkins, J. G. (1992). *Hypnoanalytic techniques*. New York: Irvington.

Weiser, J. (1993). *Phototherapy techniques*. San Francisco, CA: Jossey-Bass.

Wilner, R. S., & Rau, J. H. (1976). Family systems drawings. *Family Therapy, 3,* 245–267.

Wilson, L. (1999). Art Therapy with an anxious 12-year-old girl. In J. A. Rubin (Ed.), *Art therapy: An introduction* (pp. 341–349). New York: Brunner/Mazel.

Wilson, L. (2001). Symbolism and art therapy. In J. A. Rubin (Ed.), *Approaches to art therapy* (2nd ed., pp. 40–53). New York: Brunner-Routledge.

Wilson, M. (2003). Art therapy in addictions treatment: Creativity and shame reduction. In C. A Malchiodi (Ed.), *Handbook of art therapy* (pp. 281–293). New York: Guilford Press.

Winnicott, D. W. (1971a). *Playing and reality*. New York: Basic Books.

Winnicott, D. W. (1971b). *Therapeutic consultations in child psychiatry*. New York: Basic Books.

Winnicott, D. W. (1989). The squiggle game. In C. Winnicott, R. Shepherd, & M. David (Eds.), *Psycho-analytic explorations/D. W. Winnicott* (pp. 299–317). Cambridge, MA: Harvard University Press. (Original work published 1964–1968)

Wolf, R. (1976). The Polaroid technique: Spontaneous dialogues from the unconscious. *Art Psychotherapy, 3,* 197–214.

Index

About the Author

J udith A. Rubin, PhD, ATR-BC, has been an art therapist for more than 40 years. She is the author of *Child Art Therapy: Understanding and Helping Children Grow through Art* (2005, third edition; first and second editions 1978 and 1984, respectively), *The Art of Art Therapy* (1984), *Art Therapy: An Introduction* (1999), *My Mom and Dad Don't Live Together Anymore* (2002); and editor of *Approaches to Art Therapy: Theory and Technique* (2001, second edition; first edition 1987).

She was the Art Lady for the first three years of *Mister Rogers' Neighborhood* (PBS), and was inspired by Fred Rogers to make films and, more recently, videotapes. Her early films are *We'll Show You What We're Gonna Do! Art for Multiply-Handicapped Blind Children* (1972); *Children and the Arts: A Film about Growing* (1973); and *The Green Creature Within: Art and Drama in Group Psychotherapy with Adolescents* (1984, with Eleanor C. Irwin). Her recent videotapes are *Art Therapy Has Many Faces* (2004) and *Beyond Words: Art Therapy with Older Adults* (2004).

A licensed psychologist, Dr. Rubin is clinical assistant professor in the Department of Psychiatry, University of Pittsburgh, and emeritus faculty at the Pittsburgh Psychoanalytic Institute. She is also a past president and honorary life member of the American Art Therapy Association.

About the DVD-ROM

Introduction

This appendix provides you with information on the contents of the DVD that accompanies this book. For the latest and greatest information, please refer to the ReadMe file located at the root of the DVD.

System Requirements

- A computer with a processor running at 120 Mhz or faster
- At least 32 MB of total RAM installed on your computer; for best performance, we recommend at least 64 MB
- A DVD-ROM drive

  * NOTE: Many of the video files on this DVD-ROM are in MP4 format. This format is playable with "Apple Quicktime" software. If you need to install Apple Quicktime onto your computer, visit **http://www.quicktime.com** to download a free copy.

Using the DVD with Windows

To install the items from the DVD to your hard drive, follow these steps:

1. Insert the DVD into your computer's DVD-ROM drive.
2. The DVD-ROM interface will appear. The interface provides a simple point-and-click way to explore the contents of the DVD.

If the opening screen of the DVD-ROM does not appear automatically, follow these steps to access the DVD:

1. Click the Start button on the left end of the taskbar and then choose Run from the menu that pops up.
2. In the dialog box that appears, type **d:\setup.exe.** (If your DVD-ROM drive is not drive d, fill in the appropriate letter in place of *d*.) This brings up the DVD Interface described in the preceding set of steps.

What's on the DVD

The following sections provide a summary of the software and other materials you'll find on the DVD.

Content

The attached companion DVD contains almost 500 image files, which have been carefully chosen and edited in order to bring the text alive for the reader. Since this book is about the use of art in therapy, it will come as no surprise that about 160 are of artwork, some of them color versions of the black and white reproductions in the book. About 230 show individuals of all ages creating with art media in a variety of clinical settings.

Perhaps most unusual are the video files—over 200 of them—in which the reader can hear and see what goes on when people use art in their clinical work. Although the majority of these are brief, one is a 10-minute excerpt from an interview by Natalie Rogers, daughter of psychologist Carl Rogers, in which a young woman uses drawings to help define her identity.

NOTE: Many of the video files on this DVD-ROM are in MP4 format. This format is playable with "Apple Quicktime" software. If you need to install Apple Quicktime onto your computer, visit **http://www.quicktime.com** to download a free copy.

Customer Care

If you have trouble with the DVD-ROM, please call the Wiley Product Technical Support phone number at (800) 762-2974. Outside the United States, call 1(317) 572-3994. You can also contact Wiley Product Technical Support at **http://www.wiley.com/techsupport**. John Wiley & Sons will provide technical support only for installation and other general quality control items. For technical support on the applications themselves, consult the program's vendor or author.

To place additional orders or to request information about other Wiley products, please call (877) 762–2974.

CUSTOMER NOTE:

IF THIS BOOK IS ACCOMPANIED BY SOFTWARE, PLEASE READ THE FOLLOWING BEFORE OPENING THE PACKAGE.